McGraw-Hill Education

PTCE

REVIEW

McGraw-Hill Education

PTCE

REVIEW

KRISTY MALACOS

New York Chicago San Francisco Athens London Madrid
Mexico City Milan New Delhi Singapore Sydney Toronto

1 2 3 4 5 6 7 8 9   LHS   25 24 23 22 21 20

ISBN   978-1-260-47005-5
MHID   1-260-47005-9

e-ISBN 978-1-260-47006-2
e-MHID   1-260-47006-7

McGraw Hill products are available at special quantity discounts for use as premiums and sales promotions, or for use in corporate training programs. To contact a representative, please visit the Contact Us pages at www.mhprofessional.com.

Contents

McGraw-Hill Education

PTCE
REVIEW

Introduction: Pharmacy Technicians and the PTCE

Congratulations on choosing to become a pharmacy technician! This book will help you prepare for the Pharmacy Technician Certification Exam (PTCE). Each chapter is broken down into corresponding domains from the certification exam. Before we get started on test content, let's take a minute to review the pharmacy technician role and potential job opportunities. We'll also review the PTCE itself to make sure you are prepared for the structure and requirements of this exam.

After reading Chapter 1, you will be able to:

- Explain the role of the pharmacy technician and importance to the healthcare team

- Identify different career paths for pharmacy technicians

- Understand the requirements and preparation needed to become a certified pharmacy technician

- Describe the content of the PTCE and requirements for continuing education

- Recognize strategies for exam preparation

The Pharmacy Technician

A pharmacy technician is an integral part of the healthcare team and helps serve patients by supporting the pharmacist through the completion of a variety of important tasks. The role of the pharmacy technician is dependent upon practice setting, but typically includes filling prescriptions or medication orders; working with insurance companies to troubleshoot or gain approval of coverage;

compounding IVs, chemotherapy, or nonsterile products; and being an active customer service agent of the pharmacy.

Pharmacy technicians working in the community setting are based in a retail pharmacy. The pharmacy may be part of a large chain or smaller independent store. In the community setting, pharmacy technicians may input and fill prescriptions. They may investigate insurance rejections; work on inventory, including over-the-counter (OTC) drugs; or wait on customers and ring out verified prescriptions.

Institutional pharmacy technicians practice in hospitals or long-term care facilities. Hospital pharmacy technicians may compound IVs, repack unit dose medications, fill and maintain automated dispensing cabinets, and stock crash carts. Hospital technicians may interact with patients less than community pharmacy technicians, but instead may interact more with nursing staff and other healthcare providers. Pharmacy technicians may also compound chemotherapy in hospitals or in a designated cancer center. Long-term-care pharmacy technicians may also compound IVs and repack unit dose medications in larger packages for nursing home patients. They may also fill orders for facilities or be part of the customer service team who helps answer nursing questions or direct orders to each facility.

Other places pharmacy technicians may work is in a nuclear, compounding, or specialty pharmacy. Nuclear pharmacy technicians compound radiopharmaceuticals to be used for diagnostic testing or cancer treatment. Compounding technicians compound both sterile and nonsterile preparations for patient-specific use. These technicians often require additional training for compounding technique and calculations. Specialty pharmacy is a growing area involving the dispensing of high-dollar drugs used to treat complex disease states, such as multiple sclerosis. Pharmacy technicians working in specialty pharmacy will review prescriptions and work with insurance providers on authorization for patient coverage.

Mail-order pharmacies are an additional place for pharmacy technicians to work. In this setting, pharmacy technicians may package large amounts of medication to be shipped using packaging machines. Technicians may also review prescriptions, assess insurance coverage, and work on authorizations to have medications filled.

Pharmacy technicians and pharmacists are in high demand in many settings, and because of this, the role of the technician is expanding to allow more time for the pharmacist to provide patient-centered care. Pharmacy technicians may take medication histories for patients upon admission to a hospital and reconcile home medication lists with what is currently prescribed. This process is known as medication reconciliation (med rec), and med rec techs are becoming more popular with the increase in patient safety this role can provide. Additionally, community pharmacy technicians are becoming more active in medication therapy management (MTM). MTM is a service that pharmacists provide to patients where medications that are currently prescribed are reviewed to ensure the best outcome is achieved from the treatment. Technicians can assist with this process by monitoring MTM databases, examining patients' adherence to medications, and notifying pharmacists of potential compliance issues. Because of this expansion of responsibilities, it is essential that pharmacy technicians have sufficient training and certification.

Certified Pharmacy Technician

The state in which you will practice will determine requirements for certification, registration, or licensure. Certification is the completion or passing of a designated standard, such as an exam, from an established nongovernmental organization. Pharmacy Technician Certification is offered through the Pharmacy Technician Certification Board (PTCB) and the National Healthcareer Association (NHA). The PTCB uses the Pharmacy Technician Certification Exam (PTCE) for certification, and the NHA uses the Exam for the Certification of Pharmacy Technicians (ExCPT).

Registration is registering with an organization, such as with a board of pharmacy, who may require pharmacy technicians to register annually. Licensure is the regulation of a profession by a governmental body. Some states may require pharmacy technicians to register or be licensed to practice. You should check your state requirements when preparing to become certified as a pharmacy technician.

PTCE Overview

The PTCE is divided into four knowledge domains, with specific content areas within each domain. Following are the four domains and the percentage of the PTCE dedicated to each domain.

KNOWLEDGE DOMAIN	% OF PTCE CONTENT	NUMBER OF QUESTIONS (OUT OF 90)
Medications	40	36
Federal Requirements	12.5	11
Patient Safety and Quality Assurance	26.25	24
Order Entry and Processing	21.25	19

The Medications domain comprises the largest portion of the exam at 40 percent of content and also contains the most knowledge areas. The breakdown of the Medications content of the PTCE follows.

- Generic names, brand names, and classifications of medications
- Therapeutic equivalence
- Common and life-threatening drug interactions and contraindications (e.g., drug–disease, drug–drug, drug–dietary supplement, drug–laboratory, drug–nutrient)
- Strengths/dose, dosage forms, routes of administration, special handling and administration instructions, and duration of drug therapy
- Common and severe medication side effects, adverse effects, and allergies
- Indications of medications and dietary supplements
- Drug stability (e.g., oral suspensions, insulin, reconstitutables, injectables, vaccinations)
- Narrow therapeutic index (NTI) medications

- Physical and chemical incompatibilities related to nonsterile compounding and reconstitution
- Proper storage of medications (e.g., temperature ranges, light sensitivity, restricted access)

The Federal Requirements domain consists of laws, standards, and regulations related to pharmacy practice, including controlled substances. The five areas within this domain follow.

- Federal requirements for handling and disposal of nonhazardous, hazardous, and pharmaceutical substances and waste
- Federal requirements for controlled substance prescriptions (i.e., new, refill, transfer) and Drug Enforcement Administration (DEA) controlled substance schedules.
- Federal requirements (e.g., DEA, Federal Drug Administration [FDA]) for controlled substances (i.e., receiving, storing, ordering, labeling, dispensing, reverse distribution, take-back programs, and loss or theft of)
- Federal requirements for restricted drug programs and related medication processing (e.g., pseudoephedrine, risk evaluation and mitigation strategies [REMS])
- FDA recall requirements (e.g., medications, devices, supplies, supplements, classifications)

The Patient Safety and Quality Assurance domain consists of content areas concerning patient safety and error prevention strategies and reporting methods. The areas for this domain follow.

- High-alert/risk medications and look-alike/sound-alike (LASA) medications
- Error prevention strategies (e.g., prescription or medication order to correct patient, Tall Man lettering, separating inventory, leading and trailing zeros, bar code usage, limit use of error-prone abbreviations)
- Issues that require pharmacist intervention (e.g., drug utilization review [DUR], adverse drug event [ADE], OTC recommendation, therapeutic substitution, misuse, adherence, post-immunization follow-up, allergies, drug interactions)
- Event reporting procedures (e.g., medication errors, adverse effects, and product integrity, MedWatch, near miss, root-cause analysis [RCA])
- Types of prescription errors (e.g., abnormal doses, early refill, incorrect quantity, incorrect patient, incorrect drug)
- Hygiene and cleaning standards (e.g., handwashing, personal protective equipment [PPE], cleaning counting trays, countertop, and equipment)

The Order Entry and Processing domain consists of areas related to prescription processing, including calculations, equipment for drug administration, and lot numbers and expiration dates. The areas for this domain follow.

- Procedures to compound nonsterile products (e.g., ointments, mixtures, liquids, emulsions, suppositories, enemas)
- Formulas, calculations, ratios, proportions, alligations, conversions, sig codes (e.g., b.i.d.k, t.i.d., Roman numerals), abbreviations, medical terminology, and symbols for days supply, quantity, dose, concentration, dilutions

- Equipment/supplies required for drug administration (e.g., package size, unit dose, diabetic supplies, spacers, oral and injectable syringes)
- Lot numbers, expiration dates, and National Drug Code (NDC) numbers
- Procedures for identifying and returning dispensable, nondispensable, and expired medications and supplies (e.g., credit return, return to stock, reverse distribution)

Preparing for the PTCE

The Pharmacy Technician Certification Exam (PTCE) is a computer-based exam consisting of 90 total questions, of which 80 are scored and 10 are unscored. The exam is multiple choice, and each question has four possible choices with one correct answer. You have two hours total to take the exam, with 10 minutes being dedicated to a pre-exam tutorial and post-exam survey. The cost to take the PTCE is $129. After passing the exam, you would earn the Certified Pharmacy Technician (CPhT) credential. To be eligible for the PTCE requires completion of one of two pathways. One pathway is completion of a PTCB-approved education or training program. The second pathway is equivalent work experience (minimum of 500 hours) as a pharmacy technician. You must also disclose any criminal and state board of pharmacy registration or licensure actions, and be compliant with all PTCB certification policies. If you have met these criteria, you can apply to take the exam by creating an account with the PTCB. Once approved, you can schedule your exam.

Exams are taken at designated testing centers year-round. To prepare for the PTCE, you can use this book you're currently reading, and also check out some of the PTCB online content for practice. After completion of the exam, you will know if you passed immediately on the screen, though you will not get your official score report until two to three weeks later. You will be able to download your certificate through the PTCB website.

As a CPhT, you will have specified requirements to maintain your credentials. You must complete a minimum of 20 hours of continuing education (CE) every two years. These 20 hours must include 1 hour in pharmacy law and 1 hour in patient safety. The PTCB also requires that the CE earned must be pharmacy-technician-specific, which can be earned through CE with a designation of "T".

So now you know what pharmacy technicians do and where they work. You know how to apply to become certified and what is required for certification. This book will help you prepare for the exam by breaking down the contents of each domain throughout the next four chapters. You will be able to study the material and then test your skills through practice questions and exams.

Let's get started in preparing for the PTCE!

CHAPTER 2

Medications

PTCE Knowledge Domain: Medications   40% of Exam

Knowledge Areas:

- Generic names, brand names, and classifications of medications

- Therapeutic equivalence

- Common and life-threatening drug interactions and contraindications (e.g., drug–disease, drug–drug, drug–dietary supplement, drug–laboratory, drug–nutrient)

- Strengths/dose, dosage forms, routes of administration, special handling and administration instructions, and duration of drug therapy

- Common and severe medication side effects, adverse effects, and allergies

- Indications of medications and dietary supplements

- Drug stability (e.g., oral suspensions, insulin, reconstitutables, injectables, vaccinations)

- Narrow therapeutic index (NTI) medications

- Physical and chemical incompatibilities related to nonsterile compounding and reconstitution

- Proper storage of medications (e.g., temperature ranges, light sensitivity, restricted access)

After reading Chapter 2 you will be able to:

- Recognize pharmacology principles, including absorption, distribution, metabolism, and elimination

- Identify the brand and generic names and drug class for the top 200 drugs

- Understand drug interactions and the impact on patient safety

- Describe dosage forms and routes of administration, and drug stability

- Recognize medication that have a narrow therapeutic index (NTI)

- Understand the proper storage of medications, including temperature ranges, light-sensitivity requirements, and restricted access

In this chapter, we review the brand and generic names and drug classifications of the top 200 prescribed medications. We also review side effects and indications of these drugs. This chapter also reviews drug interactions and stability as well as dosage forms and routes of administration. It is important to start with some basic pharmacology principles. This will help you understand drug interactions, side effects, and stability of medications later on in the chapter.

Pharmacology is the study of the effect of and mechanism of action of drugs. There are two divisions of pharmacology, known as **pharmacokinetics** and **pharmacodynamics**. Pharmacokinetics is the study of movement of drugs, or specifically, the absorption, distribution, metabolism, and elimination or excretion processes. Absorption, distribution, metabolism, and elimination/excretion are collectively known as ADME. Pharmacodynamics is study of the effect a drug has on the body.

Let's review the ADME processes more in depth:

A	**Absorption**	Process of the drug entering the bloodstream and circulation
D	**Distribution**	Dispersion of a drug to cells and tissue in the body
M	**Metabolism**	Breakdown of the drug into smaller components that can be excreted
E	**Elimination**	Removal of the metabolized drug from the body

Absorption and **distribution** are the ways into the body, whereas **metabolism** and **elimination** are the ways out. Recognizing the ADME properties will help you understand drug action, such as why a medication administered intravenously works more quickly than a drug taken by mouth—the faster the drug can enter the bloodstream (absorption) and be distributed, the quicker the onset of action. It will also help you understand drug interactions and how impacting metabolism can lead to adverse effects and toxicity.

Generic Names, Brand Names, and Classifications of Medications

After a drug is approved by the FDA, it possesses three naming conventions: chemical, generic, and brand names.

DRUG NAME	DESCRIPTION	EXAMPLE
Chemical name	Complex name derived from molecular structure of drug	(RS)-2-[4-(2-methylpropyl) phenyl] propanoic acid
Generic name	Assigned by the US Adopted Name Council (USAN)	Ibuprofen
Brand name	Given by drug company and protected by a patent, may also be known as trade name	Advil®

The **chemical name** is determined while the drug is being designed and investigated. The drug is then assigned a **generic name** by USAN by following a naming convention that identifies the active ingredient in the drug. This naming convention specifies the drug class. A drug class is a group of drugs that are similar in action or treat the same disease. For example, ACE inhibitors used to treat blood pressure all end in *-pril* (lisinopril, quinapril, enalapril).

The following are a few examples of drug classes identified through the drug stem named by USAN. As we review the top 200 drugs, these are identified with each class.

DRUG STEM	CLASS	EXAMPLE
-azepam	Benzodiazepine (antianxiety)	alprazolam (Xanax)
-caine	Local anesthetic	lidocaine (Xylocaine)
cef-	Cephalosporin (antibiotic)	cefdinir (Omnicef)
-cillin	Penicillins (antibiotic)	amoxicillin (Amoxil)
-olol	Beta blocker	propranolol (Inderal LA)
-oxacin	Antibiotic (fluoroquinolone)	levofloxacin (Levaquin)
-prazole	Antiulcer	pantoprazole (Protonix)
-pril	ACE inhibitor	lisinopril (Prinivil)
-sartan	ARB (angiotensin II receptor blocker)	olmesartan (Benicar)
-statin	Antihyperlipidemic (HMG-CoA reductase inhibitors)	simvastatin (Zocor)
-vir	Antiviral	oseltamivir (Tamiflu)

After the generic name is selected, the drug company can give the drug a brand or trade name. The **brand name** does not need to follow a naming convention and is often designed to be appealing to patients or help them remember what the drug is treating. For example, the brand name Lipitor is used to treat high cholesterol or "lipids" in the body. This can help both prescribers and patients remember names.

Once a brand name is developed, it is protected by a patent for a specific period of time. The purpose in a drug patent is to allow the drug company to sell the drug without a generic competitor. This helps the drug company recover some of the costs of drug development. After a patent has expired, other manufacturers are permitted to develop a generic version of the brand name drug. The FDA must also approve generic drugs, but it is through an accelerated process and takes less time and resources to complete, which allows generic drugs to be sold at a cheaper price. Generic drugs must have the same active ingredient and meet the same standards for quality and safety as the brand name drug. Generic drugs are permitted to have different inactive ingredients, and for patients who are sensitive to dyes and fillers, this may result in different side effects of generic medications versus the brand name.

Top 200 Drug Generic and Brand Names and Drug Class

Learning the top 200 most frequently prescribed drugs is an important component of the PTCE and also for becoming a successful pharmacy technician. You'll find the following table to be helpful for learning and remembering generic and brand names, as well as the drug class for each of the most commonly prescribed drugs. Remember that the top 200 drugs is subject to change each year with the changes in prescribing and new drug development, but this will make you knowledgeable about the 200 most frequently prescribed drugs.

Top 200 Most Frequently Prescribed Drugs		
GENERIC NAME	**BRAND NAME**	**DRUG CLASS**
lisinopril	Zestril, Prinivil	Antihypertensive—ACE inhibitor
atorvastatin	Lipitor	Antihyperlipidemic—HMG-CoA reductase inhibitor
levothyroxine	Synthroid, Levoxyl, Levothroid	Thyroid hormone
metformin	Glucophage	Antidiabetic—biguanide
amlodipine	Norvasc	Antihypertensive—calcium channel blocker
metoprolol tartrate	Lopressor	Antihypertensive—beta blocker
omeprazole	Prilosec	Antiulcer agent—proton pump inhibitor
simvastatin	Zocor	Antihyperlipidemic—HMG-CoA reductase inhibitor
losartan potassium	Cozaar	Antihypertensive—angiotensin II receptor blocker (ARB)
albuterol	Proventil	Bronchodilator
gabapentin	Neurontin	Anticonvulsant
hydrochlorothiazide	Microzide	Diuretic—thiazide
hydrocodone with acetaminophen	Norco	Narcotic analgesic
sertraline	Zoloft	Antidepressant—selective serotonin reuptake inhibitor (SSRI)
fluticasone	Flonase	Corticosteroid
montelukast	Singulair	Leukotriene inhibitor
furosemide	Lasix	Diuretic—loop

Top 200 Most Frequently Prescribed Drugs *(continued)*

GENERIC NAME	BRAND NAME	DRUG CLASS
amoxicillin	Amoxil	Antibiotic—penicillin
pantoprazole	Protonix	Antiulcer agent—proton pump inhibitor
escitalopram	Lexapro	Antidepressant—selective serotonin reuptake inhibitor (SSRI)
alprazolam	Xanax	Antianxiety—benzodiazepine
prednisone	Deltasone	Oral corticosteroid
buproprion	Wellbutrin	Antidepressant
pravastatin	Pravachol	Antihyperlipidemic—HMG-CoA reductase inhibitor
acetaminophen	Tylenol	Analgesic
citalopram	Celexa	Antidepressants—selective serotonin reuptake inhibitor (SSRI)
dextroamphetamine/ amphetamine	Adderall	Stimulant
ibuprofen	Motrin	Non-steroidal anti-inflammatory drug (NSAID)
carvedilol	Coreg	Antihypertensive—beta blocker
trazodone	Desyrel	Antidepressant
fluoxetine	Prozac	Antidepressant—selective serotonin reuptake inhibitor (SSRI)
tramadol	Ultram	Narcotic analgesic
insulin glargine	Lantus	Insulin
clonazepam	Klonopin	Antianxiety—benzodiazepine
tamsulosin	Flomax	Alpha blocker
atenolol	Tenormin	Antihypertensive—beta blocker
potassium	Klor-Con, K-Dur	Mineral and electrolyte replacement
meloxicam	Mobic	Non-steroidal anti-inflammatory drug (NSAID)
rosuvastatin	Crestor	Antihyperlipidemic—HMG-CoA reductase inhibitor
clopidogrel	Plavix	Antiplatelet
propranolol	Inderal	Antihypertensive—beta blocker
aspirin	Ecotrin	Antipyretic, analgesic
cyclobenzaprine	Flexeril	Muscle relaxant
lisinopril with hydrochlorothiazide	Prinzide, Zestoretic	Antihypertensive—combination agent
glipizide	Glucotrol	Antidiabetic—sulfonyurea
duloxetine	Cymbalta	Antidepressant—serotonin and norepinephrine reuptake inhibitor (SNRI)
methylphenidate	Ritalin	Stimulant
ranitidine	Zantac	Antiulcer agent—histamine (H2) antagonists
venlafaxine	Effexor	Antidepressant—serotonin and norepinephrine reuptake inhibitor (SNRI)

(continued)

Top 200 Most Frequently Prescribed Drugs (continued)

GENERIC NAME	BRAND NAME	DRUG CLASS
zolpidem	Ambien	Hypnotic
warfarin	Coumadin	Anticoagulant
oxycodone	Oxycontin	Narcotic analgesic
ethinyl estradiol, norethindrone	Junel, Lo-Estrin	Oral contraceptive
allopurinol	Zyloprim	Antigout
ergocalciferol	Drisdol	Vitamin D_2 analogs
insulin aspart	Novolog	Insulin
azithromycin	Zithromax	Antibiotic—macrolide
metronidazole	Flagyl	Antibiotic
loratadine	Claritin	Antihistamine
lorazepam	Ativan	Antianxiety—benzodiazepine
estradiol	Climara, Estrace	Hormone—estrogen
ethinyl estradiol, norgestimate	Ortho Tri-Cyclen	Oral contraceptive
lamotrigine	Lamictal	Anticonvulsant
glimeperide	Amaryl	Antidiabetic—sulfonyurea
fluticasone propionate/salmeterol	Advair	Combination corticosteroid and beta agonist
cetirizine	Zyrtec	Antihistamine
losartan with hydrochlorothiazide	Hyzaar	Antihypertensive—combination agent
paroxetine	Paxil	Antidepressant—selective serotonin reuptake inhibitor (SSRI)
spironolactone	Aldactone	Diuretic—potassium sparing
fenofibrate	Tricor	Antihyperlipidemic—fibric acid derivative
naproxen	Aleve, Naprosyn	Non-steroidal anti-inflammatory drug (NSAID)
pregabalin	Lyrica	Anticonvuslant
insulin human	Regular Insulin	Insulin
budesonide, formoterol	Symbicort	Combination corticosteroid and beta agonist
diltiazem	Cardizem	Antihypertensive—calcium channel blocker
quetiapine	Seroquel	Antipsychotic
topiramate	Topamax	Anticonvulsant
bacitracin, neomycin, polymixin B	Neosporin	Topical antibiotic
clonidine	Catapres	Antihypertensive—alpha agonist
buspirone	Buspar	Antianxiety agent

Top 200 Most Frequently Prescribed Drugs *(continued)*

GENERIC NAME	BRAND NAME	DRUG CLASS
latanoprost	Xalatan	Glaucoma agent
tiotropium	Spiriva	Bronchodilator
ondansetron	Zofran	Antiemetic
lovastatin	Mevacor	Antihyperlipidemic—HMG-CoA reductase inhibitor
valsartan	Diovan	Antihypertensive—angiotensin II receptor blocker (ARB)
finasteride	Proscar	5-alpha reductase inhibitor
amitriptyline	Elavil	Antidepressant—tricyclic
esomeprazole	Nexium	Antiulcer agent—proton pump inhibitor
tizanidine	Zanaflex	Muscle relaxant
alendronate	Fosamax	Bisphosphonate
lisdexamfetamine dimesylate	Vyvanse	Stimulant
ferrous sulfate	Feosol	Iron supplement
apixaban	Eliquis	Direct oral anticoagulants (DOAC)
diclofenac	Voltaren	Non-steroidal anti-inflammatory drug (NSAID)
sitagliptin	Januvia	Antidiabetic—DPP-4 inhibitor
folic acid	Folvite	Vitamin supplement
sumatriptan	Imitrex	Serotonin receptor agonists (Triptan)
ethinyl estradiol, drospirenone	Yasmin, Yaz	Oral contraceptive
hydroxyzine	Vistaril, Atarax	Antihistamine
oxybutynin	Ditropan	Overactive bladder agent
triamterene with hydrochlorothiazide	Maxzide, Dyazide	Antihypertensive—combination agent
cephalexin	Keflex	Antibiotic—cephalosporin
triamcinolone	Aristocort, Kenalog, Nasacort	Corticosteroid
benazepril	Lotensin	Antihypertensive—ACE inhibitor
hydralazine	Apresoline	Vasodilator
celecoxib	Celebrex	Cyclooxygenase-2 (COX-2) inhibitors
ciprofloxacin	Cipro	Antibiotic—fluoroquinolone
ropinirole	Requip	Antiparkinson agents
rivaroxaban	Xarelto	Direct oral anticoagulants (DOAC)
levetiracetam	Keppra	Anticonvulsant
isosorbide mononitrate	Imdur	Nitrates
aripiprazole	Abilify	Antipsychotic

(continued)

Top 200 Most Frequently Prescribed Drugs (continued)

GENERIC NAME	BRAND NAME	DRUG CLASS
doxycycline	Vibramycin	Antibiotic—tetracycline
insulin detemir	Levemir	Insulin
famotidine	Pepcid	Antiulcer agent—histamine (H2) antagonists
amoxicillin with clavulanate	Augmentin	Antibiotic—penicillin
methotrexate	Trexall	Antirheumatic agent
hydrocodone bitartrate	Hysingla	Narcotic analgesic
mirtazapine	Remeron	Antidepressant
nifedipine	Procardia XL	Antihypertensive—calcium channel blocker
sulfamethoxazole with trimethoprim	Bactrim	Antibacteria —sulfonamide
enalapril	Vasotec	Antihypertensive —ACE inhibitor
docusate	Colace	Stool softener
insulin lispro	Humalog	Insulin
pioglitazone	Actos	Antidiabetic—glitazones
divalproex	Depakote	Anticonvulsant
donepezil	Aricept	Anti-alzheimer agent
hydroxychloroquine	Plaquenil	Antirheumatic agent, antimalarial
prednisolone	Orapred	Oral corticosteroid
thyroid	Armour Thyroid	Thyroid hormone
guanfacine	Intuniv	Stimulant
testosterone	Depo-Testosterone, AndroGel	Hormone testosterone
valsartan with hydrochlorothiazide	Diovan HCT	Antihypertensive—combination agent
ramipril	Altace	Antihypertensive—ACE Inhibitor
diazepam	Valium	Antianxiety—benzodiazepine
ethinyl estradiol, levonorgestral	Alesse, Aviane, Tri-Levlen, Seasonique	Oral contraceptive
clindamycin	Cleocin	Antibiotic
gemfibrozil	Lopid	Antihyperlipidemic—fibric acid derivative
metformin with sitagliptin	Janumet	Antidiabetic—combination agent
baclofen	Lioresal	Muscle relaxant
norethindrone	Camila, Errin, Heather	Progestins, oral contraceptive
temazepam	Restoril	Benzodiazepine
nitroglycerin	Nitroquick	Nitrate

Top 200 Most Frequently Prescribed Drugs (continued)

GENERIC NAME	BRAND NAME	DRUG CLASS
nebivolol	Bystolic	Antihypertensive—beta blocker
verapamil	Calan, Isoptin	Antihypertensive—calcium channel blocker
timolol	Timoptic	Ophthalmic beta blocker (glaucoma agent)
promethazine	Phenergan	Antiemetic
benzonatate	Tessalon	Antitussive
memantine	Namenda	Alzheimer's disease agent
doxazosin	Cardura	Alpha blocker
ezetimibe	Zetia	Cholesterol absorption inhibitor
valacyclovir	Valtrex	Antiviral
beclometasone	Qvar	Corticosteroid
hydrocortisone	Cortaid, Cortizone	Topical corticosteroid
morphine	MS Contin, Roxanol	Narcotic analgesic
risperidone	Risperdal	Antipsychotic
methylprednisolone	Medrol	Oral corticosteroid
omega-3-acid ethyl esters	Lovaza	Lipid regulating drug
oseltamivir phosphate	Tamiflu	Antiviral
amlodipine with benazepril	Lotrel	Antihypertensive—combination agent
meclizine	Antivert	Antiemetic
polyethylene glycol 3350	GoLytely, Miralax	Laxative
liraglutide	Victoza	Antidiabetic—GLP-1 agonist
desogestrel, ethinyl estradiol	Apri, Mircette	Oral contraceptive
levofloxacin	Levaquin	Antibiotic—fluoroquinolone
acyclovir	Zovirax	Antiviral
brimonidine	Alphagan	Glaucoma agent
digoxin	Digitek	Antiarrhythmic
adalimumab	Humira	Monoclonal antibody
cyanocobalamin	Vitamin B12	Vitamin supplement
magnesium	Uromag	Magnesium supplement
albuterol sulfate with ipratropium bromide	Combivent, Duoneb	Combination bronchodilator
chlorthalidone	Thalitone	Diuretic—thiazide
glyburide	Diabeta, Micronase	Antidiabetic—sulfonylurea
levocetirizine	Xyzal	Antihistamine

(continued)

Top 200 Most Frequently Prescribed Drugs (continued)

GENERIC NAME	BRAND NAME	DRUG CLASS
carbamazepine	Tegretol	Anticonvulsant
ethinyl estradiol, etonogestrel	Nuvaring	Contraceptive
methocarbamol	Robaxin	Muscle relaxant
pramipexole dihydrochloride	Mirapex	Dopamine agonist
lithium	Lithobid, Eskalith	Bipolar disorder agent
dicyclomine	Bentyl	Antispasmodic
fluconazole	Diflucan	Antifungal
nortriptyline	Pamelor	Antidepressant—tricyclic
carbidopa/levodopa	Sinemet	Antiparkinson agents
nitrofurantoin	Macrobid	Antibiotic
mupirocin	Bactroban	Topical antibiotic
acetaminophen, butalbital, caffeine	Fioricet	Barbituate
lansoprazole	Prevacid	Antiulcer agent—proton pump inhibitor
dexmethylphenidate	Focalin XR	Stimulant
budesonide	Pulmicort	Corticosteroid
mirabegron	Myrbetriq	Overactive bladder agent
canagliflozin	Invokana	Antidiabetic—SGLT-2 inhibitor
menthol	Bengay, Icyhot	Topical analgesic
terazosin	Hytrin	Alpha blocker
progesterone	Prometrium	Hormone—progesterone
amiodarone	Cordarone	Antiarrhythmic
mometasone	Nasonex	Nasal corticosteroid
cefdinir	Omnicef	Antibiotic—cephalosporin
atomoxetine	Strattera	Selective norepinephrine reuptake inhibitor
linagliptin	Tradjenta	Antidiabetic—DPP-4 inhibitor

Use this top 200 drug list to quiz yourself on brands, generics, and drug classes for the PTCE!

Dosage Forms and Routes of Administration

Dosage forms are broken down into solid, liquid, and semisolid forms. Solid dosage forms include tablets and capsules. Both are convenient methods of administration and storage for patients. However, the onset of action can be delayed when taking oral tablets due to the first pass through the stomach. When medications are taken orally, absorption does not occur until the small intestine. To help speed up the absorption time, tablets have been modified into different forms, listed as follows.

Tablet Type	
Buccal	Administered between gum and cheek to dissolve and absorb into blood vessels in the mouth
Chewable	Chewed and not swallowed and absorbed through lining of the mouth
Effervescent	Dissolves in water and reacts to give off carbon dioxide, which causes a fizz
Enteric-coated	Coated tablet designed to prevent breakdown in the stomach so it can be absorbed in the intestine; cannot be crushed or chewed
Film-coated	Coated tablet that is designed to mask a foul taste of a tablet
Orally disintegrating tablet (ODT)	Dissolves on tongue and is absorbed through blood vessels in the tongue
Sublingual	Placed under tongue to dissolve and is absorbed through blood vessels under the tongue

Capsules are also frequently used for oral administration. They are made of a gelatin shell that makes it easier to swallow. Inside of the shell is the drug or active ingredient. You can open the capsule, and some can be sprinkled onto food or dissolved in a liquid.

There are also dosage forms that are not designed to release the drug immediately. These dosage forms can sometimes decrease the amount of doses needed in one day. You will often see these abbreviated after the medication name. For example, Ambien CR has a different release mechanism than Ambien, which is designed to both help initiate sleep and sustain sleep.

DRUG ABBREVIATION	TYPE OF MODIFIED RELEASE
CD	Controlled delivery
CR	Controlled release
DR	Delayed release
ER	Extended release
LA	Long acting
SR	Sustained release
TR	Timed release
XL, XR	Extended release

Lozenges or troches are another type of solid dosage form that are sweetened or flavored to help medication slowly dissolve locally to the throat or mouth. Additional solid dosage forms include powders, such as those ground for topical treatment or aerosol. Patches are also considered a solid dosage form and are applied transdermally to the skin, which allows the medication to absorb directly into the bloodstream.

Liquid dosage forms can be administered orally but can also be used topically for cleansing or irrigation.

Liquid Dosage Forms	
Irrigation	Continuous flow of solution used to wash wounds, bladder, or eyes
Enema	Solution injected into the rectum typically used for bowel cleansing or to deliver specific medication
Solution	Liquid in which drug is completely dissolved
Syrup	Thick liquid sweetened with sugar
Elixir	Sweetened liquid and sometimes contains alcohol
Suspension	A mixture in which the drug does not fully dissolve in liquid and must be shaken well before administration

Semisolid dosage forms are those that are not fully solid or liquid. These are mostly administered topically.

Semisolid Dosage Forms	
Cream	Emulsion of oil and water, which tends to be less greasy than ointment
Gel	Jelly-like substance that is neither a liquid nor a solid
Lotion	Thinnest composition of all semisolid forms and is administered topically
Ointment	Protects the skin as a barrier to liquid and has a greasy texture
Suppository	Solid at room temperature and designed to melt at body temperature after insertion

Routes of Administration

Most medications are given via one of three routes of administration: oral, parenteral, or topical.

Oral Routes

Oral routes of administration include any dose given by mouth (PO). This is the most commonly prescribed route for prescriptions, as it is most convenient for patients. If a more rapid route is needed, medications can be given via the buccal route (dissolved in the cheek) or sublingual route (dissolved under the tongue).

Parenteral Routes

Any route that is parenteral bypasses the intestines and goes directly into the bloodstream. Though the onset of action is quicker with parenteral routes, injections are more painful and can be a source of infection.

Parenteral Routes of Administration	
IA	Intrarterial → injected into the artery
ID	Intradermal → injected into the top layer of the skin; often used for skin testing, such as TB tests
IM	Intramuscular → injected into the muscle; most vaccines administered IM
IV	Intravenous → injected into the vein
Intra-articular	Injected into a joint
Intrathecal	Injected into the spinal column
Subcut	Subcutaneous → injected directly under the skin, such as insulin

Medications given IV can be administered in different ways depending on the drug, infusion time, and volume to be infused.

IV Infusion	
IV bolus	Drug administered over a quick period, often to bring a patient's blood concentration to a therapeutic level quickly (loading dose)
IV push	Syringe of medication that is pushed into the IV line
IV piggyback (IVPB)	Smaller volume of fluid administered IV, typically less than 250mL
Continuous infusion	Larger volume parenteral (LVP), infusion over 250mL, which is typically administered over a longer period of time

Topical Routes

A medication administered topically is applied to a mucous membrane, such as the eye or ear, or to the skin. Topical routes also include into the nose, rectally, or vaginally.

Topical Routes of Administration	
Nasal	Administered through the nostril such as an allergy spray
Nebulized	Using a machine to help administer medication into the lungs by creating a mist to inhale
Otic	Administered into the ear
Ophthalmic	Administered into the eye
Rectal	Inserted into the rectum, such as a suppository or enema
Vaginally	Inserted into the vagina, such as a suppository or irrigation

The strength of a medication is the amount of **active ingredient** within the drug and dosage form. This is typically expressed in terms of mcg, mg, or g for solids, and mg/mL for liquids. Many drugs are available in more than one strength and dosage form. For example, acetaminophen is available as 325mg and 500mg tablets, 1,000mg/100mL IV solution, and 160mg/5mL oral suspension.

The duration of drug therapy is the amount of time a patient needs to take the drug for the entire treatment. **Chronic** conditions are those in which an illness persists for a long time, such as months, years, or even the rest of your life, such as diabetes or hypertension. **Acute** conditions are those with a rapid onset and resolves quickly, such as a cold or viral infection. **Compliance** can also be a factor in the duration of drug therapy. If a patient does not follow their course of treatment, the disease may persist longer than expected.

The **indication** of a drug is the use of a drug in treating a disease. For example, the indication for paroxetine (Paxil) is depression. Use of a medication for diseases or treatment outside of their FDA-approved indication is considered "off-label" use. The next section gives a brief review of the body system for each drug system. It also highlights indications for the top 200 medications and special dosing and administration considerations, side effects, dosages, contraindications, and interactions.

Cardiovascular System and Drugs

The cardiovascular system includes the heart and blood vessels networked through the body. The heart pumps nutrient-rich, oxygenated blood through the arteries and the veins carry deoxygenated blood back to the heart. Capillaries are the small vessels where the exchange of gases (oxygen and carbon dioxide) occurs between arteries and veins.

The heart has two chambers on the top (atria) and two chambers on the bottom (ventricles). These chambers are separated by valves, which open and close to allow blood to flow in the right direction. The left ventricle is the largest chamber and pumps blood through the aorta to the rest of the body. The right ventricle pumps blood through the right atrium to the lungs to become oxygenated. This blood then returns back through the left atrium and into the left ventricle to continue the circulation. This beating of the heart is controlled through an electrical conduction system. Heartbeats are recorded through EKG or ECG (electrocardiogram) and can identify abnormal rhythms.

When the heart is pumping, there is pressure created by the force of the blood pushing against the blood vessels. There are two values to this pressure: systolic pressure, which is the pressure when the heart is pumping, and diastolic pressure, or the pressure when the heart is relaxed. A normal blood pressure is 120/80 mm Hg, with the systolic reading being the top value and the diastolic the lower value.

There are many disorders of the heart that can be treated with medication. It is helpful to have an understanding of cardiovascular diseases when studying medications for treatment. A description of cardiac-related disorders follows.

Disorders of the Cardiovascular System	
Angina	Lack of oxygen that causes chest pain
Arrhythmia	Abnormal rhythm of the heart
Atrial fibrillation (AFib)	Irregular, rapid heartbeat
Atherosclerosis	Buildup of plaque and cholesterol that causes hardening of the arteries
Blood clots	Moving clot (embolus) or stationary clot (thrombosis) in a blood vessel
Congestive heart failure (CHF)	Accumulation of fluid in the body, resulting from the inability of the heart to pump sufficiently
Hypertension	High blood pressure
Hyperlipidemia	High cholesterol
Myocardial infarction (MI)	Lack of oxygen and blood leading to a heart attack
Pulmonary embolism (PE)	Moving clot that travels to the lungs
Venous thromboembolism (VTE)	Blood clot in the deep veins, usually legs, that may travel to the lungs and cause a PE

The following are the drug classes that are reviewed individually for treatment of cardiovascular diseases. Many of these classes are affiliated with a USAN drug stem that is helpful when remembering what class each drug belongs to.

CARDIAC DRUG CLASS	STEM	TOP 200 DRUG EXAMPLES
ACE inhibitor	*-pril*	lisinopril, benazepril, ramipril, enalapril
Alpha agonist		clonidine
Alpha blocker	*-azosin*	doxazosin, terazosin
Angiotensin II receptor antagonists (ARBs)	*-sartan*	losartan, valsartan
Antiarrhythmic		amiodarone, digoxen
Anticoagulant		warfarin
Anticoagulant—direct oral anticoagulants	*-xaban*	apixaban, rivaroxaban
Platelet inhibitor	*-grel*	clopidogrel
Beta blocker	*-olol*	atenolol, carvedilol, metoprolol, nebivolol, propranolol
Calcium channel blocker		amlodipine, diltiazem, nifedipine, verapamil
Cholesterol absorption inhibitor	*-imibe*	ezetimibe

(continued)

CARDIAC DRUG CLASS	STEM	TOP 200 DRUG EXAMPLES
Diuretic		hydrochlorothiazide, furosemide, spironolactone, chlorthalidone
Fibric acid derivative	-fibrate	fenofibrate, gemfibrozil
Lipid regulating agent		omega-3-acid ethyl esters
Antihyperlipidemics (HMG-CoA reductase inhibitors)	-statin	atorvastatin, simvastatin, lovastatin, pravastatin, rosuvastatin
Nitrates		isosorbide mononitrate, nitroglycerin
Vasodilator		hydralazine

These drug classes to treat disorders of the cardiovascular system are reviewed to include the following:

- Mechanism of action
- Side effects
- Special handling and administration instructions
- Drug interactions
- Indications
- Dosage form
- Dosage and duration of therapy

Angiotensin-Converting Enzyme (ACE) Inhibitor	
Mechanism of action	Inhibit ACE, which prevents the conversion of angiotensin I to angiotensin II; this results in vasodilation (expansion of blood vessel to allow blood to flow more easily)
Side effects	Dry cough, hypotension, headache, dizziness
Special instructions	Must not be taken during pregnancy, may cause fetal mortality
Drug interactions	Potassium supplements (may induce hyperkalemia), NSAIDs (reduce effectiveness of ACE inhibitor)

GENERIC NAME	INDICATION	DOSAGE FORM	DOSAGE
benazepril	Hypertension	Tablet	5mg–40mg PO QD
enalapril	Hypertension, congestive heart failure (CHF)	Tablet and injection	2.5mg–20mg PO QD, 1.25mg IV
lisinopril	Hypertension, CHF (as adjunct)	Tablet, given in one daily dose	2.5mg–40mg PO QD
ramipril	Hypertension, CHF	Tablet and capsule	1.25mg–10mg PO QD/ BID

Alpha Agonists

Mechanism of action	Stimulate alpha receptors in the brain, which results in lowered blood pressure and heart rate
Side effects	Dry mouth, dizziness, headache, fatigue, impotence
Special instructions	Dose must be tapered to avoid withdrawal (do not stop abruptly)
Drug interactions	Tricyclic antidepressants

GENERIC NAME	INDICATION	DOSAGE FORM	DOSAGE
clonidine	Hypertension and hypertensive emergencies	Tablet Transdermal patches	0.1mg–0.3mg PO BID 0.1mg/24hr transdermally to 0.3mg/24hr transdermally Q7D

Alpha Blockers

Mechanism of action	Block alpha receptors in the sympathetic nervous system, which prevents norepinephrine from causing vessel contraction and keeps vessels opened and relaxed
Side effects	Dizziness, headache, fatigue
Special instructions	Take first dose at bedtime to avoid dizziness from standing; do not take with liver impairment
Drug interactions	Other hypertensive agents (increased hypotensive effect)

GENERIC NAME	INDICATION	DOSAGE FORM	DOSAGE
doxazosin	Hypertension, benign prostatic hyperplasia	Tablet and XL (ER)	1mg–8mg PO QD 4mg and 8mg XL PO QD
terazosin	Hypertension, benign prostatic hyperplasia	Capsules	1mg–5mg PO QHS

Angiotensin II Receptor Antagonists (ARBs)

Mechanism of action	Block angiotensin II receptors, which prevents vasoconstriction
Side effects	Dizziness, headache
Special instructions	Do not take if pregnant
Drug interactions	NSAIDs and COX-2 inhibitors (celecoxib)

GENERIC NAME	INDICATION	DOSAGE FORM	DOSAGE
losartan	Hypertension, diabetic nephropathy	Tablet	50mg–100mg PO QD
valsartan	Hypertension, CHF, reduce morbidity following myocardial infarction (MI)	Tablet	80mg–320mg PO QD

Antiarrhythmic Agents

Mechanism of action	Modify electrical conduction and force of contraction in heart muscle
Side effects	Cardiogenic shock, cardiac arrest, CHF, nausea, vomiting, blurred vision
Special instructions	Do not take OTC cough and cold medication, laxatives, or antidiarrheals before consulting physician, do not take if pregnant
Drug interactions	Warfarin, grapefruit juice, Saint John's wort

GENERIC NAME	INDICATION	DOSAGE FORM	DOSAGE
amiodarone	Ventricular fibrillation, unstable tachycardia	Tablet Injection	400mg PO QD 150mg infused over 10 minutes, then slow infusion of 360mg over 6 hours
digoxen	CHF, atrial fibrillation, atrial flutter	Tablet Capsule Injection	0.125mg–5mg PO QD 0.1mg/mL–0.25mg/mL

Antiarrhythmic Agents

Mechanism of action	Modify electrical conduction and force of contraction in heart muscle
Side effects	Cardiogenic shock, cardiac arrest, CHF, nausea, vomiting, blurred vision
Special instructions	Do not take OTC cough and cold medication, laxatives, or antidiarrheals before consulting physician; do not take if pregnant
Drug interactions	Warfarin, grapefruit juice, Saint John's wort

GENERIC NAME	INDICATION	DOSAGE FORM	DOSAGE
warfarin	Adjunct to reduce risk of systemic embolism after MI, prophylaxis and treatment of thromboembolic disorders, and complications arising from atrial fibrillation or valve replacement	Tablets	2mg–10mg PO QD or in two divided doses

Anticoagulants—Direct Oral Anticoagulants (DOAC)

Mechanism of action	Inhibit factor Xa in the clotting cascade
Side effects	Bleeding, thrombocytopenia
Special instructions	Can be taken without regard to meals
Drug interactions	Saint John's wort, NSAIDs

GENERIC NAME	INDICATION	DOSAGE FORM	DOSAGE
apixaban	Deep vein thrombosis (DVT), nonvalvular atrial fibrillation, prophylaxis of DVT, treatment of pulmonary embolism (PE)	Tablets	2.5mg–5mg PO BID
rivaroxaban	DVT, nonvalvular atrial fibrillation, prophylaxis of DVT, treatment of PE	Tablets	15mg–20mg PO QD with meals

Platelet Inhibitors

Mechanism of action	Bind to and modify platelet receptors, which inhibits platelet aggregation
Side effects	Upper respiratory infection, chest pain, headache, flu-like symptoms, dizziness, back pain, abdominal pain
Special instructions	Can be taken with or without meals; must alert provider before elective surgery; contraindicated with liver failure, pregnancy, and active bleeding
Drug interactions	NSAIDs, may interfere with metabolism of phenytoin and warfarin

GENERIC NAME	INDICATION	DOSAGE FORM	DOSAGE
clopidogrel	Reduction of atherosclerotic events (MI, stroke)	Tablets	75mg PO QD

Beta Blockers	
Mechanism of action	Block beta-1 receptors, which decreases heart rate and cardiac output
Side effects	Dizziness, fatigue, drowsiness, bradycardia, and hypotension
Special instructions	Should not be taken by patients with asthma; for patients with diabetes—may mask symptoms of hypoglycemia; avoid abrupt withdrawal
Drug interactions	Clonidine, NSAIDs, verapamil

GENERIC NAME	INDICATION	DOSAGE FORM	DOSAGE
atenolol	Hypertension, acute MI, renal impairment	Tablet Injection	50mg–100mg PO QD 5mg/10mL infusion over 5 minutes
carvedilol	Hypertension, CHF, left ventricular dysfunction	Tablet Capsule	12.5mg PO BID, may increase to 25mg
metoprolol	Hypertension, angina, CHF	Tablet Injection	(Succinate) 25mg–100mg PO QD (up to 400mg/day) (Tartrate) 100mg PO QD (up to 450mg per day) (Tartrate) 25mg–50mg IV Q6H
nebivolol	Hypertension	Tablet	1.25mg–2.5mg PO QD up to 10mg/day
propranolol	Hypertension, arrhythmia, angina, migraines, MI	Tablets Capsules (SR) Injection Oral Solution	80mg to 640mg per day in divided doses

Calcium Channel Blockers	
Mechanism of action	Inhibit calcium movement, which reduces electrical conduction of the heart, causing relaxation of muscles and less effort to pump the heart
Side effects	Edema, flushing, headache, fatigue
Special instructions	OTC cough and cold medications should not be taken before consulting prescriber
Drug interactions	Carbamazepine, simvastatin, atorvastatin, pravastatin

GENERIC NAME	INDICATION	DOSAGE FORM	DOSAGE
amlodipine	Hypertension, angina	Tablet	2.5mg–5mg PO QD, may increase to 10mg PO QD
diltiazem	Hypertension, angina, atrial fibrillation	Tablet 12-hr capsules (SR) 24-hr capsules (CD) and tablets (LA) Injection	120mg–240mg PO QD/BID, may increase to 360mg/day 10mg/hr to 15mg/hr IV continuous infusion
nifedipine	Hypertension, angina	Capsules SR tablets	30mg–90mg PO QD
verapamil	Hypertension, angina, tachyarrhythmia	Tablets Tablets (SR) Capsules (SR) Capsules (DR) Injection	80mg PO Q6–8hr, may increase to total of 480mg per day in divided doses

Cholesterol Absorption Inhibitors	
Mechanism of action	Inhibit the absorption of cholesterol at the small intestine, which decreases amount of cholesterol circling in the bloodstream and delivered to the liver
Side effects	Myalgia, abnormality in liver enzymes
Special instructions	Do not take concurrently with a statin for patients who have liver disease; do not take if you are pregnant or nursing
Drug interactions	Gemfibrozil and fenofibrate

GENERIC NAME	INDICATION	DOSAGE FORM	DOSAGE
ezetimibe	Adjunctive therapy with diet for reduction of total cholesterol	Tablet	10mg PO QD

Diuretics	
Mechanism of action	Increase excretion of water
Side effects	Increased urination, dizziness, thirst, muscle cramps
Special instructions	Should be taken in the morning to avoid frequent urination at bedtime
Drug interactions	ACE inhibitors (with potassium-sparing diuretics), digoxin (thiazide and loop diuretics)

GENERIC NAME	INDICATION	DOSAGE FORM	DOSAGE
chlorthalidone	Edema associated with CHF, hypertension	Tablet	25mg–100mg PO QD
furosemide	Edema associated with CHF, hypertension	Tablets Oral solution Injection	20mg–80mg PO QD 20mg–50mg IM/IV over 2 minutes
hydrochlorothiazide	Edema associated with CHF, hypertension	Capsules Tablets	25mg–100mg PO QD
spironolactone	Edema associated with CHF, hypertension, hypokalemia, hyperaldosteronism	Tablets	100mg PO QD, may increase to 200mg PO QD

Antihyperlipidemic—Fibric Acid Derivatives	
Mechanism of action	Increase elimination and breakdown of lipids, which lowers triglycerides
Side effects	Muscle pain, cold symptoms
Special instructions	Must not be taken with hepatic or renal dysfunction; may cause liver toxicity and blurred vision
Drug interactions	Avoid use with statins, may increase action of warfarin

GENERIC NAME	INDICATION	DOSAGE FORM	DOSAGE
fenofibrate	As adjunctive therapy to diet to reduce cholesterol	Tablets	48mg–145mg PO QD with meals
gemfibrozil	Treatment of patients with hyperlipidemia at risk for pancreatitis	Tablets	600mg PO BID 30 minutes prior to morning and evening meal

Lipid Regulating Agents	
Mechanism of action	Reduce synthesis of triglycerides
Side effects	Belching, dyspepsia, and taste perversion
Special instructions	Should be taken with meals; must not take if allergic to fish
Drug interactions	Anticoagulants (may increase bleeding)

GENERIC NAME	INDICATION	DOSAGE FORM	DOSAGE
omega-3-acid ethyl esters	As an adjunct to diet to reduce triglycerides in patients	Capsule	1g PO QID

Antihyperlipidemic—HMG-COA Reductase Inhibitors (Statins)

Mechanism of action	Inhibit HMG-COA reductase, which is responsible for the synthesis of cholesterol
Side effects	Constipation, muscle pain, dyspepsia
Special instructions	Should be taken at bedtime (cholesterol is produced at night); avoid overexposure to sunlight (photosensitivity); do not take while pregnant or with active liver disease
Drug interactions	Grapefruit juice

GENERIC NAME	INDICATION	DOSAGE FORM	DOSAGE
atorvastatin	Hyperlipidemia, reduce risk of MI	Tablet	10mg–80mg PO QD
lovastatin	Hyperlipidemia, to slow progression of coronary atherosclerosis, prevention of coronary artery disease	Tablet	10mg–40mg PO QD
pravastatin	Hyperlipidemia, reduce risk of MI	Tablet	10mg–80mg PO QHS
rosuvastatin	Hyperlipidemia	Tablet	5mg–40mg PO QD
simvastatin	Hyperlipidemia	Tablet	5mg–80mg PO QD

Nitrates

Mechanism of action	Relax vascular muscle, which reduces oxygen demand and lowers pressure
Side effects	Headache, nausea, vomiting, flushing of face and neck
Special instructions	Nitroglycerin should be dispensed and stored in original glass container
Drug interactions	Sildenafil (Viagra) causes hypotensive effect

GENERIC NAME	INDICATION	DOSAGE FORM	DOSAGE
isosorbide mononitrate	Angina prophylaxis	Tablets	30mg–120mg PO QAM
nitroglycerin	Prophylaxis, management, and treatment of angina	Sublingual tablet Injection	0.4mg dissolved under tongue Q5min up to 3 times in 15 minutes 5mcg/min IV infusion titration

Vasodilators	
Mechanism of action	Relax vascular smooth muscle
Side effects	Tachycardia, heart palpitations, headache
Special instructions	Avoid OTC cough and cold agents without consulting prescriber; do not discontinue therapy without first discussing with provider
Drug interactions	Beta blockers

GENERIC NAME	INDICATION	DOSAGE FORM	DOSAGE
hydralazine	Hypertension	Tablet	25mg PO QID
		Injection	20mg–40mg IM/IV

The following are medications that are a combination of two different drugs used for the treatment of hypertension. Most include a diuretic to help with fluid retention or contain two different drug classes to reduce blood pressure through different mechanisms.

Combination Medications

GENERIC NAME	INDICATION	DOSAGE FORM	DOSAGE
amlodipine and benazepril	Hypertension	Capsule	2.5mg/10mg to 10mg/40mg PO QD
lisinopril and hydrochlorothiazide	Hypertension	Tablet	10mg/12.5mg to 20mg/25mg PO QD
losartan and hydrochlorothiazide	Hypertension	Tablet	50mg/12.5mg to 100mg/25mg PO QD
triamterene and hydrochlorothiazide	Hypertension, edema associated with CHF	Capsule Tablet	37.5mg/25mg to 75mg/50mg PO BID
valsartan and hydrochlorothiazide	Hypertension	Tablet	80mg/12.5mg to 320mg/25mg PO QD

Gastrointestinal System and Drugs

The gastrointestinal (GI) system begins with the mouth and continues down the esophagus into the stomach. Food that travels to the stomach is broken down by acid. From the stomach, food enters the small intestine. This is where absorption occurs. After the nutrients have been absorbed, the food then passes to the large intestine, also known as the colon, where water is reabsorbed back into the body. This prepares the food for excretion through the rectum and out the anus. Additional organs to aid in digestion include the gallbladder, which stores bile for fat digestion, and the liver, which produces and secretes bile. The pancreas also has important functions in protein, fat, and starch digestion, and also releases insulin into the blood.

Many disorders that affect the GI system are caused by lifestyle factors, such as poor diet or obesity. The following are disorders can impact the GI system.

Disorders of the GI System	
Constipation	Difficulty in emptying the bowels
Crohn's disease	Inflammation of the digestive tract, leading to abdominal pain, diarrhea, fatigue, weight loss, and malnutrition
Diarrhea	Loose stools, which may be caused by an infection or by a disorder such as Crohn's disease
Flatulence	Gas buildup in the abdominal area
Gastroesophageal reflux disease (GERD)	Also known as heartburn, burning pain in the upper abdomen and chest caused by a reflux of acidic contents of the stomach into the esophagus
Nausea	Feeling or urge to vomit, sometimes associated with vertigo or dizziness
Ulcer	A sore formed in the stomach or small intestine caused by hypersecretion of acid
Vomiting	Also known as emesis, occurs when the stomach or brain is triggered to eject matter from the stomach

The following drug classes are reviewed individually for treatment of GI disorders.

GI DRUG CLASS	STEM	TOP 200 DRUG EXAMPLES
Antiemetic		meclizine, ondansetron, promethazine
Antimotility agents		dicylomine
Antiulcer agent—histamine (H2) Antagonist	*-tidine*	famotidine, ranitidine
Monoclonal antibody	*-mab*	adalimumab
Antiulcer agent—proton pump inhibitor	*-prazole*	esomeprazole, lansoprazole, omeprazole, pantoprazole
Laxative and stool softener		bisacodyl and milk of magnesia (OTC), polyethylene glycol 3350

These drug classes to treat disorders of the GI system are reviewed to include the following:

- Mechanism of action
- Side effects
- Special handling and administration instructions
- Drug interactions
- Indications
- Dosage form
- Dosage and duration of therapy

Antiulcer Agent—Histamine (H2) Antagonists	
Mechanism of action	Inhibit histamine binding at H2 receptors in gastric cells in the stomach that suppresses acid secretion
Side effects	Headache, dizziness, constipation, and abdominal pain
Special instructions	Full course of therapy should be finished; take with food or milk if stomach upset occurs; avoid in renal impairment
Drug interactions	Warfarin

GENERIC NAME	INDICATION	DOSAGE FORM	DOSAGE
famotidine	Short-term treatment of ulcer, treatment of GERD	Tablet Oral suspension Injection	20mg–40mg PO BID for 6 to 12 weeks 10mg/mL IV Q12H up to 40mg/day
ranitidine	Short-term treatment of ulcer, treatment of GERD	Tablets Syrup Injection	150mg PO BID or 300mg PO QHS 50mg/2mL IM or IV Q6to8H

Antiulcer Agent—Proton Pump Inhibitors (PPI)	
Mechanism of action	Inhibit the proton pump in the gastric cells, which inhibits acid secretion into the stomach
Side effects	Headache, diarrhea or constipation, flatulence
Special instructions	Should be taken at least 60 minutes prior to eating
Drug interactions	Diazepam, phenytoin, and warfarin

GENERIC NAME	INDICATION	DOSAGE FORM	DOSAGE
esomeprazole	Healing of erosive esophagitis, treatment of GERD, reduction in occurrence of ulcers, adjunct in *H. pylori* infection	Capsules (DR) Injection	20mg–40mg PO QD × 4 to 8 weeks 20mg–40mg IV over 10 to 30 minutes
lansoprazole	Gastric ulcers, healing of erosive esophagitis, GERD	Capsules (DR) Orally disintegrating tablets (Solutab) Injection	15mg–30mg PO QD before meal × 4 weeks 30mg infusion
omeprazole	Treatment of ulcer, healing of erosive esophagitis, treatment of GERD, adjunct in *H. pylori* infection	Capsules (SR)	20mg–40mg PO QD × 4 to 8 weeks
pantoprazole	Treatment of erosive esophagitis associated with GERD	Tablets (DR) Injection	20mg–40mg PO QD × 8 weeks 40mg/mL infusion QD × 7 to 10 days

Monoclonal Antibodies	
Mechanism of action	Inactivate tumor necrosis factor (TNF), which reduces inflammation
Side effects	Numbness or tingling, headache, cold-like symptoms, redness or pain at injection site
Special instructions	Injection must be refrigerated
Drug interactions	Other biologic drugs such as disease-modifying antirheumatic drugs (DMARDS)

GENERIC NAME	INDICATION	DOSAGE FORM	DOSAGE
adalimumab	Crohn's disease, ulcerative colitis	Injection	40mg/0.8mL subcutaneously every other week

Antiemetics	
Mechanism of action	Prevent nausea and vomiting by blocking receptors in the brain
Side effects	Drowsiness, dry mouth
Special instructions	Avoid alcohol; patients with asthma or glaucoma should not take
Drug interactions	If taken with other depressants can increase CNS depression

GENERIC NAME	INDICATION	DOSAGE FORM	DOSAGE
meclizine	Control of vertigo, motion sickness, not indicated in children under 12	Tablets Chewable tablets	12.5mg and 25mg PO up to 100mg per day (in divided doses) 25mg PO up to QID
ondansetron	Prevention of nausea and vomiting associated with chemotherapy, nausea and vomiting associated with radiotherapy, postoperative nausea and vomiting	Tablets Orally disintegrating tablets (ODT) Oral solution Injection	8mg PO TID 2mg/mL slow IV push or infusion over 30 minutes
promethazine	Control of motor sickness, control of nausea and vomiting, sedation	Tablets Syrup Suppositories Injection	12.5mg–25mg Q4–6HR PRN 25mg PO or PR, may repeat in 2 hours 25mg/mL and 50mg/mL IVPB over 30 minutes

Antispasmodics	
Mechanism of action	Block acetylcholine from binding on smooth muscle, which decreases spasm
Side effects	Dry mouth, difficulty urinating, constipation, bloating, or stomach pain
Special instructions	Should be taken 30 minutes before meals; should not be taken by patients with urinary tract obstruction or BPH
Drug interactions	Haloperidol

GENERIC NAME	INDICATION	DOSAGE FORM	DOSAGE
dicyclomine	Treatment of irritable bowel syndrome	Capsule Tablet Syrup Injection	10mg–20mg PO TID/QID, 30 minutes before meals 20mg IM QID

Laxatives and Stool Softeners	
Mechanism of action	Promote evacuation of bowel through increase in motility or fluid stimulation
Side effects	Electrolyte imbalance, diarrhea, nausea
Special instructions	Must drink plenty of water to avoid dehydration; should not be taken with renal insufficiency
Drug interactions	Furosemide

GENERIC NAME	INDICATION	DOSAGE FORM	DOSAGE
bisacodyl (stimulant laxative)	Constipation	Tablet Suppository	5mg–15mg PO QD 10mg rectally daily
docusate (stool softener)	Constipation	Tablets Capsules Enema	50mg–300mg PO QD (sodium) 240mg (calcium) PO QD Insert one enema 1 to 3 times daily
magnesium hydroxide (milk of magnesia) (saline laxative)	Constipation, antacid for indigestion	Liquid	30mL–60mL PO QD
polyethylene glycol 3350 (bowel evacuant)	Constipation and irregular bowel movements	Powder	Powder—17g dissolved in 8oz of liquid

Respiratory System and Drugs

The respiratory system is comprised of the organs that allow us to breathe in oxygen and exhale carbon dioxide. This process starts when oxygen enters our nose or mouth and travels through our sinuses. Sinuses are hollow cavities in the skull that create a mucous layer that protects our nose from dirt and infectious agents traveling in the air. Because of this first-line protection, sinuses often become infected, which can lead to drainage, blockage, and an increase in pressure in the head.

Airflows from the sinuses to the windpipe or trachea, which branches into bronchi. Bronchi extend into the lungs and branch further into bronchioles. The end of each bronchiole is covered with air sacs, known as alveoli. This is where gas exchange occurs, when blood is pumped to the lungs from the heart. In the alveoli, the carbon dioxide is removed from the blood and exhaled, while the oxygen from the air we breathe is exchanged into the blood.

The following are respiratory disorders, which are typically caused by either an infection or a chronic disease.

Disorders of the Respiratory System	
Asthma	Narrowing and swelling of airways; symptoms include wheezing, coughing, and shortness of breath
Chronic obstructive pulmonary disease (COPD)	Obstruction of airflow that is irreversible; comprised of chronic bronchitis (inflammation of lining of the airways) and emphysema (destruction of alveoli caused by smoking, environmental pollution or infection)
Cough and cold	Respiratory tract infection most commonly caused by a virus; characterized by sneezing, itchy throat, coughing (either dry or productive), rhinorrhea (runny nose) and fever; symptoms are often treated by OTC agents

The following are the drug classes that are reviewed individually for treatment of respiratory disorders.

RESPIRATORY DRUG CLASS	STEM	TOP 200 DRUG EXAMPLES
Antihistamine	-ine	cetirizine, hydroxyzine, levocetirizine, loratidine
Antitussive		benzonatate
Bronchodilator	-terol	albuterol, tiotropium, albuterol and ipratropium (combination agent)
Corticosteroid	-olone	beclometasone, fluticasone, mometasone, triamcinolone
Combination corticosteroid and beta agonist		fluticasone and salmeterol, budesonide and formoterol
Decongestant		OTC
Expectorant		OTC
Leukotriene inhibitor	-lukast	montelukast

These drug classes to treat disorders of the respiratory system are reviewed to include the following:

- Mechanism of action
- Side effects
- Special handling and administration instructions
- Drug interactions
- Indications
- Dosage form
- Dosage and duration of therapy

Bronchodilators

Mechanism of action	Activate beta-2 receptors in lungs, which dilate bronchioles
Side effects	Headache, insomnia, palpitations, nervousness
Special instructions	Shake inhalers before use; do not take if tachycardia or hypertension
Drug interactions	Some beta blockers, antidepressants (monoamine oxidase inhibitors and tricyclic)

GENERIC NAME	INDICATION	DOSAGE FORM	DOSAGE
albuterol	Bronchospasm in COPD, maintenance and prevention of bronchospasm	MDI Nebules	MDI: 2 puffs QID Inhalation solution: 2.5mg TID/QID via nebulizer
albuterol and ipratropium	COPD, bronchospasm	MDI Nebules	MDI: 2 puffs QID Inhalation solution: 3mL QID via nebulizer
tiotropium	COPD	Capsules	18mcg for use in HandiHaler QD

Corticosteroids

Mechanism of action	Reduce inflammation and swelling in airways, which lowers mucus production
Side effects	Congestion, pharyngitis, nasal irritation
Special instructions	Do not exceed prescribed dosage
Drug interactions	Other corticosteroids, lactose intolerance (some powders in inhalers contain lactose)

GENERIC NAME	INDICATION	DOSAGE FORM	DOSAGE
beclometasone	Asthma	MDI	MDI: 1 to 4 puffs BID
fluticasone	Asthma (MDI), seasonal rhinitis (nasal spray)	MDI Nasal spray	44mcg, 110mcg, 220mcg puffs BID 2 sprays in each nostril QD
mometasone	Prophylaxis and treatment of seasonal allergic rhinitis	Nasal spray	2 sprays in each nostril QD
triamcinolone	Treatment of seasonal allergic rhinitis	Nasal spray	2 sprays in each nostril QD

Leukotriene Inhibitors

Mechanism of action	Inhibit bronchoconstriction (and inflammation) by blocking leukotriene receptors in lungs
Side effects	Cough, headache
Special instructions	Take regularly, even when asymptomatic; should not be used for asthma attacks
Drug interactions	Phenobarbital

GENERIC NAME	INDICATION	DOSAGE FORM	DOSAGE
Montelukast	Prophylaxis and treatment of asthma, relief of symptoms of seasonal allergies, prevention of exercise-induced bronchoconstriction	Chewable tablets Tablets	4mg–10mg PO QPM

Combination Corticosteroid and Beta Agonists

Mechanism of action	Reduce inflammation and relaxes the muscles in the airways
Side effects	Fungal infections (thrush), upper respiratory infection
Special instructions	Rinse mouth after inhalation to avoid fungal infection
Drug interactions	Beta blockers, MAOIs, and tricyclic antidepressants

GENERIC NAME	INDICATION	DOSAGE FORM	DOSAGE
fluticasone and salmeterol	Maintenance of asthma, COPD	Diskus MDI	Diskus: 1 inhalation QD MDI: 2 puffs Q12H
budesonide and formoterol	Maintenance of asthma, COPD	MDI	1 puff Q12H

Antihistamines

Mechanism of action	Block action of histamine on receptors, which reduces symptoms of allergies
Side effects	Drowsiness, dizziness, dry mouth
Special instructions	Drinking alcohol may worsen side effects, do not take if hypertension or glaucoma
Drug interactions	Beta blockers and calcium channel blockers

GENERIC NAME	INDICATION	DOSAGE FORM	DOSAGE
cetirizine	Allergic rhinitis, uticaria	Tablet Syrup Available OTC	10mg PO QD 10mg/10mL PO QD
diphenhydramine (Benadryl)	Relief of symptoms due to hay fever, allergies, runny nose, sneezing, itchy, watery eyes, and itchy throat; also relieves symptoms of common cold	Tablets Liquid Injection Available OTC	25mg PO Q4–6H 12.5mg/5mL PO Q4–6H 50mg/1mL IM or IV up to 400mg/day Also available in combination cough and cold preparations
hydroxyzine	Pruritis, contact dermatitis, symptomatic relief of anxiety, sedative for generic anesthesia	Capsules Tablets Syrup Injection	25mg–50mg PO up to QID 10mg/5mL PO QID 25mg/mL–50mg/mL IV QD/BID
loratadine	Allergic rhinitis, uticaria	Tablet Available OTC	10mg PO QD
levocetirizine	Allergic rhinitis, uticaria	Tablet Available OTC	5mg PO QPM

Antitussives	
Mechanism of action	Inhibit cough by numbing receptors in lungs and reducing cough reflex
Side effects	Drowsiness, dizziness, headache
Special instructions	Benzonatate must be swallowed and not chewed or dissolved
Drug interactions	Medications that are also numbing

GENERIC NAME	INDICATION	DOSAGE FORM	DOSAGE
benzonatate	Relief of cough	Capsules (Perles)	100mg–200mg PO TID PRN
dextromethorphan (Delsym)	Relief of cough	Liquid Available OTC	(adults) 10mL PO BID Also available in combination cough and cold preparations

Decongestants

Mechanism of action	Constrict blood vessels within nose and sinuses to decrease swelling
Side effects	Nervousness, excitability, insomnia, lack of appetite
Special instructions	Not to be taken with hypertension; if an OTC medication is followed with a "D," this means it contains either pseudoephedrine or phenylephrine (decongestant)
Drug interactions	Antihypertensive medications, stimulants

GENERIC NAME	INDICATION	DOSAGE FORM	DOSAGE
pseudoephedrine (Sudafed)	Temporarily relieves runny nose, sneezing, itchy, watery eyes, itching of the nose or throat, nasal congestion and reduces swelling of nasal passages	Tablets Tablets (12-hour) Tablets (24-hour) Available OTC	30mg PO Q4–6H 120mg PO BID 240mg PO QD Also available in combination cough and cold preparations
phenylephrine (Sudafed PE)	Temporarily relieves runny nose, sneezing, itchy, watery eyes, itching of the nose or throat, and nasal congestion, and reduces swelling of nasal passages	Tablets Available OTC	10mg PO Q4–6H Also available in combination cough and cold preparations

Expectorants

Mechanism of action	Increase output of bronchial secretions to break up mucus and allow for productive cough
Side effects	Drowsiness, dizziness, nausea
Special instructions	Not to be taken in patients with hypertension, diabetes, or glaucoma
Drug interactions	Alcohol can increase side effects

GENERIC NAME	INDICATION	DOSAGE FORM	DOSAGE
guaifenesin (Mucinex)	Helps loosen phlegm and thin bronchial secretions in the bronchial passageway and make coughs more productive	Tablet Tablet (ER) Liquid Available OTC	200mg–400mg PO Q4H 600mg–1200mg PO BID 100mg/5mL to 200mg/5mL PO Q4H Also available in combination cough and cold preparations

Endocrine System and Drugs

The endocrine system is comprised of glands and organs that produce and secrete hormones, which helps keep the body in balance. There are 10 glands or organs in the endocrine system:

- Pituitary gland
- Thyroid gland
- Hypothalamus
- Pineal gland
- Parathyroid gland
- Adrenal gland
- Thymus gland
- Ovaries
- Tests
- Pancreas

The following lists each gland and the hormone secreted or produced. Each hormone has a site of action and function in the body that is important for physiological equilibrium.

GLAND	SECRETES OR PRODUCES	FUNCTION	SITE OF ACTION
Pituitary gland	Antidiuretic hormone (ADH) (vasopressin)	Regulates retention of water	Kidneys
	Oxytocin (OT)	Stimulates contractions during childbirth and lactation	Uterine muscle and mammary glands
	Prolactin	Induces lactation	Mammary glands
	Melanocyte-stimulating hormone	Stimulates release of melanin in skin, which increases pigmentation	Skin
	Follicle-stimulating hormone (FSH)	Stimulates growth of follicles in ovaries and testicular growth in men	Ovary and testes
	Luteinizing hormone (LH)	Causes ovulation in women, and stimulates testosterone production in men	Ovary and testes
	Thyroid-stimulating hormone (TSH)	Stimulates the thyroid to produce thyroid hormones	Thyroid
	Adrenocorticotropic hormone (ACTH)	Stimulates release of cortisol from adrenal gland in response to stress	Adrenal gland
	Growth hormone (somatotropin)	Stimulates growth and cell regeneration	Bones
Thyroid gland	Triiodothyronine (T3)	Regulates temperature, metabolism and heart rate	Bloodstream
	Thyroxine (T4)	Regulates temperature, metabolism and heart rate	Bloodstream
	Calcitonin	Reduces calcium levels in the blood (works opposite of parathyroid hormone)	Bloodstream

(continued)

GLAND	SECRETES OR PRODUCES	FUNCTION	SITE OF ACTION
Pineal gland	Melatonin	Regulates sleep/wake cycle	Bloodstream
Parathyroid gland	Parathyroid hormone (PTH)	Increases calcium levels in the blood (works opposite of calcitonin)	Bloodstream
Adrenal gland	Epinephrine (adrenaline)	Increases heart rate, muscle strength, and BP in response to stress	Bloodstream
	Norepinephrine (noradrenaline)	Helps body respond to stress and exercise (fight-or-flight response)	Bloodstream
	Cortisol	Steroid hormone released in response to stress and impacts metabolism	Bloodstream
	Aldosterone	Steroid hormone that regulates salt and water in the body and can impact blood pressure	Bloodstream causing kidney to reabsorb sodium
Thymus gland	Thymosin	Stimulates T-cell production	Bloodstream
Ovaries	Estrogen	Female reproductive system and secondary sex characteristic development	Bloodstream
	Progesterone	Thickens endometrial lining preparing for pregnancy	Bloodstream
Testes	Testosterone	Male reproductive system and secondary sex characteristic development	Bloodstream
Pancreas	Insulin	Decreases blood sugar by allowing glucose to enter cells and use for energy	Bloodstream to stimulate cells
	Glucagon	Increases blood sugar by stimulating conversion of glycogen into glucose from liver (prevents hypoglycemia)	Bloodstream to stimulate liver

The following are disorders that affect the pancreas.

DISORDER	AFFECTED ENDOCRINE GLAND	DESCRIPTION
Diabetes type I	Pancreas	The body does not produce insulin; requires insulin for treatment
Diabetes type II	Pancreas	The body does not respond to insulin so glucose is not absorbed; the pancreas is resistant to insulin

The following are drug classes for diabetes treatment.

Diabetes Treatment

ENDOCRINE SYSTEM DRUG CLASS	STEM	TOP 200 DRUG EXAMPLES
Antidiabetic—biguanide		metformin
Antidiabetic—DPP-4 inhibitor	-gliptin	linagliptin, sitagliptin
Antidiabetic—glitazone	-glitazone	pioglitazone
Antidiabetic—GLP-1agonist	-glutide	liraglutide
Antidiabetic—SGL2 inhibitor	-gliflozin	canagliflozin
Antidiabetic—sulfonyurea	gli-/gly-	glimepiride, glipizide, glyburide
Insulin		insulin aspart, insulin detemir, insulin glargine, insulin human, insulin lispro

Antidiabetic Agents	
Mechanism of action	Stimulate insulin release from pancreas or increase cell sensitivity to insulin
Side effects	Headache, nausea, dizziness
Special instructions	Most should be taken with first main meal of the day
Drug interactions	Furosemide

GENERIC NAME	INDICATION	DOSAGE FORM	DOSAGE
canagiflozin	Adjunct to diet and exercise for type II diabetes, and reduce risk of cardiovascular death in adults with type II diabetes	Tablets	100mg PO QD
glimepiride	Adjunct to diet and exercise for type II diabetes, for use in combination with insulin to lower blood glucose	Tablets	1mg–4mg PO QD, max daily dose of 8mg
glipizide	Adjunct to diet and exercise for type II diabetes	Tablets	5mg–20mg PO QD, max daily dose of 40mg
glyburide	Adjunct to diet and exercise for type II diabetes	Tablets	2.5mg–5mg PO QD/BID, max dose is 20mg/day
linagliptin	Adjunct to diet and exercise for type II diabetes	Tablets	5mg PO QD

(continued)

GENERIC NAME	INDICATION	DOSAGE FORM	DOSAGE
liraglutide	Adjunct to diet and exercise for type II diabetes, and reduce risk of cardiovascular death in adults with type II diabetes	Injection	1.2mg subcut QD, may increase to 1.8mg
metformin	Adjunct to diet and exercise for type II diabetes	Tablets	500mg PO BID, may increase up to maximum daily dose of 2550mg
pioglitazone	Adjunct to diet and exercise for type II diabetes	Tablets	15mg–30mg PO QD, up to 45mg PO QD
sitagliptin	Adjunct to diet and exercise for type II diabetes	Tablets	100mg PO QD
sitagliptin and metformin	Adjunct to diet and exercise for type II diabetes	Tablets	50mg sitagliptin/ 1000mg metformin to 100mg sitagliptin/ 1000mg metformin PO QD

Insulins	
Mechanism of action	Stimulate the uptake of glucose into cells and lowers blood glucose
Side effects	Hypoglycemia, injection-related side effects
Special instructions	Insulin and doses are highly individualized; insulin can be fast-acting, intermediate, or long-acting
Drug interactions	Corticosteroids, estrogen and oral contraceptives, levothyroxine

GENERIC NAME	INDICATION	DOSAGE FORM	DURATION OF ACTION
Insulin aspart	Treatment of type I and type II diabetes	Injection	Long-acting
Insulin detemir	Treatment of type I and type II diabetes	Injection	Intermediate
Insulin glargine	Treatment of type I and type II diabetes	Injection	Fast-acting
Insulin human	Treatment of type I and type II diabetes	Injection	Long-acting
Insulin lispro	Treatment of type I and type II diabetes	Injection	Fast-acting

The following are disorders impacting the reproductive glands.

DISORDER	AFFECTED ENDOCRINE GLAND	DESCRIPTION
Hypogonadism	Testes	Deficient production and secretion of testosterone
Hormone replacement	Ovaries	Symptoms of menopause
Menstrual dysfunction	Ovaries	Amenorrhea (absence of menstruation); dysmenorrheal (difficult or painful menstruation); endometriosis (endometrium grows outside of uterus); and abnormal bleeding

The following are drug classes for hormonal therapy.

Hormone Treatment

ENDOCRINE SYSTEM DRUG CLASS	STEM	TOP 200 DRUG EXAMPLES
Androgens	-ster-	testosterone
Hormone replacement	-estr	estradiol, ethinyl estradiol, and norethindrone
Contraceptives	-estr (estrogens) -gest (progestins)	ethinyl estradiol and desogestrel, ethinyl estradiol and drospirenone, ethinyl estradiol and etonogestrel, ethinyl estradiol and levonorgestrel, ethinyl estradiol and norethindrone, ethinyl estradiol and norgestimate, norethindrone
Progestin hormone	-gest (progestins)	norethindrone, progesterone

Androgens	
Mechanism of action	Activate androgen receptors eliciting effects of testosterone
Side effects	Facial hair growth, anxiety
Special instructions	Testosterone is a Schedule III medication because of the Anabolic Steroid Control Act; should not be used in patients with breast or prostate cancer, or who have high cholesterol or liver problems
Drug interactions	Warfarin, corticosteroids

GENERIC NAME	INDICATION	DOSAGE FORM	DOSAGE
testosterone	Deficiency of testosterone, hypogonadism	Injection	50mg–400mg IM Q4W

Hormone Replacements

Mechanism of action	Act on estrogen receptors to treat symptoms of menopause
Side effects	Abnormal bleeding during menstruation, mental depression, insomnia, weight change
Special instructions	Must be discontinued if pregnancy occurs; do not take with breast cancer
Drug interactions	Antibiotics

GENERIC NAME	INDICATION	DOSAGE FORM	DOSAGE
estradiol	Treatment of moderate to severe vasomotor symptoms associated with menopause	Tablets	1mg–2mg PO QD
ethinyl estradiol and norethindrone	Treatment of moderate to severe vasomotor symptoms associated with menopause, prevention of osteoporosis	Tablets	0.5/2.5mg tab PO QD

Contraceptive

Mechanism of action	Suppress LH and FSH, which inhibits ovulation
Side effects	Abdominal cramping, acne, weight gain
Special instructions	Do not take if pregnant, have breast cancer, or have clotting disorder
Drug interactions	Antibiotics

GENERIC NAME	INDICATION	DOSAGE FORM	DOSAGE
ethinyl estradiol and desogestrel	Prevention of pregnancy	Tablets	1 tab PO QD × 21 or 28 days
ethinyl estradiol and drospirenone	Prevention of pregnancy	Tablets	1 tab PO QD × 28 days
ethinyl estradiol and etonogestrel	Prevention of pregnancy	Vaginal ring	Insert 1 ring vaginally and leave in place for 3 weeks, then remove for 1 week
ethinyl estradiol and levonorgestrel	Prevention of pregnancy	Tablets	1 tab PO QD × 21 or 28 days
ethinyl estradiol and norethindrone	Prevention of pregnancy	Tablets	1 tab PO QD × 21 or 28 days
ethinyl estradiol and norgestimate	Prevention of pregnancy	Tablets	1 tab PO QD × 28 days
norethindrone	Prevention of pregnancy	Tablets	1 tab PO QD × 28 days

Progestin Hormones	
Mechanism of action	Prevent ovulation
Side effects	Abdominal pain, migraine headache, blurred vision
Special instructions	Do not take with known or suspected pregnancy; may worsen depression; can take with food if upset stomach
Drug interactions	Progesterone may decrease benefit of estrogen

GENERIC NAME	INDICATION	DOSAGE FORM	DOSAGE
norethindrone	Endometriosis, abnormal bleeding	Tablets	2.5mg–10mg PO QD × 5 to 10 days
progesterone	Endometrial hyperplasia, amenorrhea	Capsules	200mg PO QPM × 12 days in a 28-day cycle

The following are disorders of the thyroid, adrenal, and parathyroid glands.

DISORDER	AFFECTED ENDOCRINE GLAND	DESCRIPTION
Osteoporosis	Ovaries and parathyroid gland	Decrease in bone density; deficiency in estrogen, calcium, and vitamin D
Hypothyroidism	Thyroid gland	Low production of thyroid hormone
Hyperthyroidism	Thyroid gland	High production of thyroid hormone
Addison disease	Adrenal gland	Deficiency in cortisol and aldosterone production, which disrupts sodium and potassium regulation

The following drug classes are used to treat disorders of the parathyroid, thyroid, and adrenal glands.

Other Endocrine System Treatment

ENDOCRINE SYSTEM DRUG CLASS	STEM	TOP 200 DRUG EXAMPLES
Bisphosphonates	*-dronate*	alendronate
Thyroid hormone		levothyroxine, thyroid
Oral corticosteroids		prednisone

Bisphosphonates

Mechanism of action	Inhibit bone breakdown by osteoclasts
Side effects	Abdominal pain, flatulence, constipation
Special instructions	Must be swallowed with 8 ounces plain water immediately after rising for the day and must be 30 minutes before first food, beverage, or medication of the day
Drug interactions	Calcium and aluminum (antacids)

GENERIC NAME	INDICATION	DOSAGE FORM	DOSAGE
alendronate	Treatment and prevention of osteoporosis in postmenopausal women	Tablets	10mg PO QD or 70mg PO QW

Thyroid Hormones

Mechanism of action	Synthetic form of thyroxine (T4)
Side effects	Tachycardia, hypoglycemia, may cause hair loss in children
Special instructions	Do not discontinue therapy without speaking to prescriber; do not take if you have diabetes
Drug interactions	Anticoagulants

GENERIC NAME	INDICATION	DOSAGE FORM	DOSAGE
levothyroxine	Replacement therapy for absent thyroid function	Tablets Injection	25mcg–300mcg PO QD 100mcg–300mcg IV
thyroid	Hypothyroidism, treatment or prevention of goiter	Tablets	60mg–180mg PO QD

Oral Corticosteroids	
Mechanism of action	Suppress inflammatory response from immune system
Side effects	Upset stomach, weight gain, hypertension
Special instructions	Long-term use may cause diabetes and increase susceptibility for infection
Drug interactions	Other immunosuppressant agents

GENERIC NAME	INDICATION	DOSAGE FORM	DOSAGE
methylprednisolone	Allergic and inflammatory disease	Tablets Dosepak Injection	4mg–48mg PO QD Dosepak: 21-tablet pack with incremental increase 40mg–120mg IM
prednisone	Allergic and inflammatory disease	Tablets Oral solution	5mg–60mg PO QD
prednisolone	Allergic and inflammatory disease	Oral solution	5mg–60mg PO QD

The Nervous System and Drugs

The nervous system is composed of the brain and spinal cord (central nervous system) and the network of nerves that run through our body (peripheral nervous system). The brain releases chemicals known as neurotransmitters. Neurotransmitters act on different receptors in the brain, which coordinate responses and reactions.

The following are the neurotransmitters of the brain that can be modified by drug therapy for treatment.

Neurotransmitters	
Acetylcholine (ACH)	Activates muscles and causes smooth muscle contraction as part of the peripheral nervous system; is involved in attention and memory as part of the central nervous system
Adrenaline (epinephrine)	Produced during fight-or-flight response; increases heart rate
Dopamine (DA)	Influences mood and feelings of pleasure and motivation, helps regulate body movements
Gamma aminobutyric acid (GABA)	Inhibitory neurotransmitter, blocks and inhibits signals in the brain, reduces excitability
Glutamate	Excitatory neurotransmitter, most abundant neurotransmitter in brain, involved in learning and memory
Norepinephrine (NE) (noradrenaline)	Increases attention and responsive actions in the brain, causes blood vessels to contract and heart rate to increase
Serotonin (5-HT)	Contributes to feelings of happiness and well-being; helps regulate mood, social behavior, sleep, memory, appetite, and digestion

When the amount of neurotransmitter is too low or too high, a chemical imbalance occurs. Many disorders of the nervous system are a result of neurotransmitter imbalance. The following are disorders of the nervous system.

Disorders of the Nervous System	
Alzheimer's disease	Progressive and irreversible disorder that slowly leads to dementia, and problems with memory, thinking, and behavior; acetylcholine and glutamate appear to play a role
Anxiety	Excessive nervousness, worry, and apprehension may be caused by decrease in GABA and serotonin
Attention deficit hyperactivity disorder (ADHD)	Impacts attention, ability to sit still, self-control, and restlessness
Bipolar disorder	Mental disorder causing shifts in mood, energy, and ability to carry out everyday tasks; large swings in mood include emotional highs (mania) followed by lows (depression)
Depression	Mood disorder causing a persistent feeling of sadness and loss of interest; often caused by low levels of serotonin or low receptor levels
Epilepsy	Abnormal electrical activity in brain, which causes sensory disturbances and may include loss of consciousness or convulsions, may be caused by imbalance of GABA
Insomnia	Trouble falling and/or staying asleep
Migraines	Intense headaches, nausea and vomiting, numbness or tingling, sensitivity to light; may be caused by low level of serotonin
Parkinson's disease	Progressive disease that impacts movement with gradual onset of symptoms including tremors, rigidity of the muscles, and a slow shuffling gait; caused by deficiency of dopamine
Schizophrenia	Neurological disorder characterized by an abnormal interpretation of reality, resulting in hallucinations and delusions, thought to be associated with excess dopamine in the brain

The following are the drug classes that are reviewed individually for treatment of nervous system disorders.

NERVOUS SYSTEM DRUG CLASS	STEM	TOP 200 DRUG EXAMPLES
Antianxiety agent		buspirone
Benzodiazepines	-azepam	alprazolam, clonazepam, diazepam, lorazepam, temazepam
Selective serotonin reuptake inhibitors (SSRIs)	-traline, -oxetine	citalopram, escitalopram, fluoxetine, paroxetine, sertraline
Serotonin and norepinephrine reuptake inhibitors (SNRIs)	-faxine, -oxetine	duloxetine, venlafaxine
Tricyclic antidepressants (TCAs)	-triptyline	amitriptyline, nortriptyline
Monoamine oxidase inhibitors (MAOIs)	-giline	
Antispychotics	-tiapine, -peridone	bupropion, mirtazapine, risperidone
Bipolar disorder agents		lithium
Hypnotics	-pidem	zolpidem
Anticonvulsant (antiepileptic)	-gab, -racetam, -trigine	carbamazepine, divalproex, gabapentin, lamotrigine, levetiracetam, pregabalin, topiramate
Antiparkinson agents	-dopa	carbidopa/levodopa, ropinirole
Alzheimer's disease agents	-pezil, -mantine	donepezil, memantine
Stimulants		dexmethylphenidate, dextroamphetamine and amphetamine, guanfacine, lisdexamfetamine, methylphenidate
Selective norepinephrine reuptake inhibitors (SNRIs)		atomoxetine
Serotonin receptor agonist	-triptan	sumatriptan

These drug classes to treat disorders of the nervous system are reviewed to include the following:

- Mechanism of action
- Side effects
- Special handling and administration instructions
- Drug interactions
- Indications
- Dosage form
- Dosage and duration of therapy

Antianxiety Agents

Mechanism of action	Exact mechanism of buspirone is unknown
Side effects	Headache, dizziness, drowsiness, nervousness
Special instructions	May cause tardive dyskinesia (involuntary movements of the face or jaw)
Drug interactions	Grapefruit juice, MAOIs

GENERIC NAME	INDICATION	DOSAGE FORM	DOSAGE
buspirone	Anxiety disorder, short-term relief of anxiety symptoms	Tablets	5mg–30mg BID, can be given up to four times daily

Benzodiazepines

Mechanism of action	Increase the inhibitory effect of GABA resulting in sedative and antianxiety effects
Side effects	Drowsiness, fatigue
Special instructions	Should avoid alcohol; can be habit forming
Drug interactions	Grapefruit juice, other depressants

GENERIC NAME	INDICATION	DOSAGE FORM	DOSAGE
alprazolam	Management of anxiety and panic disorder	Tablets (IR) Tablets (ER) Orally disintegrating tablets Oral solution	0.25mg–0.5mg PO TID, may take up to 4mg total per day
clonazepam	Treatment of seizures	Tablets Orally disintegrating tablets	0.5mg PO TID, maximum daily dosage is 20mg
diazepam	Management of anxiety disorders, withdrawal from alcohol, muscle spasm, preoperative apprehension, seizures	Tablets Injection Rectal gel	2mg–10mg PO Q4H PRN 2mg–10mg IM or IV Q4H PRN 5mg–10mg rectally, max dose is 30mg
lorazepam	Management of anxiety disorders, insomnia, seizures	Tablets Injection	1mg–10mg PO QD 2mg/mL and 4mg/mL IV push
temazepam	Insomnia	Capsules	7.5mg–30mg PO 30 minutes before bedtime

Selective Serotonin Reuptake Inhibitors (SSRIs)

Mechanism of action	Block the reuptake or reabsorption of serotonin, which increases levels of serotonin in the brain
Side effects	Somnolence, impotence, insomnia, dry mouth
Special instructions	May impair cognitive and motor performance; avoid alcohol; antidepressants may increase suicidal thoughts in children and teenagers
Drug interactions	NSAIDs, aspirin, clopidogrel

GENERIC NAME	INDICATION	DOSAGE FORM	DOSAGE
citalopram	Depression	Tablet Solution	20mg PO QD, may increase to 40mg PO QD
escitalopram	Depression	Tablet Solution	10mg PO QD, may increase to 20mg PO QD
fluoxetine	Depression, obsessive-compulsive disorder, bulimia, panic disorder	Tablets Capsules Capsules (DR) Liquid	10mg–40mg PO QD Weekly dose: 90mg PO QW
paroxetine	Depression, obsessive-compulsive disorder, social anxiety disorder, panic disorder	Tablets Tablets (CR) Oral suspension	25mg–62.5mg PO QD
sertraline	Depression, obsessive-compulsive disorder, social anxiety disorder, panic disorder, premenstrual dysphoric disorder	Tablets Oral concentrate	50mg PO QD, may be increased up to 200mg/day

Serotonin and Norepinephrine Reuptake Inhibitors (SNRIs)

Mechanism of action	Block the reuptake or reabsorption of both serotonin and norepinephrine, which increases levels of both neurotransmitters in the brain
Side effects	Somnolence, impotence, insomnia, dry mouth, decreased appetite
Special instructions	May take up to 4 weeks for therapeutic effect
Drug interactions	NSAIDs, anticoagulants

GENERIC NAME	INDICATION	DOSAGE FORM	DOSAGE
duloxetine	Depression, neuropathic pain, generalized anxiety disorder	Capsule	20mg–60mg PO QD
venlafaxine	Depression, generalized anxiety disorder, social anxiety disorder	Tablets Capsules (ER) Tablets (ER)	75mg PO QD, may increase to 225mg/day

Tricyclic Antidepressants (TCAs)

Mechanism of action	Inhibit reuptake of serotonin and norepinephrine
Side effects	Drowsiness, dry mouth, urinary retention, weight gain
Special instructions	May cause drowsiness; avoid alcohol
Drug interactions	MAOIs, cimetidine

GENERIC NAME	INDICATION	DOSAGE FORM	DOSAGE
amitriptyline	Depression	Tablets	10mg–150mg PO QHS
nortriptyline	Depression	Capsules Oral solution	75mg–150mg PO QD/BID

Monoamine Oxidase Inhibitors (MAOIs)

Mechanism of action	Inhibit monoamine oxidase, which increases levels of serotonin and norepinephrine (monoamine oxidase is the enzyme that breaks down serotonin and norepinephrine in the brain)
Side effects	Dry mouth, nausea, headache, insomnia
Special instructions	MAOIs should only be used in patients who have not responded to other antidepressant therapy; must avoid tyramine-containing foods, such as aged cheese, sauerkraut, cured meat
Drug interactions	Other antidepressants—can create a dangerously high level of serotonin, known as serotonin syndrome; must wait 14 days before starting a new antidepressant therapy

Atypical Antidepressants

Mechanism of action	Affect levels of serotonin and norepinephrine in the brain
Side effects	Dry mouth, nausea, headache, insomnia
Special instructions	Can be taken at bedtime for drowsiness
Drug interactions	SSRIs

GENERIC NAME	INDICATION	DOSAGE FORM	DOSAGE
buproprion	Depression, seasonal affective disorder (SAD), management of tobacco cessation	Tablets (IR) Tablets (SR) Tablets (XL)	IR: 100mg PO TID SR: 200mg BID XL: 150mg–300mg PO QD
mirtazapine	Depression	Tablets and orally disintegrating tablets	15mg–45mg PO QHS
trazodone	Depression	Tablets	50mg–300mg PO max daily dose is 400mg

Antipsychotics

Mechanism of action	Block dopamine and serotonin receptors limiting excessive release of dopamine
Side effects	Weight gain, insomnia, tardive dyskinesia
Special instructions	Should be taken at the same time every day
Drug interactions	SSRIs, carbamazepine

GENERIC NAME	INDICATION	DOSAGE FORM	DOSAGE
aripiprazole	Schizophrenia, bipolar disorder	Tablets Orally disintegrating tablets Oral solution	10mg–15mg PO QD
quetiapine	Schizophrenia, bipolar disorder	Tablets Tablets (ER)	25mg PO BID, up to 300mg ER: 300mg PO QD with maximum dose of 800mg/day
risperidone	Schizophrenia, bipolar disorder, irritability associated with autism	Tablets Orally disintegrating tablets Oral solution Injection	1mg PO BID, maximum daily dose is 16mg 25mg–50mg IM Q2W

Bipolar Disorder Agents	
Mechanism of action	Unknown mechanism, but thought to increase serotonin release and decrease norepinephrine release
Side effects	Hand tremors, increased thirst and urination, weight gain, poor concentration, diarrhea
Special instructions	Take as directed, do not take more or less than prescribed, and do not chew or crush
Drug interactions	NSAIDs, SSRIs, ACE inhibitors, ARBs, diuretics, caffeine

GENERIC NAME	INDICATION	DOSAGE FORM	DOSAGE
lithium	Bipolar disorder, manic episodes of bipolar disorder	Tablets Tablets (ER) Capsules Solution	900mg–1,800mg PO QD in 3 or 4 divided doses

Hypnotics	
Mechanism of action	Increase effects of GABA and causes sedation
Side effects	Headache, drowsiness
Special instructions	Should be taken right before bed and should not be crushed or chewed
Drug interactions	Other depressants

GENERIC NAME	INDICATION	DOSAGE FORM	DOSAGE
zolpidem	Insomnia	Tablets Tablets (CR)	5 mg–10mg PO QHS 6.25mg–12.5mg PO QHS

Anticonvulsants	
Mechanism of action	Suppress rapid firing of neurons during seizure, increase GABA transmission
Side effects	Dizziness, unsteadiness, weight gain, rash
Special instructions	Must take as prescribed as minimal changes in dosing can impact therapy
Drug interactions	Oral contraceptives, other anticonvulsants may impact metabolism

GENERIC NAME	INDICATION	DOSAGE FORM	DOSAGE
carbamazepine	Seizure disorder	Chewable tablets Tablets Tablets (ER) Capsules (ER) Suspension	800mg–1,200mg per day in 3 or 4 divided doses
divalproex	Seizure disorder, bipolar disorder, prophylaxis of migraines	Tablets (enteric-coated) Tablets (ER) Sprinkle capsules	250mg PO TID
gabapentin	Adjunctive therapy for seizure disorder, postherpetic neuralgia	Capsules Tablets Oral solution	300mg–600mg PO TID
lamotrigine	Adjunctive therapy for seizure disorder, bipolar disorder	Chewable tablets Tablets (orally disintegrating and ER)	25mg–200mg PO QD
levetiracetam	Adjunctive therapy for seizure disorder	Tablets (IR) Tablets (ER) Oral solution	500mg PO BID
pregabalin	Adjunctive therapy for seizure disorder, fibromyalgia, neuropathic pain	Capsules	25mg–225mg PO TID
topiramate	Adjunctive therapy for seizure disorder, prophylaxis for migraines	Tablets	25mg–200mg PO QHS

Antiparkinson Agents	
Mechanism of action	Increase levels of dopamine in brain
Side effects	Somnolence, fatigue, involuntary movements, dizziness
Special instructions	Should be taken at regular intervals and the same time every day to avoid disruptions in drug concentration; avoid driving, may cause abrupt onset of sleep
Drug interactions	MAOIs

GENERIC NAME	INDICATION	DOSAGE FORM	DOSAGE
carbidopa-levodopa	Parkinson's disease	Tablets Tablets (CR)	10mg/100mg PO TID to 25mg/250mg PO TID 25mg/100mg PO BID to 50mg/200mg PO BID
ropinirole	Parkinson's disease, restless leg syndrome	Tablets Tablets (ER)	0.25mg–5mg PO TID 2mg–8mg (ER) PO QD
pramipexole dihydrochloride	restless leg syndrome	Tablets Tablets (ER)	0.125 mg/day PO 2–3 hr before bedtime initially; may be increased every 4 to 7 days up to 0.5 mg/day

Anti-Alzheimer Agents	
Mechanism of action	Prevent breakdown of acetylcholine, which increases levels in the brain
Side effects	Nausea, diarrhea, insomnia
Special instructions	Should take before bed, take at the same time every day
Drug interactions	Atropine and bentropine (drugs with anticholinergic properties)

GENERIC NAME	INDICATION	DOSAGE FORM	DOSAGE
donepezil	Mild, moderate, and severe dementia caused by Alzheimer's disease	Tablets Orally disintegrating tablets Oral solution	5mg–10mg PO QHS
memantine	Moderate and severe dementia caused by Alzheimer's disease	Tablets Oral solution	20mg PO QD

Stimulants	
Mechanism of action	Increase levels of norepinephrine, dopamine, and serotonin in the brain by blocking reuptake, which increases brain activity
Side effects	Restlessness, insomnia, anorexia, anxiety
Special instructions	Can become habit forming
Drug interactions	MAOIs can cause hypertensive crisis

GENERIC NAME	INDICATION	DOSAGE FORM	DOSAGE
dexmethylphenidate	ADHD	Tablets Capsules (ER)	2.5mg PO BID, can increase by 5mg increments per week if needed, max 20mg daily
dextroamphetamine and amphetamine	Narcolepsy, ADHD	Tablets Capsules	20mg PO QD
guanfacine	ADHD	Tablets Tablets (ER)	1mg PO QD—taken at the same time every day
lisdexamfetamine	ADHD in children 6 years and older	Capsules	30mg PO QAM, may increase up to 70mg/day
methylphenidate	ADHD in children 6 years and older, narcolepsy	Tablets Tablets (SR) Chewable tablets Capsules (CR) Solution	18mg–54mg PO QD

Selective Norepinephrine Reuptake Inhibitors	
Mechanism of action	Block reuptake of norepinephrine, which increases levels in the brain
Side effects	Restlessness, insomnia, anorexia
Special instructions	Should be taken at the same time every day; may increase suicide risk in children and adolescents
Drug interactions	MAOIs and other antidepressants

GENERIC NAME	INDICATION	DOSAGE FORM	DOSAGE
atomoxetine	ADHD	Capsules	40mg PO QD, can be increased to 80mg daily in divided doses, max 100mg daily

Serotonin Receptor Agonists	
Mechanism of action	Activate serotonin receptors, which constricts blood vessels in the brain
Side effects	Numbness, drowsiness, tightness in chest, flushing
Special instructions	Cannot be used for prophylactic migraine therapy; should take as soon as symptoms of migraine appear
Drug interactions	MAOIs

GENERIC NAME	INDICATION	DOSAGE FORM	DOSAGE
Sumatriptan	Treatment of migraines	Tablets Injection Nasal spray	25mg–100mg PO at onset 6mg subcut at onset 5mg and 20mg intranasal at onset

The Urinary System and Drugs

The urinary (renal) system is responsible for eliminating waste, regulating blood pressure, and controlling the level of electrolytes in the blood. Blood is transported to the kidneys via the renal arteries. The kidneys contain a million small units called nephrons, and each nephron completes the processes of filtration, reabsorption, and secretion. It is through this process that the kidneys help regulate blood pressure through filtration (in the glomerulus), removal of waste through secretion, and blood volume through reabsorption.

Each nephron also contains a renal tubule, which contains the proximal convoluted tubule, loop of Henle, distal convoluted tubule, and connecting tubule. Each segment of tubule completes excretion of substances or secretion back into the bloodstream. Diuretics act on specific portions of the tubule, which impacts reabsorption and can help reduce blood pressure.

Following this filtration, reabsorption, and secretion, the urine exits each kidney through the ureters. These tubes connect the kidneys to the bladder. Urine is stored in the bladder until the body is ready for excretion. The urethra connects the bladder to external body for excretion. This tube is much longer in men than women. This often leads to more frequent urinary tract infections in women, due to the short proximity of the urethra to the bladder. The following are disorders of the urinary system.

Disorders of the Urinary System	
Benign prostatic hyperplasia (BPH)	Prostate gland enlargement, can block urine flow
Overactive bladder	Uncontrolled need to suddenly urinate
Hypertension	High blood pressure

The following drug classes are reviewed individually for treatment of nervous system disorders.

URINARY SYSTEM DRUG CLASS	STEM	TOP 200 DRUG EXAMPLES
Alpha blockers	-azosin	doxazosin, tamsulosin, terazosin
5-alpha reductase inhibitor	-steride	finasteride
Overactive bladder agents		oxybutynin, mirabegron
Diuretic—loop	-semide	furosemide
Diruetic—potassium sparing		spironolactone
Diuretic—thiazide	-thiazide	hydrochlorothiazide, chlorthalidone

These drug classes to treat disorders of the urinary system are reviewed to include the following:

- Mechanism of action
- Side effects
- Special handling and administration instructions
- Drug interactions
- Indications
- Dosage form
- Dosage and duration of therapy

Alpha Blockers	
Mechanism of action	Block alpha receptors, which causes vasodilation
Side effects	Dizziness, headache, fatigue
Special instructions	Take dose at bedtime to avoid dizziness when standing
Drug interactions	Other hypertensive agents

GENERIC NAME	INDICATION	DOSAGE FORM	DOSAGE
doxazosin	Hypertension, BPH	Tablet XL tablet (ER)	1mg–8mg PO QD 4mg and 8mg XL PO QD
tamsulosin	BPH	Capsules	0.4mg PO QD following same meal daily
terazosin	Hypertension, BPH	Capsules	1mg–10mg PO QHS

5-Alpha Reductase Inhibitors

Mechanism of action	Inhibit 5-alpha reductase, which is the enzyme that metabolizes testosterone
Side effects	Impotence, abnormal ejaculation, breast tenderness
Special instructions	Women who plan to become pregnant should not handle or be exposed to semen from man who is taking
Drug interactions	Warfarin, digoxin, propranolol

GENERIC NAME	INDICATION	DOSAGE FORM	DOSAGE
finasteride	BPH, alopecia (men only)	Tablets	5mg PO QD

Overactive Bladder Agents

Mechanism of action	Inhibit receptors involved in contraction of urinary muscles
Side effects	Difficulty urinating, sweating less than usual, dry mouth
Special instructions	Avoid prolonged exposure to hot weather
Drug interactions	Atropine, antihistamines, dicyclomine

GENERIC NAME	INDICATION	DOSAGE FORM	DOSAGE
oxybutynin	Overactive bladder	Tablets Tablets (ER) Syrup	5mg PO QD, may increase to maximum of 30mg per day
mirabegron	Overactive bladder	Tablets (ER)	25mg–50mg PO QD

Loop Diuretics

Mechanism of action	Inhibit sodium and chloride reabsorption in the loop of Henle, resulting in increased urine output
Side effects	Photosensitivity, muscle cramps, dizziness, hyponatremia, hypochloremia
Special instructions	Take in morning, avoid excessive exposure to sunlight
Drug interactions	Lithium, NSAIDs

GENERIC NAME	INDICATION	DOSAGE FORM	DOSAGE
Furosemide	Treatment of edema associated with CHF or renal dysfunction, hypertension, pulmonary edema	Tablets Oral solution Injection	20mg–80mg PO QD, may increase 20–40mg up to 600mg 40mg IV push over 1–2 minutes

Potassium-Sparing Diuretics

Mechanism of action	Inhibit effect of aldosterone, which increases secretion of sodium and water
Side effects	Dry mouth, dizziness and unsteadiness, amenorrhea
Special instructions	Take in morning; avoid in patients in hepatic failure
Drug interactions	Must not be taken with ACE inhibitors—can lead to hyperkalemia

GENERIC NAME	INDICATION	DOSAGE FORM	DOSAGE
Spironolactone	Edema associated with CHF, hypertension, hypokalemia, hyperaldosteronism	Tablets	100mg PO QD, may increase to 200mg PO QD

Thiazide Diuretics

Mechanism of action	Inhibit reabsorption of sodium and chloride at distal renal tubule
Side effects	Dry mouth, fast or irregular heartbeat, muscle pain or weakness
Special instructions	Take in morning; avoid excessive exposure to sunlight
Drug interactions	Lithium, diabetes drugs (may cause hyperglycemia)

GENERIC NAME	INDICATION	DOSAGE FORM	DOSAGE
chlorthalidone	Adjunctive therapy in edema associated with CHF or renal dysfunction, hypertension	Tablets	25mg–100mg PO QD
hydrochlorothiazide	Adjunctive therapy in edema associated with CHF or renal dysfunction, hypertension	Tablets	25mg–100mg PO QD
lisinopril and hydrochlorothiazide	Hypertension	Tablets	10mg lisinopril/12.5mg hydrochlorothiazide to 20mg lisinopril/25mg hydrochlorothiazide PO QD
losartan and hydrochlorothiazide	Hypertension	Tablets	50mg losartan/12.5mg hydrochlorothiazide to 100mg losartan/25mg hydrochlorothiazide PO QD
triamterene and hydrochlorothiazide	Hypertension, adjunctive therapy in edema associated with CHF or renal dysfunction	Tablets Capsules	37.5mg triamterene/25mg hydrochlorothiazide to 75mg triamterene/50mg hydrochlorothiazide PO QD/BID
hydrochlorothiazide and valsartan	Hypertension	Tablets	80mg valsartan/12.5mg hydrochlorothiazide to 320mg valsartan/25mg hydrochlorothiazide PO QD

The Immune System and Drugs

The immune system consists of many structures that help protect the body from pathogens (bacteria, virus, or other organism) and aid in immunity. As mentioned earlier, the thymus gland produces T-cells, which play an essential role in the immune response. T-cells are a type of lymphocyte, or white blood cell, and help kill foreign cells or regulate the immune response. The lymph system also plays a role in immunity by circulating lymph (clear fluid made of white blood cells) through the body to lymph nodes and other organs that help fight infection. If a pathogen is recognized in the lymph fluid, the nodes produce more white blood cells causing them to swell. Lymph nodes are located in clusters throughout the body, including the neck, armpit, and groin. The spleen also aids in immunity by filtering old red blood cells and storing platelets and white blood cells. Disorders of the immune system are typically a result of an infection, allergic reaction, or autoimmune reaction.

Disorders of the Immune System	
Infection	Foreign substance or pathogen enters the body and causes harm, typically one of the following: ■ Bacterium ■ Virus ■ Fungus
Overactive Immune System	Hypersensitivity to allergens, including dust, mold, pollen, or food. ■ Asthma → can be triggered by allergens ■ Eczema → itchy skin rash caused by allergic dermatitis ■ Allergic rhinitis → sneezing, runny nose, and sniffling
Autoimmune Disease	Disease in which the body attacks healthy tissue, including: ■ Diabetes type 1 → attacks cells in pancreas ■ Rheumatoid arthritis → attacks joints ■ Lupus → attacks various body tissues, including lungs, kidneys, and skin
AIDS	Acquired immunodeficiency syndrome caused by the human immunodeficiency virus (HIV), which damages the immune system and prevents the body from fighting infections

The following are the drug classes are reviewed individually for treatment of immune system disorders.

ANTI-INFECTIVE DRUG CLASS	STEM	TOP 200 DRUG EXAMPLES
Antibiotic—cephalosporin	*ceph-, cef-*	cephalexin, cefdinir
Antibiotic—Fluoroquinolone	*-oxacin*	ciprofloxacin, levofloxacin
Antibiotic—macrolide	*-mycin*	azithromycin
Antibiotic—penicillin	*-cillin*	amoxicillin, amoxicillin with clavulanate
Antibiotic—sulfonamide	*-sulfa*	sulfamethoxazole and trimethoprim
Antibiotic—tetracycline	*-cycline*	doxycycline
Antibiotic		clindamycin, metronidazole, nitrofurantoin
Antiviral	*-vir*	acyclovir, valacyclovir, oseltamivir
Antifungal	*-conazole*	fluconazole
Topical corticosteroid	*-cort-*	hydrocortisone
Topical antibiotic		neomycin/bacitracin/polymixin B, mupirocin

These drug classes to treat disorders of the special senses are reviewed to include the following:

- Mechanism of action
- Side effects
- Special handling and administration instructions
- Drug interactions
- Indications
- Dosage form
- Dosage and duration of therapy

Antibiotic—Cephalosporins	
Mechanism of action	Disrupt the synthesis of the bacterial cell wall, causing cell death
Side effects	Nausea, vomiting, diarrhea, rash
Special instructions	Complete full course of antibiotic therapy; cephalosporins are cross-sensitive with penicillins by 5%–10%
Drug interactions	Oral contraceptives

GENERIC NAME	INDICATION	DOSAGE FORM	DOSAGE
cephalexin	Cystitis, infections due to *E. coli*, streptococci, staphylococci, *H. influenzae*	Capsules Tablets Oral suspension	250mg–1000mg PO Q6H
cefdinir	Community-acquired pneumonia, pharyngitis, tonsillitis, skin infection, otitis media	Capsules Oral suspension	600mg PO daily in 1 or 2 doses

Antibiotic—Fluoroquinolones	
Mechanism of action	Inhibit enzymes required for bacterial DNA synthesis, causing bacterial cell death
Side effects	Nausea, vomiting, dizziness, headache
Special instructions	Complete full course of antibiotic therapy; may cause ruptures in shoulder, hand, and Achilles tendons (black box warning)
Drug interactions	NSAIDs, corticosteroids, antidepressants, warfarin

GENERIC NAME	INDICATION	DOSAGE FORM	DOSAGE
ciprofloxacin	Sinusitis, infectious diarrhea, bone and joint infections respiratory tract infections, pneumonia, cystitis, UTI, anthrax	Tablets Tablets (extended release) Oral suspension Injection	250mg–500mg PO Q12H × 7–21 days (depending on infection type)
levofloxacin	Pneumonia, sinusitis, chronic bronchitis, prostatitis, UTI, anthrax	Tablets Oral solution Injection	500mg PO QD × 7 days

Antibiotic—Macrolides

Mechanism of action	Inhibit formation of bacterial proteins, ceasing bacterial growth
Side effects	Nausea, vomiting, ringing in ears (tinnitus)
Special instructions	Do not take with liver impairment, do not take antacids within 2 hours before or after administration
Drug interactions	Antacids, amiodarone

GENERIC NAME	INDICATION	DOSAGE FORM	DOSAGE
azithromycin	Sinusitis, otitis media, pneumonia, pharynitis, skin infections, gonorrhea	Tablets Oral suspension Injection	500mg on first day, than 250mg once daily for 4 days (ZPAK)

Antibiotic—Penicillins

Mechanism of action	Inhibit final step in bacterial cell wall production, killing the bacteria
Side effects	Nausea, vomiting, diarrhea, rash
Special instructions	Do not take with liver impairment; cross-sensitivity with cephalosporin allergy is 5%–10%
Drug interactions	Methotrexate

GENERIC NAME	INDICATION	DOSAGE FORM	DOSAGE
amoxicillin	Ear, nose and throat infections; infections of the genitourinary tract (urinary and reproductive); lower respiratory infections, *H. pylori* (causing ulcer); anthrax; endocarditis	Tablets Chewable tablets Capsules Oral suspension	250mg–500mg PO Q8H or 500mg–750mg PO Q12H
amoxicillin and clavulanate	Lower respiratory tract infection, COPD, sinusitis, animal bite wounds, skin abscess	Tablets Chewable tablets Tablets (ER) Oral suspension	500mg amoxicillin/125mg clavulanate tablet PO Q8H or 875mg amoxicillin/125mg clavulanate tablet PO Q12H

Antibiotic—Sulfonamides	
Mechanism of action	Interfere with bacterial synthesis of folic acid, which is required for bacterial growth
Side effects	Photosensitivity, rash, diarrhea, nausea
Special instructions	Avoid sunlight during therapy
Drug interactions	Warfarin, lisinopril, methotrexate

GENERIC NAME	INDICATION	DOSAGE FORM	DOSAGE
sulfamethoxazole and trimethoprim	UTI, otitis media, traveler's diarrhea	Tablets—regular strength Tablets—double strength Oral suspension Injection	800mg sulfamethoxazole/160mg trimethoprim Q12H × 10 to 14 days

Antibiotic—Tetracyclines	
Mechanism of action	Inhibit bacterial protein synthesis, stopping growth
Side effects	Loss of appetite, nausea, vomiting, diarrhea, photosensitivity
Special instructions	Avoid sunlight during therapy; should not be used in children under 8 (tooth staining)
Drug interactions	Antacids, calcium supplements, carbamazepine

GENERIC NAME	INDICATION	DOSAGE FORM	DOSAGE
doxycycline	Rocky mountain spotted fever, chlamydia, gonorrhea, respiratory tract infection, anthrax	Tablets Capsules Oral syrup Oral suspension Injection	100mg PO Q12H

Antibiotics	
Mechanism of action	Inhibit bacterial growth or causes bacterial cell death
Side effects	Nitrofurantoin may cause urine discoloration
Special instructions	Clindamycin should be taken with a full glass of water to avoid irritation
Drug interactions	Metronidazole must not be taken with alcohol

GENERIC NAME	INDICATION	DOSAGE FORM	DOSAGE
metronidazole	Bacterial vaginosis, pelvic inflammatory disease, skin or soft tissue infection, surgical prophylaxis	Tablets Capsules Tablets (extended release) Injection	250mg–500mg PO TID × 7 days
clindamycin	Osteomyelitis, pelvic inflammatory disease, postpartum endometritis, skin and soft tissue infections, toxic shock syndrome	Capsules Injection	150mg–450mg PO Q6H 150mg–600mg IM, IV Q6H, max dose of 600mg/dose IM
nitrofurantoin	Cystitis, bacteriuria	Capsules Macrocrystal capsules Suspension	100mg PO Q12H × 7 days

Antivirals	
Mechanism of action	Terminate growing viral DNA to inhibit growth
Side effects	Nausea, vomiting, diarrhea, fatigue
Special instructions	Take as soon as possible after symptoms present; can cause renal injury—do not take with renal impairment, drink water to avoid crystallized stones
Drug interactions	Shingles vaccine, varicella vaccine

GENERIC NAME	INDICATION	DOSAGE FORM	DOSAGE
acyclovir	Genital herpes, treatment for chickenpox, treatment of herpes zoster (shingles)	Capsules Tablets Ointment Cream Oral suspension Injection	200mg PO Q4H while awake (5 times daily) × 10 days
oseltamivir	Treatment of influenza who have had symptoms for no more than 48 hours, prophylaxis of influenza	Capsules Oral suspension	75mg PO QD (prophylaxis) 75mg PO BID (treatment) for 5 days 30–60mg PO BID (pediatric)
valacyclovir	Genital herpes, treatment of herpes zoster (shingles), treatment of cold sores	Tablets	1g PO BID × 10 days

Antifungals	
Mechanism of action	Inhibit the fungal enzyme preventing fungal cell growth
Side effects	Headache, dizziness, rash, nausea
Special instructions	Do not take with patients who have an arrhythmia, are pregnant or nursing
Drug interactions	Erythromycin

GENERIC NAME	INDICATION	DOSAGE FORM	DOSAGE
fluconazole	Vaginal candidiasis (yeast infection), esophageal candidiasis, oropharyngeal candidiasis	Tablets Oral suspension Injection	150mg PO × one dose

Topical Corticosteroids	
Mechanism of action	Prevent release of inflammatory substances, reducing inflammation
Side effects	Local itching or burning, crusting of skin, thinning of skin causing easy bruising
Special instructions	Do not use around the eyes
Drug interactions	Systemic corticosteroids

GENERIC NAME	INDICATION	DOSAGE FORM	DOSAGE
hydrocortisone	Relief of inflammatory and pruritic manifestations of dermatoses, hemorrhoids	Ointment Cream Rectal cream, foam, and gel Lotion	Apply to affected area BID/TID

Topical Antibiotics	
Mechanism of action	Inhibit bacterial cell wall synthesis
Side effects	Burning or stinging
Special instructions	Do not use around the eyes
Drug interactions	None known

GENERIC NAME	INDICATION	DOSAGE FORM	DOSAGE
mupirocin	Prevention of topical infections from minor cuts, scrapes or burns	Ointment Nasal ointment Cream	Apply 1 to 3 times daily to affected area
bacitracin, neomycin, and polymyxin B	Prevention of topical infections from minor cuts	Ointment	Apply 1 to 3 times daily to affected area

The Musculoskeletal System and Drugs

The musculoskeletal system consists of muscles, bones, joints and other supportive structures to provide stability and movement for the body. The following are the main structures of the system and potential disorders.

Structure of the Musculoskeletal System	
Joint	Connection between two bones, includes hinge (elbows, ankles, knees), ball-and-socket (shoulder and hip) and pivot (neck and vertebrae); surrounded by synovial fluid for movement
Bursa	Sac that contains synovial fluid, helps facilitate motion between joints
Cartilage	Padding that covers the ends of long bones for protection, such as in the knee
Ligament	Connects a joint to a bone
Tendon	Connects a muscle to a bone
Muscle	Voluntary (conscious control) and involuntary (unconscious control) that permits movement, including: Smooth muscle → involuntary, lining of organs Cardiac muscle → involuntary, heart Skeletal muscle → voluntary, attached to bones to control movement

The following are the disorders of the musculoskeletal system.

Disorders of Muscles and Joints	
Arthritis	Inflammation of the joints
Fever	Body temperature above 99°F
Gout	Complex form of arthritis caused by excessive uric acid, affects the joints—most specifically that of the big toe
Inflammation	Localized condition of reddening, swelling, and hotness, which is often painful
Pain	Distressful feeling caused by damaging stimuli
Spasm	Involuntary muscle contractions
Sprain	Stretch or tear in a ligament
Strain	Overstretching of muscle
Tendonitis	Inflammation of the tendon

The following are the drug classes are reviewed individually for treatment of musculoskeletal system disorders.

MUSCULOSKELETAL DRUG CLASS	STEM	TOP 200 DRUG EXAMPLES
Non-steroidal anti-inflammatory Drugs (NSAIDs)	-ac, -profen	diclofenac, ibuprofen, meloxicam, naproxen
Narcotic analgesic		acetaminophen with hydrocodone, hydrocodone, morphine, oxycodone, tramadol
Nonnarcotic analgesic		acetaminophen, aspirin
Topical analgesic		menthol
Muscle relaxants		cyclobenzaprine, baclofen, methocarbamol, tizanidine
Cyclooxygenase-2 (COX-2) inhibitors	-coxib	celecoxib
Antigout		allopurinol
Antirheumatic agent	-trexate	methotrexate, hydroxychloroquine

These drug classes to treat disorders of the special senses are reviewed to include the following:

- Mechanism of action
- Side effects
- Special handling and administration instructions
- Drug interactions
- Indications
- Dosage form
- Dosage and duration of therapy

Non-Steroidal Anti-inflammatory Drugs (NSAIDs)	
Mechanism of action	Inhibit enzyme (cyclooxygenase) which decreases production of prostaglandins (cause inflammation) and lowers inflammation
Side effects	Nausea, indigestion, stomach ulcer, tinnitus
Special instructions	NSAIDs have antipyretic, anti-inflammatory, and analgesic effects
Drug interactions	Aspirin, diuretics, beta blockers, warfarin

GENERIC NAME	INDICATION	DOSAGE FORM	DOSAGE
diclofenac	Rheumatoid arthritis, osteoarthritis, ankylosing spondylitis, pain	Tablets (extended release) Tablets (enteric-coated)	50mg PO TID–QID, 75mg PO BID, or 100mg PO QD
ibuprofen	Mild to moderate pain, dysmenorrheal; rheumatoid arthritis and osteoarthritis	Tablets Injection	200mg–800mg PO TID–QID
meloxicam	Rheumatoid arthritis, osteoarthritis	Tablets Oral suspension	5mg–15mg PO QD
naproxen	Mild to moderate pain, ankylosing spondylitis Rheumatoid arthritis, osteoarthritis, relief of acute gout	Tablets	500mg PO BID

Narcotic Analgesics	
Mechanism of action	Binds to opioid receptors in the brain and alters perception of pain
Side effects	Drowsiness, dizziness, constipation, nausea, vomiting, headache
Special instructions	May become habit forming; narcotic analgesics are scheduled drugs; when discontinuing therapy, dose should be tapered down to avoid symptoms of withdrawal
Drug interactions	Alcohol and other CNS depressants

GENERIC NAME	INDICATION	DOSAGE FORM	DOSAGE
acetaminophen with hydrocodone	Moderate to severe pain	Tablets Elixir Oral solution	1–2 tablets PO Q4–6hrs PRN Max dose of acetaminophen is 4000mg/day
hydrocodone	Severe pain	Tablet (extended release 24 hr) Capsule (extended release 12 hr)	20mg PO QD or 10mg Q12H
morphine	Moderate to severe pain	Tablet (extended release) Capsules (extended release 24 hr) Injection Oral solution suppository	10mg PO Q4H PRN, may increase up to 30mg PO Q4H

(continued)

GENERIC NAME	INDICATION	DOSAGE FORM	DOSAGE
oxycodone	Management of chronic moderate to severe pain when alternative treatments are inadequate	Tablets (controlled release) Capsules Capsules (ER12 hr) Oral concentrate	5mg–15mg PO Q4–6hr PRN
tramadol	Moderate to severe pain	Tablets Tablet (extended release) Capsule (extended release)	50mg–100mg PO Q4–6hr max dose is 400mg/day

Non-Narcotic Analgesics	
Mechanism of action	Reduce production of prostaglandins, lowering inflammation
Side effects	Liver toxicity (acetaminophen), tinnitus, stomach pain, and coughing up blood (aspirin)
Special instructions	To prevent liver damage: max dose for healthy adult for acetaminophen is 4,000mg/day; renal or liver impairment should be max 3,000mg/day.
Drug interactions	Warfarin, NSAIDS (aspirin)

GENERIC NAME	INDICATION	DOSAGE FORM	DOSAGE
acetaminophen	Mild to moderate pain, fever	Tablet Tablet (extended release) Tablet chewable Caplet Caplet (ER) Capsule Oral liquid Oral solution Oral suspension Injection Suppository	325mg–650mg PO Q4H PRN—must not exceed 4,000mg/day Pediatric: dosing based off weight—10mg/kg/dose to 15mg/kg/dose Q4–6hr PRN
aspirin	Pain, inflammation, fever, vascular indications	Caplet Caplet (enteric coated) Capsule (ER) Tablet Tablet chewable Tablet (enteric coated) Suppository	325mg to 1g Q4–6hr PRN max dose 4000mg/day (antipyretic and analgesic) Tablet should be chewed for a rapid onset

Topical Analgesics	
Mechanism of action	Dilate blood vessels to create cold sensation, leads to analgesic effect
Side effects	Burning sensation, stinging
Special instructions	For topical use only, do not use on open wounds or cuts
Drug interactions	Avoid use with other anesthetics

GENERIC NAME	INDICATION	DOSAGE FORM	DOSAGE
Menthol	Topical anesthetic	Cream, gel, lotion, patch	Apply film or patch up to QID

Muscle Relaxants	
Mechanism of action	Inhibit transmission of muscle reflexes
Side effects	Drowsiness, dizziness, headache, dry mouth
Special instructions	Avoid use in geriatric patients
Drug interactions	Alcohol and other CNS depressants

GENERIC NAME	INDICATION	DOSAGE FORM	DOSAGE
baclofen	Multiple sclerosis	Oral solution Injection Intrathecal solution Tablet	5mg PO TID, may increase up to 20mg PO QID
cyclobenzaprine	Relief of skeletal muscle spasm or pain	Tablets Capsules	5mg PO TID, can increase to 10mg TID
methocarbamol	Muscle spasm, tetanus	Tablets Injection	1.5g PO QID for up to 3 days, then decrease dose 1g–2g IM or IV
tizanidine	Muscle spasm and pain	Capsule Tablet	2mg–4mg PO Q6–12hr PRN

COX-2 Inhibitors	
Mechanism of action	Inhibit cyclooygenase-2 (COX2), which inhibits prostaglandin production, leading to reduced inflammation
Side effects	Peripheral edema, diarrhea, dyspepsia
Special instructions	Lowest effective dose should be used for the shortest duration of time; due to increased risk of cardiovascular events—avoid in patients with cardiovascular disease
Drug interactions	Ketorolac, NSAIDs

GENERIC NAME	INDICATION	DOSAGE FORM	DOSAGE
celecoxib	Ankylosing spondylitis, rheumatoid arthritis, osteoarthritis, management of acute pain and dysmenorrhea	Capsules	200mg PO QD or 100mg PO BID

Antigout	
Mechanism of action	Inhibit enzyme responsible for uric acid production, which lowers uric acid in the body
Side effects	Rash, nausea, and vomiting
Special instructions	Should be administered after meals
Drug interactions	Amoxicillin

GENERIC NAME	INDICATION	DOSAGE FORM	DOSAGE
allopurinol	Gout, prevention of kidney stones	Tablets Injection	100mg PO QD, max up to 800mg/day

Antirheumatic Agents	
Mechanism of action	Mechanism is unknown for treatment of arthritis, but inhibits DNA synthesis
Side effects	Stomach upset and nausea, dizziness, chest pain, hypotension, alopecia, burning sensation of skin
Special instructions	Take with food or milk for upset stomach; do not exceed maximum dose—can cause permanent vision loss (hydroxychloroquine)
Drug interactions	Loop diuretics, sulfonamide antibiotics, beta blockers

GENERIC NAME	INDICATION	DOSAGE FORM	DOSAGE
hydroxychloroquine	Rheumatoid arthritis, malaria, lupus	Tablets	200mg–400mg PO QD 400mg PO QW (malaria)
methotrexate	Treatment of breast cancer, control of psoriasis, treatment of rheumatoid arthritis, head and neck cancer, lymphoma, osteosarcoma	Tablets Injection Oral solution	10mg–25mg PO QW

Special Senses and Drugs

The special senses system includes the organs devoted to our senses of vision, hearing, balance, taste, and smell. These organs include the eyes, ears, nose, and throat. Medications used in the ear and eye can be solutions, suspensions, or ointments. Ophthalmic medications are able to be administered into the ear, but otic medications must never be used in the eye, due to the pH of otic solutions burning if administered in the eye. Medications given through the intranasal route are administered through a nasal spray, which is a solution that forms a mist when sprayed into the nose. Medications for the throat are typically lozenges or sprays that act as a numbing agent to treat pain, such as benzocaine.

You can review some common senses disorders that follow.

Disorders of the Special Senses	
Conjunctivitis	Inflammation of the conjunctiva (membrane that covers front of eye), which causes redness and itching; highly contagious, known as pink eye
Glaucoma	High pressure in the eye, which can destroy the optic nerve and lead to blindness
Otitis media	Infection of the middle ear
Pharyngitis	Inflammation of the pharynx or throat

The following drug classes are reviewed individually for treatment of special sense disorders.

SENSES DRUG CLASS	STEM	TOP 200 DRUG EXAMPLES
Glaucoma agent		brimonidine, latanoprost
Ophthalmic beta blocker	-olol	timolol
Topical antibiotics for eye and ear		bacitracin; neomycin; polymyxin B, ciprofloxacin (otic and ophthalmic)

These drug classes to treat disorders of the special senses are reviewed to include the following:

- Mechanism of action
- Side effects
- Special handling and administration instructions
- Drug interactions
- Indications
- Dosage form
- Dosage and duration of therapy

Glaucoma Agents	
Mechanism of action	Reduce intraocular pressure within the eye
Side effects	Blurred vision; stinging or burning; may increase or change the pigmentation of the iris or eyelid skin, or change the length of the eyelashes
Special instructions	If administering with other ophthalmic drugs, administer at least 5 minutes apart; remove contact lenses before administering, and wait 15 minutes before reinserting
Drug interactions	Ophthalmic NSAIDs (latanoprost); CNS depressants such as alcohol, oxycodone, or zolpidem (brimonidine)

GENERIC NAME	INDICATION	DOSAGE FORM	DOSAGE
brimonidine	Glaucoma, elevated intraocular pressure, and ocular redness	Ophthalmic solution	One drop into affected eye every 6 to 8 hours, up to 4 times daily
latanoprost	Elevated intraocular pressure	Ophthalmic solution	One drop into affected eye QPM
timolol	Elevated intraocular pressure in patients with glaucoma	Ophthalmic solution, gel-forming solution	One drop into affected eye BID

Topical Antibiotics for Eye and Ear	
Mechanism of action	Prevent growth of bacteria in eye and ear
Side effects	Stinging and burning in eye after administration, headache
Special instructions	Otic solution should be warmed in hands for 1 minute prior to administration
Drug interactions	No known drug interactions

GENERIC NAME	INDICATION	DOSAGE FORM	DOSAGE
Bacitracin; Neomycin; Polymyxin B	Treatment of ophthalmic infection caused by bacteria	Ophthalmic ointment	Apply to affected eye every 3 to 4 hours × 7 to 10 d
Ciprofloxacin (ophthalmic)	Bacterial conjunctivitis, corneal ulcer	Solution and ointment	1 to 2 drops into eye q2h while awake × 2 d
Ciprofloxacin (otic)	Otitis externa	Solution and suspension	Instill 1 drop into affected ear BID × 7 d

Dietary Supplements

Vitamins are essential substances that the body does not produce and we must instead get from our diet. Most vitamins are available as a supplement OTC, but some are prescribed for deficiencies.

The following are the most common vitamins with their drug name, function, and what food source contains a higher concentration.

VITAMIN	NAME	FUNCTION	FOOD SOURCE
A	retinol	Essential for vision	Fish, liver, mango, carrot, sweet potato, broccoli
B_1	thiamin	Enables body to use carbohydrates for energy	Yeast, beef, pork, whole grains, cauliflower, oranges
B_2	riboflavin	Energy production, cellular growth, metabolism of fats	Eggs, milk, liver, green vegetables, grains, and cereals (fortified)
B_3	niacin (nicotinic acid)	Converts carbohydrates into glucose, metabolizes fats and proteins	Poultry, beef, fish, nuts, legumes, and grains
B_5	pantothenate (Pantothenic acid)	Breaks down fats and carbohydrates for energy; promotes health skin, hair, and eyes	Poultry, fish, whole grains, eggs, milk, legumes, mushrooms, avocado, and broccoli
B_6	pyridoxine	Metabolism of protein	Fish, liver, potatoes

(continued)

VITAMIN	NAME	FUNCTION	FOOD SOURCE
B₇	biotin	Metabolism of protein	Liver, peanuts, pork, salmon, avocado, sardines, raspberries, bananas, and mushrooms
B₉	folate (folic acid)	Proper brain function, essential during pregnancy, red blood cell production	Spinach (leafy green vegetables), asparagus, turnips, beets, brussels sprouts, liver, beans
B₁₂	cyanocobalamin	Red blood cell formation, neurological function	Fish, poultry, eggs, milk
C	ascorbic acid	Growth and repair of tissue (wound healing through collagen), antioxidant	Citrus fruits, tomatoes and tomato juice, potatoes, peppers, kiwi, broccoli, strawberries
D₂	ergocalciferol	Helps body absorb calcium and phosphorus	Salmon, tuna, eggs, mushrooms
D₃	cholecalciferol	Helps body absorb calcium and phosphorus	Salmon, tuna, some dairy (fortified)
E	tocopherols	Antioxidant, protects cells from free radical damage	Nuts, seeds, vegetable oil, soybeans, corn
K	phytonadione	Blood clotting	Spinach, asparagus, broccoli, legumes, eggs

Some vitamins are prescribed frequently and indicated for treatment of disease. The following are the most commonly prescribed vitamins and the indication for each.

VITAMINS	INDICATIONS	TOP 200 DRUG EXAMPLES
Vitamin D	Osteoporosis, vitamin D insufficiency	ergocalciferol
Vitamin B₁₂	Vitamin B₁₂ deficiency, pernicious anemia	cyanocobalamin
Vitamin B₉	Anemia, supplement to be taken during pregnancy	folic acid

Minerals are also needed in the body in small amounts for proper functioning. They can be taken as an OTC supplement or prescribed as well. Each mineral has a specific function in the body.

The following are the most common minerals in our body and the source of food in which they're found.

MINERAL	FUNCTION	FOOD SOURCE
calcium	Bone and teeth formation	Dairy
iodine	Thyroid hormone development	Table salt, seafood
iron	Oxygen transport	Eggs, green vegetables, liver, meat, nuts, whole grains
magnesium	Nerve and muscle function, bones	Eggs, green vegetables, fish, milk, nuts
potassium	Regulation of heartbeat, nerve and muscle function	Cereal, coffee, fruit, meat, vegetables
sodium	Regulation of body fluids, pH balance, nerve and muscle electrical transmission	Processed foods, salt

Some minerals are prescribed and indicated for treatment of disease. The following are the most commonly prescribed minerals and the indication of each.

MINERAL	INDICATIONS	TOP 200 DRUG EXAMPLES
iron	Iron deficiency anemia	ferrous sulfate
magnesium	Magnesium dietary supplement, antacid	magnesium
potassium	Treatment of hypokalemia, hypertension, arrhythmia	potassium

Herbal supplements are nutrients extracted from a plant or natural source for a therapeutic benefit. Although the FDA does require testing for safety, these products are not required to prove effectiveness. Herbal supplements may also interact with prescription medications, and a lack of research prevents data on all potential interactions.

The following are common herbal supplements and the proposed use of each. Keep in mind, each labeled bottle of supplement will state that "these statements have not been evaluated by the Food and Drug Administration." This means the FDA does not stand by the health claims of the manufacturer.

SUPPLEMENT	USES
aloe vera	Topical use for burns and psoriasis; oral use for constipation
black cohosh	Menopausal symptoms such as hot flashes, night sweats, or vaginal dryness
chamomile	Taken orally for sleeplessness and anxiety, can be used topically for skin issues
chondroitin	Arthritis, often taken with glucosamine
cranberry	UTI prevention
echinacea	Treats cold and flu symptoms
flaxseed	Source of fiber, lowers cholesterol
gingko	Memory issues, tinnitus
glucosamine	Arthritis, often taken with chondroitin
melatonin	Insomnia
peppermint	Nausea, indigestion, bowel problems
saw palmetto	Benign prostatic hypertrophy (enlarged prostate)
St. John's wort	Depression, anxiety, and sleep disorder

Drug Interactions

Drug interactions occur when one drug or substance alters the action of another drug. This can produce unexpected side effects, toxic concentrations, or lack of effectiveness of a drug. Drug interactions can be harmful and include interactions with both OTC and supplements.

There are several different types of drug interactions that can occur. The following is a list of the different interactions and examples of each type.

INTERACTION	DESCRIPTION	EXAMPLE
Drug–drug	One drug impacts another drug	May be additive, antagonistic, potentiated, or synergistic
Additive drug–drug	Two drugs given together have the same effect if each were taken separately	Acetaminophen and aspirin = pain relief of each drug
Antagonistic drug–drug	One drug reduces effect or inhibits another drug; often used for antidotes	Naloxone and oxycodone = naloxone blocks the opioid receptors and inhibits the effect of oxycodone
Potentiated drug–drug	Two drugs given together causes an increase in duration or prolonging of one of the drugs	Amoxicillin and clavulanate = clavulanate potentiates the action of amoxicillin and increases inhibition of bacterial growth
Synergistic drug–drug	Two drugs given together results in an effect greater than just the sum of the two drugs	Aspirin and warfarin = greater effect of anticoagulation leads to excessive bleeding
Drug–disease	Disease alters ADME properties of a drug	A patient with chronic kidney disease who takes a drug excreted by the kidneys could get a toxic buildup
Drug–dietary supplement	Interaction with a drug and dietary supplement that results in a greater or diminished effect	St. John's wort and sertraline = St. John's wort can prevent the elimination of serotonin causing a dangerously high level in the body
Drug–laboratory	Drug alters results of laboratory tests, leading to false-positive or false-negative results	Cephalexin can cause a false positive urine glucose test
Drug–nutrient	An interaction between a drug and nutrients from vitamins and minerals consumed through food or drink	Grapefruit juice and simvastatin = grapefruit juice prevents the breakdown of statins and can lead to an increase in toxic accumulation

Therapeutic Equivalence

Therapeutic equivalence is defined by the FDA as drug products that can be substituted and produce the same clinical effect and have the same safety profile. Certain requirements must be met before a drug can be considered therapeutically equivalent, including:

- Must contain the same active ingredient
- Must be the same dosage form, route of administration, and strength
- Clinical effect and safety profile are the same when administered to patients under same conditions as specified in labeling
- **Bioequivalence** is demonstrated

If all the listed criteria are met, the FDA will assign an A-rated therapeutic equivalence (TE) code. These TE codes are published in the FDA Orange Book. The Orange Book consists of all drugs that are approved as therapeutically equivalent and given an A-code. A drug product the FDA does not deem to be therapeutically equivalent is given a B-code.

While there are many different TE codes based on the dosage form, the following are some examples of A- and B-rated TE codes that are listed in the FDA Orange Book.

TE CODE	DESCRIPTION
AB	Product meets necessary bioequivalence requirements (any potential problems have been resolved)
AP	Injectable solutions
AT	Topical products
BC	Extended-release dosage forms (bioequivalence data not submitted)
BD	Active ingredient or dosage form with documented bioequivalence problems
BT	Topical products with bioequivalence issues

Narrow Therapeutic Index (NTI)

If a drug has a narrow therapeutic index (NTI), a small difference in dosing could lead to a major therapeutic failure or adverse reaction that could be life-threatening. NTI drugs often have requirements for generic substitution, because if there are any even minor differences in bioequivalence, it could result in toxic effects or a lack of effectiveness, leading to treatment failure. Treatment failure itself can be life-threatening, as many of these medications are anticonvulsants, and if dosing is not precise, seizures may not be controlled. If a prescriber is going to modify a treatment regimen, it will often be in very small incremental dosages to avoid potential adverse effects.

The following are frequently prescribed drugs with an NTI:

GENERIC	BRAND	DRUG CLASS
carbamzepine	Tegretol	Anticonvulsant
digoxin	Digitek	Antiarrhythmic
levothyroxine	Levoxyl, Levothroid	Thyroid hormone
lithium	Lithobid	Bipolar disorder agent
phenytoin	Dilantin	Anticonvulsant
warfarin	Coumadin	Anticoagulant
theophylline	Theo-24	Xanthines

Drug Stability

Drug stability refers to the capacity of a product to retain its established strength, quality, and purity. This includes chemical, physical, and therapeutic properties. The following factors can affect drug stability:

- Temperature—high temperature can accelerate drug breakdown
- pH—too alkaline (basic) or acidic can influence how quickly a drug degrades
- Light—can cause reactions that break down drug; some drugs are photosensitive and must be protected from light (packaged in amber vial)
- Moisture—water can induce reactions, which can degrade a drug

A drug shelf life or expiration date is determined by the manufacturer of the medication and indicates the time a drug will be stable if it is stored under appropriate conditions. This is different from a beyond-use-date (BUD), which is determined by the pharmacy compounding the medication and is based on sterility and stability information from pharmacy standards. A BUD is the date or time a compounded product is no longer stable or sterile and may not be dispensed to a patient.

Reconstituted Medications

The stability of a drug can also depend on the dosage form. Solid dosage forms are more stable than liquid dosage forms, and this is demonstrated in reconstitutables such as oral suspensions or reconstituted injections. These medications are in a powder form that then becomes liquid after adding a **diluent.** Reconstitution occurs when a diluent, or liquid used to dilute or reconstitute, is added to a powder, forming a liquid.

Oral suspensions have an expiration date from the manufacturer on the bottle, and once the diluent is added, the BUD is significantly shorter. The BUD is the amount of time the suspension will be stable, assuming that the medication was stored properly. To maximize shelf life, oral suspensions and reconstituted injections are not reconstituted until needed for patient treatment. This helps keep good-dated inventory available for use.

Oral suspensions can often be stored at room temperature, though some require refrigeration. The following are frequently prescribed oral suspensions and storage and stability for each.

DRUG	STORAGE REQUIREMENT	STABILITY
amoxicillin	Room temperature or refrigerated	14 days
amoxicillin with clavulanate	Refrigerated	10 days
azithromycin	Room temperature	10 days
cephalexin	Refrigerated	14 days
cefdinir	Room temperature	10 days

Whether reconstituting an oral suspension or injection, the required volume of diluent is indicated on the label. It is very important the diluent chosen and volume used for reconstitution are the same as what is indicated on the label or in the product package insert. Oral suspensions are typically reconstituted with distilled water, while injections may use sterile water or sodium chloride as a diluent.

Not all injectable drugs require reconstitution. Liquid injectable drugs are available as solutions or suspensions and as single-dose vials (SDV) or multiple-dose vials (MDV). SDVs do not contain a preservative and are therefore used for one patient or treatment. Once an SDV is opened, it must be used within 6 hours (if opened in an ISO class 5 hood). If an SDV is opened outside of a hood, it must be used within 1 hour.

Ampules are also single use and do not contain a preservative. They are a glass container that is designed to be broken at the neck. The medication inside is removed using a filter needle, to protect against any residual glass that may have fallen in the contents. As soon as the ampule is open, it is exposed to air, and the stability is limited.

MDVs do contain a preservative, and this prevents the growth of microbials. MDVs, once opened, typically have a BUD of 28 days, though this may depend on the drug. Pharmacy technicians are often responsible for reviewing MDVs on nursing units to ensure the BUD has been properly dated on each vial after opening. As long as the patient dose from an MDV is not drawn up in the patient's room, the remaining contents of the vial may be used on another patient. If the MDV is opened or a dose drawn in the patient treatment area, the vial could become contaminated when the needle is inserted. This could potentially spread infection to others receiving the drug.

Insulin

Insulin vials are similar to MDVs in that they are stable until the expiration date on the vial before opening. After opening, most are good for 28 days, though there are some insulin types that have a longer BUD. The stability of insulin is dependent upon the storage conditions and the time since opening.

The following are top prescribed insulins and stability dating for each.

INSULIN	STABILITY UNOPENED STORED IN REFRIGERATOR	STABILITY UNOPENED STORED AT ROOM TEMPERATURE	STABILITY AFTER OPENING (ROOM TEMPERATURE OR REFRIGERATED)
Insulin aspart (Novolog)	Expiration date on label	28 days	28 days
Insulin lispro (Humalog)	Expiration date on label	28 days	28 days
Insulin regular (Humulin R)	Expiration date on label	31 days	31 days
Insulin glargine (Lantus)	Expiration date on label	28 days	28 days
Insulin detemir (Levemir)	Expiration date on label	42 days	42 days
Insulin regular (Novolin R)	Expiration date on label	42 days	42 days—do not refrigerate

Vaccinations

Vaccine stability depends on the dosage form and storage conditions. Vaccines are available in SDVs, MDVs, syringes, and reconstitutable vials, and storing each properly is an important part in vaccine protection for patients. The package insert of vaccines will define the BUD after opening. SDVs and syringes expire based on the expiration date assigned by the manufacturer. Vaccines that are MDV are typically still good until the expiration date of the manufacturer after opening. It's always important to check the vaccine package insert to determine the BUD. Vaccines that are reconstituted should be prepared immediately prior to administration to avoid limitations in BUD.

The following are a few commonly administered vaccines and BUDs (assuming appropriate storage conditions).

VACCINE	BRAND NAME	DOSAGE FORM	BUD
Measles, mumps, rubella	M-M-R II	Reconstituted vial	8 hours after reconstitution
Pneumococcal 13-valent	Prevnar 13	SDV and prefilled syringe	Manufacturer expiration date
Pneumococcal 23-valent	Pneumovax	SDV and prefilled syringe	Manufacturer expiration date
Tetanus, diphtheria, pertussis (Tdap)	Boostrix, Adacel	Single dose syringe	Manufacturer expiration date
Varicella	Varivax	Reconstituted vial	30 minutes after reconstitution
Zoster	Shingrix	Reconstituted vial	6 hours after reconstitution

Storage of Medications

An important component to maintaining drug stability is ensuring medications are stored properly. This includes storing in the appropriate temperature range, light and moisture precautions, and whether the drug should have restricted access.

Each drug has a specified temperature range indicated on the packaging to avoid loss of stability. For example, a drug that is intended to be stored at room temperature will have a labeling that states:

> Store at Controlled Room Temperature
> 20°C to 25°C (68°F–77°F) (See USP)

The USP standards for temperature ranges are defined as follows:

STORAGE	RANGE (C)	RANGE (F)
Freezer	−25°C to −10°C	−13°F to 14°F
Refrigerator (cold)	2°C to 8°C	36°F to 46°F
Cool	8°C to 15°C	46°F to 59°F
Controlled room temperature	20°C to 25°C	68°F to 77°F
Warm	30°C to 40°C	86°F to 104°F

In addition to temperature ranges, light and moisture sensitivity are important to consider when storing medications. Some medications require dispensing in the original manufacturer's packaging to protect from light sensitivity. Amber bottles, such as those generally used in a retail pharmacy, help minimize exposure to light and can protect against light degradation. Nitroglycerin is a medication that must be dispensed in original packaging. If a medication is light sensitive, it will be indicated on the labeling such as:

> Warning: Keep these tablets in original container.
> Close tightly immediately after use to prevent loss of potency.

Similar to light sensitivity, if a medication is moisture sensitive, it will degrade in the presence of liquid. For these medications, a **desiccant** is used as a drying agent. This absorbs any moisture that could potentially degrade the medication. When a desiccant is packaged with a medication, the original packaging should be dispensed. If a medication is moisture sensitive, it will be indicated on the labeling such as:

> Warning: Moisture sensitive tablets—do not remove from container until immediately prior to administration.

or

> Store at Controlled Room Temperature
> 20°C–25°C (68°F–77°F) and protect from moisture

Another aspect of drug storage is restricting access to medications that are not in their final dosage form and require compounding before administering to a patient. One example of this is concentrated electrolytes in a hospital. If these medications were stocked in a nursing unit outside of the pharmacy, the consequence of a medication error could be deadly. These include:

- Hypertonic sodium chloride 3%
- Potassium chloride 2mEq/mL

- Magnesium sulfate 50%
- Sodium bicarbonate 8.4%
- Sodium chloride 23.4% solution

Other restricted access would include controlled substances, which will be discussed more in Chapter 3, and hazardous drugs, which will be discussed more in Chapter 4.

Incompatibility

Drug stability can also be impacted by compatibility of drugs and the containers in which they are compounded. Incompatibility occurs when a drug reacts with a solution or diluent, the container it's compounded in, or with another drug. There are two types of incompatibility: physical and chemical.

A **physical incompatibility** is the interaction of two or more substances that results in a change in color, odor, taste, viscosity, or physical structure. An example of this would be a precipitate forming when two substances are mixed that are incompatible. Physical incompatibility can also include the insolubility or immiscibility of two substances. For example, when compounding creams, lotions, or ointments, if the active ingredient is not soluble, it would result in a physical incompatibility and the active ingredient would not be distributed evenly throughout the compound.

A **chemical incompatibility** is a reaction between two or more substances that causes a change in the chemical properties of a drug. Chemical incompatibilities are often unseen but can be observed through a temperature or color change due to oxidation. Change in pH or release of gas (effervescence) can also occur. Chemical incompatibilities can be dangerous to patients due to potential toxicity of the compounded medication. It can also cause treatment failure through ineffectiveness if the chemical reaction renders the drug inactive. A chemical incompatibility could occur in a compound with a light-sensitive ingredient not stored in a light-resistant container. The light could cause a breakdown in the medication, causing a lack of effectiveness.

When compounding medications, part of the master formula record is to monitor for signs of incompatibility. Ensuring the proper diluent is selected for compounding can help prevent incompatibility. Also, some medications are sensitive to polyvinyl chloride (PVC), which is the main component of IV bags. PVC-free IV bags are available for medications that may adhere to the PVC and not disperse within the fluid. Nitroglycerin is an example of this and must be dispensed in a glass container.

Review Questions

The following questions help you review the chapter. Test your knowledge by working through the next 50 questions to test yourself and identify any areas you may need to review.

1. The generic name for Hytrin is
   A. budesonide
   B. mupirocin
   C. labetalol
   D. terazosin

2. The drug class of meclizine is
   A. ACE inhibitor
   B. antiemetic
   C. antiviral
   D. Alzheimer's disease agent

3. Which of the following is the name brand of aripiprazole?
   A. Lotensin
   B. Bactroban
   C. Abilify
   D. Seroquel

4. A smaller volume of fluid administered IV, typically less than 250mL, is known as
   A. IV piggyback
   B. IV push
   C. large volume parenteral
   D. IM injection

5. Which route of administration involves the use of a machine to create a mist for medication inhalation into the lungs?
   A. nebulized
   B. otic
   C. nasal
   D. ophthalmic

6. Which of the following drugs is available as a sublingual tablet?
   A. hydralazine
   B. nitroglycerin
   C. metoprolol
   D. lisinopril

7. Which of the following is indicated to treat vertigo?

   A. polyethylene glycol 3350
   B. dicylomine
   C. pantoprazole
   D. meclizine

8. Which of the following is used for allergic and inflammatory disease and is dispensed in a Dosepak with a 21-day treatment?

   A. alendronate
   B. prednisone
   C. methylprednisolone
   D. estradiol

9. Which of the following is indicated for treatment of narcolepsy and ADHD?

   A. sumatriptan
   B. dextroamphetamine and amphetamine
   C. lorazepam
   D. esomeprazole

10. Which of the following is indicated for overactive bladder?

    A. hydrochlorothiazide
    B. spironolactone
    C. oxybutynin
    D. finasteride

11. Which of the following is indicated to treat UTI, otitis media, and traveler's diarrhea?

    A. mupirocin
    B. sulfamethoxazole and trimethoprim
    C. doxycycline
    D. clindamycin

12. Which of the following inhibits COX-2?

    A. celecoxib
    B. methotrexate
    C. allopurinol
    D. cyclobenzaprine

13. A coated tablet designed to bypass the stomach and dissolve in the small intestine is

    A. chewable
    B. buccal
    C. enteric coated
    D. sublingual

14. Which type of dosage form is a thick liquid sweetened with sugar?

    A. irrigation
    B. suspension
    C. syrup
    D. enema

15. Which dosage form is solid at room temperature and melts at body temperature?

    A. suppository
    B. ointment
    C. gel
    D. cream

16. If a medication should be stored refrigerated, what temperature range would this be?

    A. −13°F to 14°F
    B. 36°F to 46°F
    C. 68°F to 77°F
    D. 86°F to 104°F

17. A technician compounding a cream notices the active ingredient powder is not dispersed throughout and is not dissolving into the base. What type of incompatibility might this be?

    A. physical
    B. chemical
    C. therapeutic
    D. desiccant

18. A drug packaged with a desiccant should be protected from

    A. light
    B. moisture
    C. sodium chloride
    D. amber bottle

19. TDAP contains which of the following vaccines?

    A. tetanus, diphtheria, and pneumococcal

    B. measles, mumps, and rubella

    C. varicella, diphtheria, and pertussis

    D. tetanus, diphtheria, and pertussis

20. Within how many days must most multi-dose vials be used after opening?

    A. 7

    B. 14

    C. 28

    D. 30

21. Which of the following would require a diluent to become a liquid?

    A. suspension

    B. syrup

    C. elixir

    D. ODT

22. An A-rated code in the FDA Orange Book means the drug is

    A. an injectable

    B. therapeutically equivalent

    C. a topical product

    D. not therapeutically equivalent

23. When one drug reduces the effect or inhibits another drug, this is a(n)

    A. additive drug–drug interaction

    B. antagonistic drug–drug interaction

    C. potentiated drug–drug interaction

    D. synergistic drug–drug interaction

24. Which of the following supplements can help prevent UTIs?

    A. flaxseed

    B. saw palmetto

    C. melatonin

    D. cranberry

25. A medication used to treat glaucoma would

    A. reduce secretion from the eye

    B. reduce stinging in the eye

    C. reduce pressure within the eye

    D. increase blood pressure

26. A generic medication that ends in -*olol* is which type of medication?
    A. benzodiazepine
    B. cephalosporin
    C. ACE inhibitor
    D. beta blocker

27. Amlodipine is used to treat
    A. high cholesterol
    B. high blood pressure
    C. diabetes
    D. thyroid disorder

28. The generic for Zoloft is
    A. albuterol
    B. omeprazole
    C. sertraline
    D. pantoprazole

29. Rosuvastatin is which type of drug?
    A. antihypertensive—beta blocker
    B. antihyperlipidemic—HMG-CoA reductase inhibitor
    C. antiplatelet
    D. antihypertensive—calcium channel blocker

30. A buccal tablet is administered between the
    A. gum and cheek
    B. tongue and throat
    C. skin and muscle
    D. tongue and roof of mouth

31. A solution used to wash wounds or bladders is a(n)
    A. enema
    B. suspension
    C. irrigation
    D. elixir

32. A medication administered IM is injected into the
    A. skin
    B. muscle
    C. vein
    D. artery

33. Which of the following drugs must be very carefully prescribed and has an NTI?

    A. lithium
    B. diphenhydramine
    C. lisinopril
    D. spironolactone

34. Ferrous sulfate is used to treat

    A. hypokalemia
    B. iron deficiency anemia
    C. indigestion
    D. hypertension

35. Vitamin B_{12} is also known as

    A. ergocalciferol
    B. folic acid
    C. phytonadione
    D. cyanocobalamin

36. Latanoprost is indicated to treat

    A. bacterial conjunctivitis
    B. elevated intraocular pressure
    C. corneal ulcer
    D. otitis media

37. Hydroxychloroquine can be used to treat malaria and

    A. breast cancer
    B. rheumatoid arthritis
    C. macular degeneration
    D. diabetes

38. Which of the following is given as one 150mg dose PO to treat vaginal candidiasis?

    A. hydrocortisone
    B. fluconazole
    C. tetracycline
    D. cephalexin

39. Metronidazole has a significant interaction if taken with

   A. alcohol

   B. water

   C. milk

   D. grapefruit juice

40. Photosensitivity is a side effect of which medication?

   A. hydrocodone

   B. sulfamethoxazole and trimethoprim

   C. docusate

   D. dicyclomine

41. Tamsulosin is indicated to treat

   A. overactive bladder disorder

   B. alopecia

   C. UTI

   D. BPH

42. Which medication is indicated for the treatment of migraines?

   A. atomexetine

   B. calcitonin

   C. sumatriptan

   D. levalbuterol

43. Dementia caused by Alzheimer's disease can be treated with

   A. carbidopa/levodopa

   B. donepezil

   C. quetiapine

   D. amitriptyline

44. Divalproex is in which class of drugs?

   A. antiparkinson agent

   B. nitrate

   C. antirheumatic agent

   D. anticonvulsant

45. The generic name of Lotensin is

   A. enalapril

   B. benazepril

   C. donepezil

   D. lisinopril

46. A drug with an ending of -*statin* belongs to which class?
    A. fibric acid derivative
    B. lipid regulating agent
    C. antihyperlipidemics (HMG-CoA reductase inhibitors)
    D. nitrates

47. Ezetimibe is indicated for
    A. edema associated with CHF
    B. myalgia
    C. lupus
    D. adjunctive treatment for reduction of cholesterol

48. Which of the following can be used to treat nausea and vomiting associated with chemotherapy?
    A. adalimumab
    B. ondansetron
    C. esomeprazole
    D. guaifenesin

49. Which of the following is available as an MDI and nasal spray?
    A. tiotropium
    B. albuterol
    C. fluticasone
    D. triamcinolone

50. Temazepam is indicated to treat
    A. depression
    B. insomnia
    C. ADHD
    D. dementia

Answer Key

1. **D**

   The generic name of Hytrin is terazosin.

2. **B**

   Meclizine is an antiemetic drug, which is used to prevent nausea and vomiting.

3. **C**

   Abilify is the name brand of aripiprazole.

4. **A**

   IV piggyback is a small volume of fluid, usually under 250mL, that is administered IV.

5. **A**

   Nebulized treatments are administered through a nebulizer for inhalation.

6. **B**

   Nitroglycerin is available as a sublingual tablet to dissolve under the tongue.

7. **D**

   Meclizine is indicated to treat vertigo.

8. **C**

   Methylprenisolone is indicated for the treatment of allergic and inflammatory disease, and is available as a 21-tablet tapering Dosepak.

9. **B**

   Dextroamphetamine and amphetamine are indicated for treatment of narcolepsy and ADHD.

10. **C**

    Oxybutynin is indicated for treatment of overactive bladder.

11. **B**

    Sulfamethoxazole and trimethoprim is indicated to treat UTI, otitis media, and traveler's diarrhea.

12. **A**

    Celecoxib inhibits COX-2.

13. **C**

    Enteric-coated tablets are designed to prevent breakdown in the stomach so they can be absorbed in the intestine and cannot be crushed or chewed.

14. **C**

    Syrup is a thick liquid sweetened with sugar.

15. **A**

A suppository is solid at room temperature and designed to melt at body temperature after insertion.

16. **B**

Refrigerated is in the temperature range 36°F to 46°F, or 2°C to 8°C.

17. **A**

Physical incompatibility can occur if the active ingredient is not soluble and would not be evenly distributed throughout the compound.

18. **B**

If a medication is moisture sensitive, it will degrade in the presence of liquid. For these medications, a desiccant is used as a drying agent. This absorbs any moisture that could potentially degrade the medication.

19. **D**

Tetanus, diphtheria, and pertussis is a vaccine called TDAP.

20. **C**

MDVs, once opened, typically have a BUD of 28 days.

21. **A**

Reconstitution occurs when a diluent, or liquid used to dilute or reconstitute, is added to a powder, forming a liquid, such as when a suspension is reconstituted.

22. **B**

The FDA will assign an A-rated therapeutic equivalence (TE) code if a drug is therapeutically equivalent.

23. **B**

An antagonistic drug–drug interaction is when one drug reduces the effect of or inhibits another drug.

24. **D**

Cranberry can be used to treat and prevent UTIs.

25. **C**

A medication used to treat glaucoma reduces intraocular pressure within the eye.

26. **D**

A beta blocker ends in *-olol* such as metoprolol or propranolol.

27. **B**

Amlodipine is a calcium channel blocker used to treat hypertension.

28. **C**

The generic for Zoloft is sertraline.

29. **B**

Rosuvastatin is an antihyperlipidemic—HMG-CoA reductase inhibitor. These drugs all end in *-statin*.

30. **A**

A buccal tablet is administered between the gum and cheek to dissolve and absor⁻¹ into blood vessels in the mouth.

31. **C**

An irrigation is a continuous flow of solution used to wash wounds, bladders, or eyes.

32. **B**

IM is intramuscular, which is injected into the muscle.

33. **A**

Lithium is a bipolar disorder agent that has a narrow therapeutic index (NTI).

34. **B**

Ferrous sulfate is used to treat iron deficiency anemia.

35. **D**

Vitamin B_{12} is also known as cyanocobalamin.

36. **B**

Latanoprost is indicated to treat elevated intraocular pressure, as seen in glaucoma.

37. **B**

Hydroxychloroquine can be used to treat malaria and rheumatoid arthritis. It can also be used to treat lupus.

38. **B**

Fluconazole is an antifungal medication used to treat vaginal candidiasis as a once 150mg PO dose.

39. **A**

Metronidazole must not be taken with alcohol.

40. **B**

Sulfamethoxazole and trimethoprim can cause photosensitivity.

41. **D**

Tamsulosin is indicated to treat BPH.

42. **C**

Sumatriptan is indicated for the treatment of migraines.

43. **B**

Donepezil can be used to treat mild, moderate, and severe dementia caused by Alzheimer's disease

44. **D**

    Divalproex (Depakote) is an anticonvulsant.

45. **B**

    Benazepril is the generic of Lotensin.

46. **C**

    Antihyperlipidemics (HMG-CoA reductase inhibitors) end in -*statin*.

47. **D**

    Ezetimibe is indicated as adjunctive therapy with diet for reduction of total cholesterol.

48. **B**

    Ondansetron is indicated for the prevention of nausea and vomiting associated with chemotherapy.

49. **C**

    Fluticasone is available as both an MDI (Flovent) and nasal spray (Flonase).

50. **B**

    Temazepam is indicated for the treatment of insomnia.

CHAPTER 3

Federal Requirements

PTCE Knowledge Domain: Medications	12.5% of Exam

Knowledge Areas:

- Federal requirements for handling and disposal of nonhazardous, hazardous, and pharmaceutical substances and waste

- Federal requirements for controlled substance prescriptions (i.e., new, refill, transfer) and DEA controlled substance schedules

- Federal requirements (e.g., DEA, FDA) for controlled substances (i.e., receiving, storing, ordering, labeling, dispensing, reverse distribution, take-back programs, and loss or theft of)

- Federal requirements for restricted drug programs and related medication processing (e.g., pseudoephedrine, risk evaluation and mitigation strategies [REMS])

- FDA recall requirements (e.g., medications, devices, supplies, supplements, classifications)

After reading Chapter 3 you will be able to:

- Understand federal requirements for controlled substance prescriptions, including new prescriptions, refills, and transfers

- Describe each DEA controlled substance schedule and examples of each

- Explain federal requirements for receiving, storing, ordering, labeling, and dispensing controlled substances

- Describe the process for loss or theft of controlled substances

- Understand reverse distribution and take-back programs for controlled substances

- Describe FDA risk evaluation and mitigation strategies (REMS), and review REMS for specific medications

- Understand the Combat Methamphetamine Epidemic Act of 2005 and the impact of pseudoephedrine dispensing

- Differentiate between FDA recalls, including medications, devices, supplies, and supplements

- Recognize federal requirements for handling and disposing of nonhazardous and hazardous drugs, as well as pharmaceutical waste

Federal oversight has long had a place in pharmacy practice. Implementation of many laws and standards has helped protect the safety of both patients and pharmacy employees. This chapter focuses on federal requirements for controlled substances as well as restricted drug programs. It also highlights safe practices in drug handling and disposal.

Controlled Substances

The Comprehensive Drug Abuse Prevention and Control Act of 1970 was created to combat the growing drug problem in America. This act included the Controlled Substance Act (CSA), which consolidated several laws regulating the prescribing, distributing, and scheduling of controlled substances. The Drug Enforcement Administration (DEA) was established in 1973, and their main mission is to enforce controlled substances laws of the United States.

Schedules of Controlled Substances

Through the CSA, five schedules were created to group controlled substances based on potential for abuse and accepted medical use. The DEA determines the schedules for controlled substances. The definitions and example medications of each schedule follow.

Schedule I (C1)

- Has no accepted medical use
- Has high potential for abuse

Example Drugs
- 3,4-methylenedioxymethamphetamine (Ecstasy)
- heroin
- lysergic acid diethylamide (LSD)
- marijuana
- psilocybin (Magic Mushrooms)

Schedule II (C2)

- Has accepted medical use, but high potential for abuse
- May lead to physical or psychological dependence

Example Drugs
- amphetamine (Adderall)
- cocaine
- codeine
- fentanyl (Duragesic)
- hydrocodone (Hysingla, Norco—with acetaminophen)
- hydromorphone (Dilaudid)
- lisdexamfetamine (Vyvanse)
- meperidine (Demerol)
- methadone
- methylphenidate (Concerta, Ritalin)
- morphine (MS Contin)
- oxycodone (Oxycontin, Percocet—with acetaminophen)

Schedule III (C3)

- Low to moderate potential for abuse
- Less abuse potential than Schedule I or II

Example Drugs
- anabolic steroids (body-building drugs)
- buprenorphine
- butalbital (Fiorinal)
- codeine combination product (Tylenol with codeine)
- ketamine

Schedule IV (C4)

- Low potential for abuse or dependence

Example Drugs
- alprazolam (Xanax)
- carisoprodol (Soma)
- chlordiazepoxide (Librium)
- clonazepam (Klonopin)
- diazepam (Valium)
- lorazepam (Ativan)
- midazolam (Versed)
- phenobarbital (Luminal)
- temazepam (Restoril)
- zolpidem (Ambien)

Schedule V (C5)

- Low potential for abuse
- Many drugs that are schedule V are used for antitussive, anticonvulsant, or antidiarrheal purposes

Example Drugs
- diphenoxylate preparations (Lomotil)
- pregabalin (Lyrica)

Prescription Requirements

Prescriptions written for a controlled substance must follow DEA requirements before it can be filled by a pharmacy. The prescription must contain the following:

- Drug name
- Strength
- Dosage form
- Quantity prescribed (written out in word format—i.e., 10 tablets [ten])
- Directions for use
- Refills, if any authorized
- Date issued
- Patient's full name
- Patient's full address
- Prescriber's full name
- Prescriber's full address
- Prescriber DEA number

The prescription must also be manually signed on the date when it was issued (if not sent electronically). Electronic prescribing of controlled substances (EPCS) is not required by the DEA, but some states require all controlled substance prescriptions to be submitted electronically. Both the prescriber and pharmacy software must be certified by the DEA to send and receive controlled substance prescriptions electronically.

DEA Number

To prescribe a controlled substance, a provider must be registered with the DEA. A physician, dentist, podiatrist, veterinarian, or midlevel (physician assistant or nurse practitioner) can be authorized to prescribe controlled substances. For the prescription to be considered valid, the provider must be prescribing the controlled substance for a legitimate medical purpose in their field of practice. For example, a dermatologist could not prescribe a controlled substance to a patient for a toothache.

Before prescribing a controlled substance, a prescriber must obtain a DEA number. The DEA number consists of two letters: the first letter identifying the type of prescriber and the second letter being the first letter of the prescriber's last name. The remaining DEA number consists of six digits and a seventh "check digit." A DEA number can be validated by following these steps.

Dr. Rachel Durham, MD, has the DEA number CD6829343.

1. First, add together the 1st, 3rd, and 5th digits.

$$6+2+3=11$$

2. Next, add the 2nd, 4th, and 6th digits.

$$8+9+4=21$$

3. Double the answer from step 2.

$$21 \times 2 = 42$$

4. Add this total to the total from step 1.

$$42+11=53$$

5. The second digit in this answer is the check digit.

$$53 = \textit{check digit} = 3$$

Not all providers can write prescriptions for controlled substances. The following are providers who can write prescriptions for controlled substances and their credentials.

PROFESSION	CREDENTIAL
Doctor of Medicine in Dentistry	DMD
Doctor of Dental Surgery	DDS
Doctor of Osteopathy	DO
Medical Doctor	MD
Midlevel Provider—Certified Nurse Practitioner	CNP
Midlevel Provider—Physician Assistant	PA
Doctor of Podiatric Medicine	DPM
Doctor of Veterinary Medicine	DVM

New, Refill, and Transfer Prescriptions for Controlled Substances

When prescribing a Schedule II controlled substance, the prescription must be handwritten or printed and signed by the prescriber. If the provider has a DEA certified electronic prescribing system, it may be sent electronically. The prescriber will validate identification with a two-factor authentication, which includes two of the following: something you know (such as a password), something you have (token or phone), and something you are (biometric—such as fingerprint).

Verbal orders for Schedule II prescriptions are discouraged, but may be accepted in emergency situations. If an emergency fill is required, the pharmacy must write out the verbal order as a valid prescription and dispense a quantity sufficient required only for the emergency period (e.g., a fill for Saturday and Sunday until the prescriber's office is open). The prescriber must then provide the pharmacy with a valid written prescription for this order within seven days. If a Schedule II prescription is faxed, it must only be used as a method to expedite prescription filling, and the original prescription must be presented upon final verification.

Schedule II prescriptions are not permitted to be refilled or transferred to another pharmacy. If a pharmacy does not have enough medication to fill the entire prescription, a partial fill may be dispensed if the remaining quantity can be given within 72 hours. After these 72 hours, if the prescription has not been picked up or is not available from the pharmacy, the patient must get a new prescription. Schedule II prescriptions may also be partially filled if needed if a prescription is written for a patient in a long-term-care facility or with a terminal illness.

Schedule III, IV, and V prescriptions may be called in verbally or faxed. Written and faxed prescriptions must be signed by the prescriber. These orders can also be sent through EPCS.

Schedule III–V prescriptions can be transferred to another pharmacy, though one time only. This rule is exempt if transferred within the same pharmacy chain. If a Schedule III–V prescription is transferred, it must meet requirements set from the DEA.

The following requirements must be met for a prescription to be transferred from a pharmacy:

- Write "VOID" on the prescription being transferred.
- Write the name, address, and DEA number of the pharmacy the prescription is being transferred to on the original prescription.
- Write the date and name of the pharmacist completing the transfer.

The following requirements must be met for a prescription to be transferred to a pharmacy:

- Date of issue of original prescription
- Original number of refills authorized
- Date of original dispensing
- Number of refills remaining and location of any previous refills
- Pharmacy name, address, and DEA number from which the prescription was transferred
- Name of the pharmacist transferring the prescription

Refills for Schedule III and IV prescriptions are permitted but limited to five refills within six months (or whichever occurs first). The following is a summary of requirements for all scheduled controlled substances.

SCHEDULE	REFILLS ALLOWED	TRANSFER ALLOWED	PARTIAL FILL ALLOWED	VERBAL OR FAXED ORDERS ALLOWED
2	No	No	Emergency only; must receive full prescription within 72 hours	In emergency only; must receive prescription within 7 days
3	Up to 5 times within 6 months	One time (unless same chain)	Yes	Yes
4	Up to 5 times within 6 months	One time (unless same chain)	Yes	Yes
5	Up to provider	One time (unless same chain)	Yes	Yes

All original controlled substance prescriptions must be filed and stored for a minimum of two years. There must be one file for Schedule II controlled substances dispensed, one file for Schedule III–V controlled substances, and a third file for noncontrolled substances dispensed. Electronic prescriptions must be retained electronically for a minimum of two years, unless the state board of pharmacy requires a longer period. All records must be readily retrievable, and if storage is limited in the pharmacy, approval must be obtained from the DEA for off-site storage.

Ordering and Receiving Controlled Substances

A new pharmacy must register with the DEA prior to ordering controlled substances. The pharmacy completes DEA Form 224, and this registration must be renewed every three years. The DEA certificate must be posted in the pharmacy.

When ordering controlled substances, DEA Form 222 is used for Schedule I or II ordering. This paper form consists of a triplicate format, with one copy being for the DEA, one copy for the manufacturer or wholesaler, and the third copy for the purchaser. The wholesaler copy is mailed to the wholesaler and the copy for the DEA is mailed to the local DEA office. DEA 222 forms must be inventoried monthly to prevent diversion or abuse of ordering.

Schedule I or II controlled substances must be ordered by a pharmacist. The form must be completed correctly for order processing. This includes only one item name per line, the number of packages and size of package for each item, and pharmacist signature. Not all pharmacists can order Schedule I and II medications upon hire. They must first be given power of attorney for ordering controlled substances before they are able to sign a DEA 222. Completed forms must be stored in the pharmacy or an approved location for a minimum of two years.

A DEA Form 224 follows.

Form-224

APPLICATION FOR REGISTRATION
Under the Controlled Substances Act

APPROVED OMB NO 1117-0014
FORM DEA-224 (04-12)
FORM EXPIRES: 01/31/2016

INSTRUCTIONS   Save time - apply on-line at *www.deadiversion.usdoj.gov*

1. To apply by mail complete this application. Keep a copy for your records.
2. Mail this form to the address provided in Section 7 or use enclosed envelope.
3. The "MAIL-TO ADDRESS" can be different than your "PLACE OF BUSINESS" address.
4. If you have any questions call 800-882-9539 prior to submitting your application.

IMPORTANT: DO NOT SEND THIS APPLICATION AND APPLY ON-LINE.

MAIL-TO ADDRESS   Please print mailing address changes to the right of the address in this box.

DEA OFFICIAL USE :

Do you have other DEA registration numbers?
☐ NO   ☐ YES

FEE FOR THREE (3) YEARS IS $731
FEE IS NON-REFUNDABLE

SECTION 1   APPLICANT IDENTIFICATION   ☐ Individual Registration   ☐ Business Registration

Name 1   (Last Name of individual -OR- Business or Facility Name)

Name 2   (First Name and Middle Name of individual - OR- Continuation of business name)

PLACE OF BUSINESS Street Address Line 1

PLACE OF BUSINESS Address Line 2

City   State   Zip Code

Business Phone Number   Point of Contact

Business Fax Number   Email Address

DEBT COLLECTION INFORMATION
Mandatory pursuant to Debt Collection Improvements Act

Social Security Number (*if registration is for individual*)

Tax Identification Number (*if registration is for business*)
Provide SSN or TIN.
See additional information note #3 on page 4.

FOR Practitioner or MLP ONLY:
Professional Degree *select from list only*   Professional School   Year of Graduation

National Provider Identification: Date of Birth (MM-DD-YYYY):

SECTION 2   BUSINESS ACTIVITY
Check one business activity box only

☐ Central Fill Pharmacy
☐ Retail Pharmacy
☐ Nursing Home
☐ Automated Dispensing System (ADS)

☐ Practitioner (DDS, DMD, DO, DPM, DVM, or MD)
☐ Practitioner Military (DDS, DMD, DO, DPM, DVM, or MD)
☐ Mid-level Practitioner (MLP) (DOM, HMD, MP, ND, NF, OD, PA, or RPH)
☐ Euthanasia Technician

☐ Ambulance Service
☐ Animal Shelter
☐ Hospital/Clinic
☐ Teaching Institution

FOR Automated Dispensing System (ADS) ONLY: DEA Registration # of Retail Pharmacy for this ADS

ADS is automatically fee-exempt. Skip Section 6 and Section 7 on page 2. You must attach a notarized affidavit.

SECTION 3   DRUG SCHEDULES
Check all that apply

☐ Schedule 2 Narcotic
☐ Schedule 2 Non-Narcotic (2N)

☐ Schedule 3 Narcotic
☐ Schedule 3 Non-Narcotic (3N)

☐ Schedule 4
☐ Schedule 5

☐ Check this box if you require official order forms - for purchase of schedule 2 controlled substances.

NEW - Page 1

A DEA Form 222 follows.

See Reverse of PURCHASER'S Copy for Instructions

No order form may be issued for Schedule I and II substances unless a completed application form has been received. (21 CFR 1305.04).

OMB APPROVAL
No. 1117-0010

TO: (Name of Supplier)   STREET ADDRESS

CITY and STATE   DATE   **TO BE FILLED IN BY SUPPLIER**
SUPPLIERS DEA REGISTRATION No.

TO BE FILLED IN BY PURCHASER

LINE No.	No of Packages	Size of Package	Name of Item	National Drug Code	Packages Shipped	Date Shipped
1						
2						
3						
4						
5						
6						
7						
8						
9						
10						

◄ LAST LINE COMPLETED   *(MUST BE 10 OR LESS)*   SIGNATURE OF PURCHASER OR ATTORNEY OR AGENT

Date Issued   DEA Registration No.   Name and Address of Registrant   3/7

Schedules

Registered as a   No. of this Order Form

DEA Form - 222
(AUGUST 2011)   **U.S. OFFICIAL ORDER FORMS - SCHEDULES I & II**
DRUG ENFORCEMENT ADMINISTRATION
SUPPLIER'S Copy 1   W

An alternative way to order Schedule I and II controlled substances is through the DEA Controlled Substance Ordering System (CSOS). CSOS reduces the number of ordering errors and increases accuracy. It is also more efficient, as it does not require time spent in the mail to the wholesaler and instead is submitted electronically for more timely and accurate validation by the supplier. This also helps pharmacies maintain a smaller inventory, because they can submit an electronic order and have the inventory replenished the next day. Records of electronic CSOS orders must also be maintained for two years.

Schedule III–V substances can be ordered be a pharmacist or pharmacy technician through the standard ordering process with a wholesaler or direct with a manufacturer. While CSOS or DEA Form 222 is required for ordering Schedule I or II controlled substances, CSOS may also be used for Schedule III–V substance ordering.

When an order for a Schedule II controlled substance is received in the pharmacy, the wholesaler invoice must be signed by the pharmacist. Each line of the CSOS receipt must also be signed by the pharmacist, indicating all controlled substances were received.

Orders for Schedules III–V can be opened and received by a pharmacist or pharmacy technician. A pharmacist is not required to sign off on these invoices. Schedule III–V invoices must be filed separate from Schedule II invoices and stored for a minimum of two years.

Storing, Labeling, and Dispensing Controlled Substances

After proper ordering and receiving is complete, the controlled substance can be put away and stored in an appropriate location. Schedule II controlled substances must be stored separately from the other noncontrolled medications. This includes within a vault or locked safe within the pharmacy. If an automated dispensing cabinet is used for storage in nursing units, the controlled substance must be in a locked cubby and not in an open matrix drawer. Retail pharmacies often have a locked cabinet for controlled substances, and only the pharmacist possesses the key to the cabinet.

Schedule III–V substances can be stored outside the locked storage of Schedule II substances or mixed into the noncontrolled inventory. Many pharmacies secure Schedule III–V with the Schedule II for additional security, though this is not a DEA requirement. It is at the discretion of the pharmacy to determine appropriate storage for Schedule III–V controlled substances.

The DEA also has requirements for manufacturers related to labeling of controlled substances. Each commercial container must have a symbol printed designating the Schedule of the controlled substances.

The following symbols are used for this labeling:

SCHEDULE	SYMBOL
Schedule I	CI
Schedule II	CII
Schedule III	CIII
Schedule IV	CIV
Schedule V	CV

In a pharmacy, when a controlled substance is dispensed to a patient, the label must contain requirements that are standard for all prescription labels, which includes:

- Pharmacy name
- Pharmacy address
- Pharmacy phone number
- Prescriber name
- Patient name

- Date prescription was filled
- Prescription number
- Medication and directions for use
- Cautionary statements (if any)

Cautionary statements for controlled substances may be applied through auxiliary labels, such as the following:

> **Controlled Substance**
> Dangerous unless used as prescribed

> **CAUTION: OPIOID**
> Risk of overdose and addiction

> **MAY CAUSE DROWSINESS OR DIZZINESS.**
> Alcohol may intensify this effect. Use care
> when operating a car or machinery.

Additionally, the FDA requires that all controlled substances in Schedules II–IV must have a label saying: *Caution: Federal law prohibits the transfer of this drug to any person other than the patient for whom it was prescribed.*

After proper labeling is completed, the medication can be dispensed to a patient. Although state law may differ in requirements for pickup, the DEA requires the prescription be dispensed to the patient or a member of the patient's household. Dispensing a controlled substance to anyone outside of this would be considered distribution and not dispensing.

Take-Back Programs and Reverse Distribution

If a pharmacy does not dispense all of a controlled substance, it may expire or outdate before it can be used. Outdated controlled substances (and all medications) must be quarantined from in-dated inventory. A pharmacy may either destroy this expired inventory or use a reverse distributor.

DEA Form 41 is submitted to the DEA if a controlled substance is destroyed. This form requires the name, strength, and dosage form of the medication destroyed, as well as the NDC of each drug. If a partial bottle is destroyed, the remaining count must be indicated. If a full bulk bottle is destroyed, the package size must also be documented and how many bottles were destroyed. The date, location, and method of destruction must be documented, and two employees must both sign the form as witnesses.

A DEA Form 41 follows.

OMB APPROVAL NO. 1117-0007   Expiration Date 10/31/2020

U. S. DEPARTMENT OF JUSTICE – DRUG ENFORCEMENT ADMINISTRATION
REGISTRANT RECORD OF CONTROLLED SUBSTANCES DESTROYED
FORM DEA-41

A. REGISTRANT INFORMATION

Registered Name:		DEA Registration Number:
Registered Address:		
City:	State:	Zip Code:
Telephone Number:		Contact Name:

B. ITEM DESTROYED
1. Inventory

	National Drug Code or DEA Controlled Substances Code Number	Batch Number	Name of Substance	Strength	Form	Pkg. Qty.	Number of Full Pkgs.	Partial Pkg. Count	Total Destroyed
Examples	16590-598-60	N/A	Kadian	60mg	Capsules	60	2	0	120 Capsules
	0555-0767-02	N/A	Adderall	5mg	Tablet	100	0	83	83 Tablets
	9050	B02120312	Codeine	N/A	Bulk	1.25 kg	N/A	N/A	1.25 kg
1.									
2.									
3.									
4.									
5.									
6.									
7.									

2. Collected Substances

	Returned Mail-Back Package	Sealed Inner Liner	Unique Identification Number	Size of Sealed Inner Liner	Quantity of Packages(s)/Liner(s) Destroyed
Examples	X		MBP1106, MBP1108 - MBP1110, MBP112	N/A	5
		X	CRL1007 - CRL1027	15 gallon	21
		X	CRL1201	5 gallon	1
1.					
2.					
3.					
4.					
5.					
6.					
7.					

Form DEA-41   *See instructions on reverse (page 2) of form.*

DEA-41 Pg. 2

C. METHOD OF DESTRUCTION

Date of Destruction:	Method of Destruction:
Location or Business Name:	
Address:	
City:	State:	Zip Code:

D. WITNESSES

I declare under penalty of perjury, pursuant to 18 U.S.C. 1001, that I personally witnessed the destruction of the above-described controlled substances to a non-retrievable state and that all of the above is true and correct.

Printed name of first authorized employee witness:	Signature of first witness:	Date:
Printed name of second authorized employee witness:	Signature of second witness:	Date:

E. INSTRUCTIONS

1. <u>Section A. REGISTRANT INFORMATION</u>: The registrant destroying the controlled substance(s) shall provide their DEA registration number and the name and address indicated on their valid DEA registration, in addition to a current telephone number and a contact name, if different from the name on the valid DEA registration.

2. <u>Section B. (1) Inventory</u>: This part shall be used by registrants destroying lawfully possessed controlled substances, other than those described in Section B(2). In each row, indicate the National Drug Code (NDC) for the controlled substance destroyed, or if the substance has no NDC, indicate the DEA Controlled Substances Code Number for the substance; if the substance destroyed is in bulk form, indicate the batch number, if available. In each row, indicate the name, strength, and form of the controlled substance destroyed, and the number of capsules, tablets, etc., that are in a full package (pkg. qty.). If destroying the full quantity of the controlled substance, indicate the number of packages destroyed (number of full pkgs.). If destroying a partial package, indicate the partial count of the capsules, tablets, etc. destroyed (partial pkg. count). If destroying a controlled substance in bulk form, indicate that the substance is in bulk form (form) and the weight of the substance destroyed (pkg. qty.). In each row, indicate the total number of each controlled substance destroyed (total destroyed).

3. <u>Section B. (2) Collected Substances</u>: This part shall be used by registrants destroying controlled substances obtained through an authorized collection activity in accordance with 21 U.S.C. 822(g). In each row, indicate whether registrant is destroying a mail-back package or an inner liner. If destroying a mail-back package, enter each unique identification number separated by a comma and/or as a list in a sequential range and total quantity of packages being destroyed. If destroying an inner liner, enter each unique identification number separated by a comma and/or as a list in a sequential range based on the size of the liners destroyed and the total quantity of inner liners being destroyed. In the case of mail-back packages or inner liners received from a law enforcement agency which do not have a unique identification number or clearly marked size, include the name of the law enforcement agency and, if known, the size of the inner liner or package. DO NOT OPEN ANY MAIL-BACK PACKAGE OR INNER LINER; AN INVENTORY OF THE CONTENTS OF THE PACKAGES OR LINERS IS PROHIBITED BY LAW AND IS NOT REQUIRED BY THIS FORM.

4. If additional space is needed for items destroyed in Section B, attach to this form additional page(s) containing the requested information for each controlled substance destroyed.

5. <u>Section C. METHOD OF DESTRUCTION</u>: Provide the date, location, and method of destruction. The method of destruction must render the controlled substance to a state of non-retrievable and meet all applicable destruction requirements.

6. <u>Section D. WITNESSES</u>: Two authorized employees must declare by signature, under penalty of perjury, that they personally witnessed the destruction of the controlled substances listed in Section B in the manner described in Section C.

7. You are not required to submit this form to DEA, unless requested to do so. This form must be kept as a record of destruction and be available by the registrant for at least two years in accordance with 21 U.S.C. 827.

A pharmacy may not be capable of, or desire to, destroy outdated controlled substances themselves. In this case, a pharmacy can dispose of expired controlled substances (and noncontrolled drugs) through a reverse distributor. A reverse distributor removes the expired inventory from a pharmacy and returns the drugs to the manufacturer. The manufacturer accepts the returns and may give credit back to the pharmacy. The reverse distributor must also be registered with the DEA. After the expired controlled substances are inventoried, a DEA form 222 must be completed. The reverse distributor then gives a copy of the triplicate form to the pharmacy, and one is mailed to the DEA for the transfer of the expired controlled substances. The reverse distributor must then complete a DEA Form 41 for any controlled substances that must be destroyed and not returned to the manufacturer.

If a patient has an outdated or unused controlled substance, it may become dangerous if these unused drugs end up in the wrong hands. Patients can dispose of these medications through take-back programs. These are designated days throughout the country that are sponsored by the DEA. A take-back day allows patients to dispose of unwanted medications safely and anonymously in a nearby location. Patients can clean out their medicine cabinets and help prevent drug abuse or misuse. Some pharmacies, hospitals, or police departments also offer medication drop boxes for year-round disposal.

Loss or Theft

In the event a pharmacy discovers there is a loss or theft of a controlled substance, they must notify the DEA within one business day of the discovery. In addition to notifying the DEA, a DEA Form 106 must also be completed. This can be completed online or downloaded and submitted to the local DEA office.

Information needed to complete a DEA Form 106 is:

- Name, address, and DEA number of the pharmacy
- Background information regarding the loss or theft (break-in, robbery, etc.)
- Estimated value of loss
- NDC and quantity of controlled substance

A DEA Form 106 follows.

REPORT OF THEFT OR LOSS OF CONTROLLED SUBSTANCES

Federal Regulations require registrants to submit a detailed report of any theft or loss of Controlled Substances to the Drug Enforcement Administration. Complete page 1, and either page 2 or 3. Make two additional copies of the completed form. Forward the original and duplicate copies to the nearest DEA Office. Retain the triplicate copy for your records. Some states may also require a copy of this report.

OMB APPROVAL
No. 1117-0001
(Expiration Date 10/23/2020)

1. Name and Address of Registrant (include ZIP Code)	2. Phone No. (Include Area Code)

3. DEA Registration Number	4. Date of Theft or Loss	5. Principal Business of Registrant (Check one)
		1 ☐ Pharmacy 5 ☐ Distributor 2 ☐ Practitioner 6 ☐ Methadone Program 3 ☐ Manufacturer 7 ☐ Other (Specify) 4 ☐ Hospital/Clinic

6. County in which Registrant is Located	7. Was Theft reported to Police? ☐ Yes ☐ No	8. Name and Telephone Number of Police Department (Include Area Code)

9. Number of Thefts or Losses Registrant has Experienced in the Past 24 Months	10. Type of Theft or Loss (Check one and complete items below as appropriate)
	1 ☐ Night Break-in 3 ☐ Employee Pilferage 5 ☐ Lost in Transit (Complete Item 14) 2 ☐ Armed Robbery 4 ☐ Customer Theft

11. If Armed Robbery, was Anyone: Killed? ☐ No ☐ Yes (How Many) _____ Injured? ☐ No ☐ Yes (How Many) _____	12. Purchase value to Registrant of Controlled Substances taken? $	13. Were any pharmaceuticals or merchandise taken? ☐ No ☐ Yes (Est. Value) $

14. IF LOST IN TRANSIT, COMPLETE THE FOLLOWING:

A. Name of Common Carrier	B. Name of Consignee	C. Consignee's DEA Registration Number

D. Was the carton received by the customer? ☐ Yes ☐ No	E. If received, did it appear to be tampered with? ☐ Yes ☐ No	F. Have you experienced losses in transit from this same carrier in the past? ☐ No ☐ Yes (How Many) _____

15. What identifying marks, symbols, or price codes were on the labels of these containers that would assist in identifying the products?

16. If Official Controlled Substance Order Forms (DEA-222) were stolen, give numbers.

17. What security measures have been taken to prevent future thefts or losses?

PRIVACY ACT INFORMATION

AUTHORITY: Section 301 of the Controlled Substances Act of 1970 (PL 91-513).
PURPOSE: Report theft or loss of Controlled Substances.
ROUTINE USES: The Controlled Substances Act authorizes the production of special reports required for statistical and analytical purposes. Disclosures of information from this system are made to the following categories of users for the purposes stated:
A. Other Federal law enforcement and regulatory agencies for law enforcement and regulatory purposes.
B. State and local law enforcement and regulatory agencies for law enforcement and regulatory purposes.
EFFECT: Failure to report theft or loss of controlled substances may result in penalties under Section 402 and 403 of the Controlled Substances Act.

In accordance with the Paperwork Reduction act of 1995, no person is required to respond to a collection of information unless it displays a valid OMB control number. The Valid OMB control number for this collection of information is 1117-0001. Public reporting burden for this collection of information is estimated to average 20 minutes per response, including the time for reviewing instructions, searching existing data sources, gathering and maintaining the data needed, and completing and reviewing the collection of information.

Freedom of Information: Please prominently identify any confidential business information per 28 CFR 16.8(c) and Exemption 4 of the Freedom of Information Act (FOIA). In the event DEA receives a FOIA request to obtain such information, DEA will give written notice to the registrant to obtain such information. DEA will give written notice to the registrant to allow an opportunity to object prior to the release of information.

FORM DEA-106 Previous editions obsolete

CONTINUE ON REVERSE

Form DEA-106 (10/23/2020) Pg. 2

LIST OF CONTROLLED SUBSTANCES LOST OR STOLEN

	Trade Name of Substance or Preparation	NDC Number	Name of Controlled Substance in Preparation	Dosage Strength	Dosage Form	Total Quantity Lost or Stolen
Examples	Desoxyn	00074-3377-01	Methamphetamine Hydrochloride	5 mg	Tablets	300
	Demerol	00409-1181-30	Meperidine Hydrochloride	50 mg/ml	Vial	150 ml
	Robitussin A-C	00031-8674-25	Codeine Phosphate	2 mg/cc	Liquid	5676 ml
1.						
2.						
3.						
4.						
5.						
6.						
7.						
8.						
9.						
10.						
11.						
12.						
13.						
14.						
15.						
16.						
17.						
18.						
19.						
20.						Express Quantity in Dosage Units, or Milliliters for Liquids

Remarks: (Optional)

I certify that the foregoing information is correct to the best of my knowledge and belief.

_____ _____ _____
Sign and Print Name   Title   Date

To help remember the DEA forms, the following is a summary of some of the DEA forms mentioned in this chapter.

FORM NUMBER	DESCRIPTION
41	Destruction of outdated or damaged controlled substances
106	Reporting a loss or theft of controlled substances
222	Ordering Schedule I or II controlled substances
224	Pharmacy registration with the DEA required for dispensing controlled substances

To prevent theft or loss, controlled substances must be counted at initial inventory and every two years thereafter. A complete count of all Schedule II substances must be completed, while the Schedule III–V may be estimated. These records of inventory must be kept for a minimum of two years, and the Schedule II inventory must be separated from III–V.

Restricted Drug Programs

Though medications must pass rigorous testing and clinical trials prior to FDA approval, some are approved or are later identified to require restrictions due to known patient safety issues. The FDA manages these through **risk evaluation and mitigation strategies (REMS)**. The manufacturer is required to develop an REMS program to accompany the new drug approval or after approval if the FDA identifies a need. Without REMS, the medication could be withdrawn from the market or not approved for manufacturing. REMS are designed to reduce the frequency and severity of adverse events by informing patients of safety concerns or requiring specific practices for safe use.

One component of REMS may be the creation of an educational handout for patients to accompany the drug. This handout, known as a **medication guide**, contains FDA-approved information for patients in an easy-to-read format to help inform patients about the potential for serious adverse events. Medication guides are dispensed when the patient picks up a prescription.

Some medication guides must be dispensed with drug classes, such as SSRIs and NSAIDs. Additionally, medication guides are required to be issued with specific drugs if:

1. Specific information could be used to prevent serious adverse events.

2. The patient should be informed regarding potential for serious known side effects.

3. Patient compliance to the directions are essential for effectiveness.

The following are some examples of drugs that require a medication guide:

BRAND	GENERIC
Abilify	aripiprazole
Accutane	isotretinoin
Actonel	risedronate
Adderall	amphetamine with dextroamphetamine
Androgel	testosterone
Ativan	lorazepam
Celebrex	celecoxib
Celexa	citalopram
Cipro	ciprofloxacin
Coumadin	warfarin
Cymbalta	duloxetine
Demerol	meperidine
Depakote	divalproex
Desyrel	trazodone
Dilantin	phenytoin
Dilaudid	hydromorphone
Effexor	venlafaxine
Eliquis	apixaban
Fioricet	acetaminophen; butalbital; caffeine
Focalin XR	dexmethylphenidate
Humira	adalimumab
Hysingla ER	hydrocodone
Invokana	canaglifozin
Janumet	metformin and sitagliptin
Januvia	itagliptin
Keppra	levetiracetam
Klonopin	clonazepam
Lamictal	lamotrigine
Lamisil	terbinafine
Levaquin	levofloxacin
Lexapro	escitalopram
Lithium	lithium carbonate
Lyrica	pregabalin
Mobic	meloxicam
Naprosyn	naproxen
Neurontin	gabapentin

(continued)

BRAND	GENERIC
Nexium	esomeprazole
Paxil	paroxetine
Plavix	clopidogrel
Prilosec	omeprazole
Protonix	pantoprazole
Prozac	fluoxetine
Restoril	temazepam
Ritalin	methylphenidate
Seroquel	quetiapine
Topamax	topiramate
Tradjenta	linagliptin
Vyvanse	lisdexamfetamine
Wellbutrin	bupropion
Xanax	alprazolam
Xarelto	rivaroxaban
Zoloft	sertraline

Although specific medications require medication guides, **patient package inserts (PPI)** contain information for patients on how to safely use a drug product. PPIs are developed by the manufacturer and are required to be dispensed with certain drug classes such as oral contraceptives or estrogen-containing products.

Requirements of a PPI include:

- Drug name
- Statement of risks versus benefits of use
- Contraindications and serious risks associated
- Warning regarding serious side effects
- Information on how to take the medication properly
- Manufacturer name and distributor
- Side effects
- Instructions on how to reduce risks
- Date of latest revision of PPI

REMS also include a goal for risk mitigation and activities or information that must be completed by the provider, patient, or pharmacist. The role for each caregiver or patient is specific to each medication. Some REMS are similar, but the key risk message and nature of the risk are different for each drug. For some medications, patients must sign an acknowledgment form that they understand the risks prior to taking the medication. Some REMS require lab testing prior to dispensing a prescription. Some REMS even require enrollment in a registry to ensure proper monitoring is completed and documentation of adverse events can occur. Additional requirements may include direct communication with the drug manufacturer and the health care provider, which includes pharmacists. Some

REMS programs require completion of a certificate prior to dispensing, such as clozapine, isotretinoin, and thalidomide.

Next, the following examples of REMS are reviewed:

- clozapine
- isotretinoin
- opioid analgesic
- suboxone
- thalidomide

Clozapine

Clozapine (Clozaril) is a medication used for the treatment of schizophrenia and has been associated with causing severe neutropenia. Neutrophils are white blood cells that help with immunity. In severe neutropenia, the neutrophil count drops to less than 500μ/L (the normal range is between 1,500μ/L and 8,000μ/L). A significant drop in neutrophils can lead to the inability to fight infections.

REMS for clozapine must be completed by the patient, pharmacist, and provider prior to initiating therapy. The provider must complete and enroll patients in the REMS program in order to prescribe the medication. Once the patient has begun treatment, the prescriber must report the absolute neutrophil count (ANC) to the REMS program to continue therapy.

Pharmacies must also certify in the clozapine REMS to both order and dispense the medication. The pharmacy must also validate the provider has been enrolled in the program and review the ANC prior to dispensing. The patient must continue regular blood tests for ANC before receiving treatment.

Isotretinoin

Isotretinoin (Accutane) is a medication used for the treatment of severe nodular acne. There is an extremely high risk of birth defects if used by female patients during pregnancy or who may become pregnant. The REMS program for isotretinoin is known as iPLEDGE. The goal of this REMS to prevent fetal exposure and inform pharmacist, providers, and patients of the potential for teratogenic effects.

Prescribers of isotretinoin must first register with iPLEDGE and may only prescribe it to patients who have registered and met all requirements of the program. Patient requirements include:

1. Two negative pregnancy tests prior to first dose

2. Monthly pregnancy tests for female patients

3. Confirmation of two forms of contraception used

4. Completion of counseling

Isotretinoin cannot be dispensed until a patient has completed these requirements. Pharmacist must also be registered with iPLEDGE in order to purchase from a wholesaler. This certification requires annual renewal, and the wholesaler will not ship the medication without an active certification. Isotretinoin must not be automatically refilled each month, as a negative pregnancy test must first be taken prior to dispensing a refill. The prescription must also be picked up within seven days of the negative pregnancy test.

Opioid Analgesic

In response to the opioid epidemic, a REMS was created by the FDA for the use of opioid analgesics in the treatment of pain. The goal of the opioid analgesic REMS is to educate providers, including pharmacists, on the treatment and monitoring of patients with pain. With an increase in education, providers will have a better understanding of pain management and the role of opioid analgesics in treatment, along with nonpharmacological treatment methods. This education also helps identify the risks of opioids, including the risk of addiction, unintentional overdose, and death.

To complete the opioid analgesic REMS, providers must complete an FDA-REMS compliant continuing education course. Patients must also be counseled on the safe use of opioid analgesics, as well as the appropriate storage and disposal methods and risks associated with use.

Suboxone

Suboxone is a combination of buprenorphine and naloxone. Buprenorphine is an opioid and naloxone blocks the effects of the opioid, including those that may lead to dependence. Suboxone is indicated to treat opioid addiction. Misuse of suboxone may lead to accidental overdose and death.

Prescribers of suboxone must first verify the patient meets appropriate criteria for treatment. Suboxone is prescribed as a limited amount and only enough to last until the next visit. Patients must have appointments scheduled to accommodate this dosing. A prescriber must also be certified to treat opioid dependence, and if prescribing suboxone for this purpose, must have an "X" number issued by the DEA.

Pharmacies must verify the prescription is written by a prescriber who is eligible for prescribing suboxone for opioid addiction. State prescription drug monitoring programs (PDMPs) must also be reviewed to identify potential behaviors of abuse and review medications for appropriate co-prescribing. Patients must be counseled and pharmacies should be aware of potential for fraudulent prescriptions or prescribing from multiple providers.

Thalidomide

Thalidomide (Thalomid) is used for the treatment of multiple myeloma. Thalidomide was once used as an antinausea agent for pregnant women and prevention of morning sickness. As a result, thousands of babies were born with severe birth defects, including deformed limbs. Due to the potential for teratogenic effects, a REMS is required for all thalidomide prescribing. The goal of this REMS is to inform patients, pharmacists, and prescribers of the potential for serious risks of thalidomide therapy.

Prescribers must first become certified and enroll in the thalomid REMS program. Patients must be counseled on benefits and risks, as well as contraception and emergency contraception. Female patients must have a negative pregnancy test before initiating therapy and before each new prescription. Providers cannot prescribe more than a 28-day supply or refills over the phone. The manufacturer must approve the provider to write prescriptions of thalidomide.

For a pharmacy to dispense thalidomide, staff training must be completed, which is provided by the manufacturer. Patients must be counseled and the prescription supplied for no more than 28 days without refills. Records must be maintained with each prescription dispensed and a completed education checklist with each patient. A pharmacy must be certified by REMS to order and dispense thalidomide.

Pseudoephedrine

The Combat Methamphetamine Epidemic Act (CMEA) of 2005 regulated retail sales of the following drugs:

- Pseudoephedrine
- Ephedrine
- Phenylpropanolamine

Each of these three medications is a common ingredient in cough and cold medications and can also be used as precursors to produce methamphetamine. Requirements and restrictions of the CMEA include:

- Daily sales not to exceed 3.6 grams
- 30-day purchase limit of no more than 9 grams
- Photo ID or proof of identity of any purchaser
- Retrievable records of all purchases to be kept for a minimum of two years
- Limit access to customers by selling behind the counter

In addition to these restrictions, the pharmacy must self-certify with the DEA each year. By completing the certification with the DEA, the pharmacy is attesting that all employees have been trained on the CMEA requirements and that the pharmacy is following all restrictions on sales, following record-keeping requirements, and tracking all purchases in a logbook.

FDA Recalls

The previous drugs are all examples of medications that have known adverse effects and how best to mitigate or prevent them. If a medication or product has been found to be defective, it may prompt a manufacturer to initiate a recall. A recall is the process of removing a product from supply or correcting a defect before use. The FDA regulates recalls, and this applies to more than medications. The following are FDA-regulated products that could be recalled:

- Medications used for humans
- Medications used for animals
- Medical devices
- Radiation-emitting products
- Vaccines
- Blood and blood products
- Transplant tissue
- Animal feed
- Cosmetics
- Most of the foods eaten in the United States

Most recalls are voluntary, meaning the manufacturer discovers a problem and recalls the product on its own. The FDA oversees the recall process and ensures a company is addressing the strategy and recall efforts appropriately.

Recalls are categorized into three classes. These are defined as follows with examples of each.

RECALL	DESCRIPTION	EXAMPLE
Class I	Dangerous or defective product that could cause serious health problems or death	Defective artificial heart valve
Class II	Products that cause a temporary health problem or slight threat	Acetaminophen 325mg is labeled as 500mg
Class III	Products that are unlikely to cause any reaction, but violate FDA labeling or manufacturing requirements	Nonorganic product being labeled as organic

As a pharmacy technician, you may help with the recall process by identifying any medications that have been recalled and removing them from pharmacy stock. These medications are quarantined, and the pharmacy will receive instructions from the manufacturer on the recall process. Some manufacturers will require the medications be sent back, while some give additional education to help correct the recall.

Hazardous Drugs

Proper handling and disposal of hazardous drugs and waste is important in both employee and patient safety. Through the Occupational Safety and Health Act of 1970, the Occupational Safety and Health Administration (OSHA) was created. OSHA helps ensure safe working conditions by establishing standards and providing education and training.

The Occupational Safety and Health Act of 1970 also established the National Institute for Occupational Safety and Health (NIOSH). NIOSH is a research agency and is part of the Centers for Disease Control and Prevention (CDC). NIOSH establishes a list of hazardous drugs and defines what makes a drug hazardous.

This list is used in most pharmacies as a reference to determine what inventory should be handled as a hazardous drug. Although many of the medications on this list are **antineoplastic medications** (chemotherapy), there are many other medications that meet the criteria for hazardous drug.

NIOSH uses six characteristics to define a hazardous drug. If a drug has one or more of these traits in either humans or animals, it is considered hazardous.

CHARACTERISTIC	DEFINITION
Carcinogenicity	Cancer causing
Teratogenicity or developmental toxicity	Causing fetal malformation
Reproductive toxicity	Interfering with normal reproduction
Organ toxicity at low doses	Causing damage to organs or organ system
Genotoxicity	Damaging to genetic information in a cell, which can cause mutations and lead to cancer
Structure or toxicity profile of new drug that mimics existing drug	If a new drug replicates another hazardous drug structure or toxicity profile, it can be assumed to also be considered hazardous

The risk of hazardous drug exposure for employees depends on the following factors:

- Entrance of drug into the body (inhaled, ingested, transdermal, etc.)
- Manipulation needed (e.g., IV needs compounding or tablet needs crushing)
- Personal protective equipment (PPE) worn when handling
- Engineering controls in place (clean room and IV hood)

In the NIOSH Hazardous Drug list, drugs are separated into three tables. Table 1 drugs must always be handled with PPE regardless of formulation. These drugs are mostly antineoplastic medications. Table 2 drugs are nonantineoplastic drugs, and if they are unopened or intact (such as tablets or capsules), they do not pose the same hazardous risk. If Table 2 medications are crushed, split, or otherwise manipulated from the final dosage form, safe handling is recommended. Table 3 drugs are nonantineoplastic also, but they are considered reproductive hazards and are also less hazardous if they are not manipulated from the final dosage form. An example of each table is listed as follows.

Table 1. Group 1: Antineoplastic drugs, including those with the manufacturer's safe-handling guidance (MSHG)

Drug	AHFS classification	MSHG	Supplemental information	Links
abiraterone	10:00 antineoplastic agents		Women who are pregnant or may be pregnant should not handle without protection (e.g., gloves); FDA Pregnancy Category X	DailyMed; DrugBank
ado-trastuzumab emtansine	10:00 antineoplastic agents	yes	Conjugated monoclonal antibody; FDA Pregnancy Category D	DailyMed; DrugBank
afatinib*	10:00 antineoplastic agents		Special warnings on contraception for females while taking and 2 weeks post-treatment; FDA Pregnancy Category D	DailyMed; DrugBank

Table 2. Group 2: Non-antineoplastic drugs that meet one or more of the NIOSH criteria for a hazardous drug, including those with the manufacturer's safe-handling guidance (MSHG)

Drug	AHFS classification	MSHG	Supplemental information	Links
abacavir	8:18.08.20 nucleoside and reverse transcriptase inhibitors		FDA Pregnancy Category C; malignant tumors observed in male and female mice and rats; genotoxic in in vivo micronucleus test	DailyMed; DrugBank
alefacept	84:92 skin and mucous membrane agents, miscellaneous		Increased frequency of malignancies observed in treated patients; FDA Pregnancy Category B	DailyMed; DrugBank
apomorphine	28:36.20.08 non-ergot-derivative dopamine receptor agonists		FDA Pregnancy Category C; genotoxic in several in vitro assays	DailyMed; DrugBank
azathioprine	92:44 immunosuppressants	yes	IARC Group 1 carcinogen†; NTP**; FDA Pregnancy Category D	DailyMed; DrugBank

Table 3. Group 3: Non-antineoplastic drugs that primarily have adverse reproductive effects

Drug	AHFS classification	Supplemental information	Links
acitretin	88:04 vitamin A	Black Box warning on adverse reproductive effects; FDA Pregnancy Category X	DailyMed; DrugBank
alitretinoin	84:92 skin and mucous membrane agents, miscellaneous	FDA Pregnancy Category D	DailyMed; DrugBank
ambrisentan	24:12:92 vasodilating agents, miscellaneous	Black Box warning on adverse reproductive effects; reduced sperm counts in patients; FDA Pregnancy Category X	DailyMed; DrugBank

Federal Requirements for Handling Pharmaceutical Substances

In addition to NIOSH and OSHA, the United States Pharmacopeia (USP) is an organization that develops standards for medications and other substances. These standards are not enforceable by USP, but are adopted by state boards of pharmacies and accrediting bodies for compliance. USP published Chapter 800 (USP<800>) Hazardous Drugs—Handling in Healthcare Settings. This chapter describes standards and best practices for handling hazardous drugs in order to protect healthcare workers and patients.

An overview of USP<800> chapters and facility requirements as follows:

- Maintain a facility-specific list of hazardous drugs reviewed annually based on the NIOSH list
- Complete an assessment of risk for medications on the hazardous drug list that defines risk of exposure and requirements for handling and manipulation
- Designate a qualified and trained person responsible for developing and implementing procedures and overseeing compliance
- Designate area for receiving, unpacking, and storing hazardous drugs
- Engineering requirements for sterile and nonsterile compounding, which include ventilation, appropriate air exchanges, and negative pressure
- Use of closed system drug-transfer devices (CSTDs) when compounding a hazardous drug
- Appropriate use of PPE for exposure reduction, including gowns, head, hair, shoe covers, and two pairs of chemotherapy-rated gloves
- Competencies and training for each personnel who handle hazardous drugs
- Procedures for packaging, transporting, and disposing of hazardous drugs
- Development of a written procedure for decontaminating, deactivating, and cleaning areas used in hazardous drug compounding and storage
- Development of a facility hazard communication plan that describes the use of safety data sheets (SDS) and hazardous drug communication

The development of a hazard communication plan is a requirement of UPS<800> and also OSHA if a facility has any hazardous chemical. This program is designed to ensure information regarding the hazards in a facility is communicated to employees. OSHA requires this program to include information regarding the labeling, handling, and disposal requirements of hazardous chemicals (including drugs). A hazardous communication program must also include steps to take if a spill occurs and an updated list of safety data sheets (SDS).

SDS contain handling requirements of hazardous drugs and chemicals. These documents are produced by the manufacturer of a chemical or drug if it is considered hazardous. OSHA requires specific information to be included in a 16-section format for standardization. The first 8 sections contain information regarding the chemical, including safe handling practices, emergency control measures, and composition. The remaining sections contain other information such as physical or chemical properties and date of last revision.

The following is a description of all 16 sections in an SDS and the contents in each:

SECTION NAME	SECTION CONTENTS
1. Identification	▪ Product identifier
	▪ Name, address, and phone number of the manufacturer, including emergency contact
	▪ Use and restrictions of the chemical
2. Hazards Identification	▪ Hazard classification and statement
	▪ Pictogram of hazard symbol
	▪ Other hazards not classified
3. Composition and Information on Ingredients	▪ Chemical name, symbol, and any identifiers, including mixtures of chemicals
	▪ If a mixture, includes concentration of all ingredients
4. First-Aid Measures	▪ Care that should be given to a person exposed to the chemical
	▪ Instructions based on route of exposure
	▪ Recommendations for immediate medical care and special treatment, if needed
5. Fire-Fighting Measures	▪ Recommendations of fire-extinguishing equipment
	▪ Any hazards that may develop from the chemical during a fire
	▪ Recommendations on special protective equipment or precautions for firefighters
6. Accidental Release Measures	▪ Response to spills, leaks, or accidental release
	▪ Cleanup practices to minimize exposure
	▪ Guidance to distinguish between large and small spills
	▪ Cleanup procedures
	▪ Personal precautions and protective equipment needed
7. Handling and Storage	▪ Precautions for safe handling
	▪ Recommendations for safe storage
8. Exposure Controls and Personal Protection	▪ Appropriate engineering controls, such as laminar flow hood
	▪ Recommendations for personal protective measures to prevent illness or injury from exposure to chemicals
	▪ Any special requirements for PPE, protective clothing, or respirators
9. Physical and Chemical Properties	▪ Physical and chemical properties of the chemical, including odor, pH, and flammability
10. Stability and Reactivity	▪ Reactivity information
	▪ Chemical stability
	▪ Hazardous reaction potential
	▪ Conditions or materials to avoid

(continued)

SECTION NAME	SECTION CONTENTS
11. Toxicological Information	■ Potential routes of exposure
	■ Description of effects of exposure, including symptoms
12. Ecological Information	■ Environmental impact of the chemical
13. Disposal Considerations	■ Recommendations of appropriate containers for disposal
	■ Recommendations for appropriate disposal methods
	■ Guidance on recycling and safe handling practices
14. Transport Information	■ Guidance on information for shipping and transporting of hazardous chemicals
15. Regulatory Information	■ Safety, health, and environmental regulations specific for the product that is not indicated anywhere else on the SDS
16. Other Information	■ Date of latest revision of the SDS

OSHA also requires PPE be available for all employees. As a pharmacy technician, PPE is worn to protect from hazardous drug exposure when compounding, receiving or unpacking, storing, and delivering hazardous drugs. PPE includes gloves, gowns, shoe covers or booties, beard and hair covers, goggles or eye shields, and a face mask. Not all PPE is typically required for receiving, storing, or delivering hazardous drugs, but employees must follow facility procedures for hazardous drug handling.

When compounding a hazardous drug, full PPE must be worn, including two pairs of chemotherapy-rated gloves. Closed system drug-transfer devices (CSTD) should be used to compound chemotherapy and other hazardous drugs. CSTDs minimize the risk of hazardous drug exposure to the employees compounding and nurses when administering to a patient. They also protect the patient from accidental spilling or leakage.

SDS also help provide information regarding the response to a hazardous drug spill. Pharmacies must have spill kits available near the compounding area, as well as where patients may be receiving hazardous drugs. USP<800> defines the minimum components required for a spill kit, which includes:

- Supplies sufficient to absorb a spill of about 1000mL
- 2 pairs of chemo-rated gloves
- Hazardous-drug-resistant gown
- Shoe covers
- Goggles or face shield
- Disposable respirator
- Spill pads and towels
- Hazardous waste disposable bag
- Scoop and container for collecting any glass fragments

A spill kit must include a NIOSH-certified respirator. OSHA requires proper fit-testing to be completed for any staff using a respirator. If an employee comes into contact with a hazardous drug through touch or inhalation, the SDS can be references for treatment.

Federal Requirements for Disposal of Nonhazardous and Hazardous Pharmaceutical Substances

Disposing of pharmaceutical waste is federally regulated by the Environmental Protection Agency (EPA), though some states have specific requirements for waste management. The Resource and Conservation Recovery Act (RCRA) gives the EPA the authority to control hazardous waste. The EPA develops regulations to ensure safe cleanup and management of waste, as well as programs that help reduce or reuse waste. The RCRA defines pharmaceutical waste as P or U-listed. These pharmaceuticals must be disposed of under hazardous waste requirements.

To dispose of nonhazardous pharmaceutical waste appropriately, several steps must be followed. It must first be segregated from biohazardous waste, which includes waste that may contain blood or other infectious substances. Sharps, such as used needles, are also included as biohazardous waste, though they must be disposed of in a hard sharps container. Pharmaceutical waste must also not include controlled substances, as these must be wasted in accordance with the DEA. The remaining waste should be disposed of by a waste removal company.

To dispose of hazardous drug waste, it must first be defined hazardous by the EPA. This waste must be disposed of separately from nonhazardous drug waste. Chemotherapy waste is divided into bulk and trace waste. Bulk chemotherapy waste includes vials of chemotherapy drugs that are not empty and items used to clean spills or PPE. Trace chemotherapy includes empty chemotherapy vials and IV bags, including tubing from patient administration. Trace chemotherapy waste must be disposed of in a yellow chemotherapy container, while bulk chemotherapy waste is disposed of in the hazardous drug container a facility uses for P- and U-listed waste.

The following is a summary of waste disposal:

WASTE TYPE	CONTENTS INCLUDED
Pharmaceutical waste	▪ Nonhazardous medications (Not P- or U-listed)
Hazardous pharmaceutical waste	▪ Hazardous medications (P- and U-listed) ▪ Packaging and half/partial doses of P- and U-listed drugs ▪ Bulk chemo waste ▪ Chemo PPE
Chemotherapy waste	▪ Trace chemo waste, including empty chemo vials, syringes, gowns, gloves, tubing, and packaging
Sharps container	▪ Needles ▪ Ampules ▪ Broken glass
Biohazardous waste	▪ Infectious waste ▪ Blood products ▪ Visibly bloody gloves ▪ Visibly bloody IV tubing ▪ Contaminated PPE ▪ Saturated gauze and bandages ▪ Closed sharps containers (not loose sharps)

Review Questions

The following questions help you review the chapter. Test your knowledge by working through the next 50 questions to test yourself and identify any areas you may need to review.

1. Which organization has oversight of controlled substance laws in the United States?
   A. FDA
   B. DEA
   C. CSA
   D. USP

2. Schedule I substances have which of the following?
   A. accepted medical use and low potential for abuse
   B. accepted medical use and high potential for abuse
   C. no accepted medical use and low potential for abuse
   D. no accepted medical use and high potential for abuse

3. Which of the following is a Schedule II substance?
   A. fentanyl
   B. heroin
   C. ketamine
   D. alprazolam

4. Which of the following is a Schedule IV substance?
   A. diazepam
   B. pregabalin
   C. meperidine
   D. oxycodone

5. Verbal orders for which schedule of controlled substances are discouraged but can be accepted in an emergency?
   A. Schedule II
   B. Schedule III
   C. Schedule IV
   D. Schedule V

6. How many times can oxycodone be refilled?
   A. 6 times in 5 months
   B. 1 time within 30 days
   C. as many times as written by prescriber
   D. no refills allowed

7. To register with the DEA, which form must be completed?

    A. 222

    B. 224

    C. 106

    D. 41

8. A DEA Form 222 or CSOS must be used to order

    A. Schedule II

    B. Schedule III

    C. Schedule IV

    D. Schedule V

9. Which symbol would be found on a bottle of Percocet?

    A. CI

    B. CII

    C. CIII

    D. CIV

10. If a controlled substance is destroyed, which form must be submitted to the DEA?

    A. 222

    B. 224

    C. 106

    D. 41

11. DEA Form 106 is completed when

    A. a pharmacy closes

    B. ordering Schedule III and IV substances

    C. loss or theft occurs

    D. reverse distribution occurs

12. FDA-required programs developed by drug manufacturers that help patients avoid potential safety issues of specific medications are known as

    A. REMS

    B. CSA

    C. USP

    D. NIOSH

13. Which of the following must be dispensed with a med guide?
    A. albuterol
    B. citalopram
    C. amoxicillin
    D. rosuvastatin

14. Which medication requires certification with iPLEDGE?
    A. clozapine
    B. thalidomide
    C. isotretinoin
    D. suboxone

15. Which medication requires REMS due to the potential for misuse causing accidental overdose and death?
    A. clozapine
    B. thalidomide
    C. isotretinoin
    D. suboxone

16. A recall that could cause serious health problems or death is which class?
    A. Class I
    B. Class II
    C. Class III
    D. Class IV

17. A medication that is teratogenic causes
    A. cancer
    B. damage to organs
    C. damage to genetic information
    D. fetal malformation

18. Which federal organization helps ensure safe working conditions?
    A. USP
    B. FDA
    C. OSHA
    D. DEA

19. Which agency defines *hazardous drug* and establishes a list of hazardous drugs?
    A. FDA
    B. OSHA
    C. USP
    D. NIOSH

20. USP<800> is a chapter published that defines standards for

    A. sterile compounding

    B. nonsterile compounding

    C. hazardous drug handling

    D. radiopharmaceuticals

21. Where should a broken ampule be disposed?

    A. hazardous waste container

    B. sharps container

    C. biohazard container

    D. chemotherapy waste container

22. Trace chemo waste, such as empty chemo vials and IV tubing, should be disposed of in the

    A. nonhazardous waste container

    B. hazardous waste container

    C. chemotherapy waste container

    D. biohazard waste container

23. Which of the following should be used when compounding chemotherapy and other hazardous drugs and when administering to patients?

    A. spill kit

    B. standard needle and syringe

    C. three pairs of chemo-rated gloves

    D. CSTD

24. A hazard communication program must include

    A. an updated list of SDS and steps to take if a spill occurs

    B. all requirements from USP<797>

    C. FDA recall information

    D. DEA inventory

25. Designating a qualified and trained person responsible for developing and implementing procedures and overseeing compliance of hazardous drugs is a requirement for

    A. USP<795>

    B. USP<797>

    C. USP<800>

    D. USP<847>

26. Which of the following was created to combat the growing drug problem in America?

    A. FDA

    B. CSA

    C. USP

    D. NIOSH

27. Methylphenidate is which schedule of controlled substance?

    A. Schedule I

    B. Schedule II

    C. Schedule III

    D. Schedule IV

28. Which of the following is a Schedule III substance?

    A. anabolic steroids

    B. oxycodone

    C. methadone

    D. alprazolam

29. Which schedule substance has low to moderate potential for abuse?

    A. Schedule I

    B. Schedule II

    C. Schedule III

    D. Schedule IV

30. Pregabalin is which schedule of controlled substance?

    A. Schedule II

    B. Schedule III

    C. Schedule IV

    D. Schedule V

31. According to federal law, if a pharmacy accepts an emergency verbal order for a Schedule II substance, when must the prescriber provide a valid written prescription?

    A. 24 hours

    B. 72 hours

    C. 7 days

    D. 30 days

32. Which of the following is required for a controlled substance prescription to be transferred to another pharmacy?

    A. number of refills remaining

    B. patient Social Security number

    C. date patient was seen by the prescriber

    D. name of technician who answered call

33. How many times could a prescription for zolpidem be refilled?

    A. no refills permitted

    B. up to 6 times in 30 days

    C. up to 5 times in 6 months

    D. up to 10 times in 180 days

34. Controlled substance prescriptions must be stored for a minimum of

    A. 30 days

    B. 180 days

    C. 1 year

    D. 2 years

35. A DEA 222 form can be completed by

    A. any pharmacy staff members

    B. a pharmacy technician only

    C. a pharmacist only

    D. a responsible pharmacist only

36. Which of the following is a benefit of CSOS?

    A. larger inventory needed

    B. slower transmission time

    C. no need for record retention

    D. more efficient and typically faster delivery

37. Ketamine would have which symbol on a stock bottle?

    A. CI

    B. CII

    C. CIII

    D. CIV

38. Removing expired or unused controlled substances from a pharmacy and returning them to the manufacturer for credit is known as

    A. take-back days
    B. reverse distribution
    C. credit/rebill
    D. diversion

39. Which drug would require a PPI?

    A. atorvastatin
    B. ethinyl estradiol and norethindrone
    C. ergocalciferol
    D. lidocaine

40. Which of the following is a handout given with certain medications that contains FDA-approved information to help patients understand the potential for serious adverse events?

    A. REMS
    B. medication guide
    C. Orange Book
    D. reverse distribution

41. Clozapine has a REMS to help prevent

    A. birth defects
    B. accidental overdose
    C. tendon rupture
    D. severe neutropenia

42. A pharmacy has 21-count boxes of pseudoephedrine with 30mg in each tablet. According to federal law, what is the maximum number of boxes that can be purchased in one day without violating the CMEA?

    A. 3 boxes
    B. 4 boxes
    C. 5 boxes
    D. 6 boxes

43. Which of the following rules must a pharmacy selling pseudoephedrine follow to comply with the CMEA?

    A. require two forms of ID of any purchaser
    B. limit access to customers by selling behind the counter
    C. daily sales not to exceed 5 grams
    D. records kept for a minimum of 6 months

44. A drug that is genotoxic causes damage to
    A. organs
    B. reproductive growth
    C. cancer
    D. genetic information in a cell

45. The RCRA gives the EPA authority to control
    A. narcotic dispensing
    B. sterile compounding
    C. recall notifications
    D. hazardous drug waste

46. Used IV tubing should be disposed of in the
    A. biohazard waste
    B. hazardous drug waste
    C. chemotherapy waste
    D. sharps container

47. Lorazepam is which schedule controlled substance?
    A. Schedule II
    B. Schedule III
    C. Schedule IV
    D. Schedule V

48. Marijuana is considered a
    A. Schedule I substance
    B. Schedule II substance
    C. Schedule III substance
    D. Schedule IV substance

49. Which schedule has a low potential for abuse and is often an antitussive, anticonvulsant, or antidiarrheal medication?
    A. Schedule II
    B. Schedule III
    C. Schedule IV
    D. Schedule V

50. After an injury, a patient who is nonhospice or in a long-term-care facility receives a prescription for a Schedule II controlled substance. The pharmacy must partially fill the order due to low inventory and all other nearby pharmacies are closed. The remaining supply must be filled fully within

A. 24 hours

B. 36 hours

C. 48 hours

D. 72 hours

Answer Key

1. **B**

   The Drug Enforcement Administration (DEA) was established in 1973, and their main mission is to enforce the controlled substances laws of the United States.

2. **D**

   Schedule I substances have no accepted medical use and a high potential for abuse.

3. **A**

   Fentanyl is a Schedule II substance.

4. **A**

   Diazepam is a Schedule IV substance.

5. **A**

   Verbal orders for Schedule II prescriptions are discouraged but may be accepted in emergency situations.

6. **D**

   Oxycodone is a Schedule II prescription and is not permitted to be refilled or transferred to another pharmacy.

7. **B**

   A new pharmacy must register with the DEA prior to ordering controlled substances. The pharmacy completes DEA Form 224, and this registration must be renewed every three years.

8. **A**

   DEA Form 222 must be used for Schedule I or II ordering.

9. **B**

   Percocet is a Schedule II substance, so the symbol used for labeling would be CII.

10. **D**

    DEA Form 41 is submitted to the DEA if a controlled substance is destroyed.

11. **C**

    In the event a pharmacy discovers there is a loss or theft of a controlled substance, they must notify the DEA within one business day of the discovery. In addition to notifying the DEA, a DEA Form 106 must also be completed. This can be completed online or downloaded and submitted to the local DEA office.

12. **A**

REMS are designed to reduce the frequency and severity of adverse events by informing patients of safety concerns or requiring specific practices for safe use.

13. **B**

Citalopram requires a medication guide. All SSRIs require med guides.

14. **C**

The REMS program for isotretinoin is known as iPLEDGE. The goal of this REMS to prevent fetal exposure and inform pharmacist, providers, and patients of the potential for teratogenic effects.

15. **D**

Suboxone is indicated to treat opioid addiction. Misuse of suboxone may lead to accidental overdose and death.

16. **A**

Class I recall is a dangerous or defective product that could cause serious health problems or death.

17. **D**

Teratogenicity causes fetal malformations.

18. **C**

OSHA helps ensure safe working conditions by establishing standards and providing education and training.

19. **D**

NIOSH establishes a list of hazardous drugs and defines what makes a drug hazardous. This list is used in most pharmacies as a reference to determine what inventory should be handled as a hazardous drug.

20. **C**

USP published Chapter 800 (USP<800>) Hazardous Drugs—Handling in Healthcare Settings. This chapter describes standards and best practices for handling hazardous drugs in order to protect healthcare workers and patients.

21. **B**

A sharps container is used for broken glass and needles.

22. **C**

Trace chemo waste, including empty chemo vials, syringes, gowns, gloves, tubing, and packaging, must be disposed of in a yellow chemo waste container.

23. **D**

Closed system drug-transfer devices (CSTD) should be used to compound chemotherapy and other hazardous drugs. CSTDs minimize the risk of hazardous drug exposure to the employees compounding and nurses when administering to a patient. They also protect the patient from accidental spilling or leakage.

24. **A**

A hazardous communication program must also include steps to take if a spill occurs and updated list of safety data sheets (SDS).

25. **C**

USP<800> requires a facility to designate a qualified and trained person responsible for developing and implementing procedures and overseeing compliance.

26. **B**

The Comprehensive Drug Abuse Prevention and Control Act of 1970 was created to combat the growing drug problem in America. This act included the Controlled Substance Act (CSA), which consolidated several laws regulating the prescribing, distribution, and scheduling of controlled substances.

27. **B**

Methylphenidate is a Schedule II substance.

28. **A**

Anabolic steroids, such as testosterone, is a Schedule III substance.

29. **C**

Schedule III has a low to moderate potential for abuse—less abuse potential than Schedule I or II.

30. **D**

Pregabalin is a Schedule V substance.

31. **C**

If an emergency fill is required, the pharmacy must write out the verbal order as a valid prescription and dispense a quantity sufficient only for the emergency period (e.g., a fill for Saturday and Sunday until the prescriber's office is open). The prescriber must then provide the pharmacy with a valid written prescription for this order within seven days.

32. **A**

    The following requirements must be met for a prescription to be transferred to a pharmacy:

    - Date of issue of original prescription
    - Original number of refills authorized
    - Date of original dispensing
    - Number of refills remaining and location of any previous refills
    - Pharmacy name, address, and DEA number from which the prescription was transferred
    - Name of pharmacist transferring the prescription

33. **C**

    Refills for Schedule III and IV prescriptions are permitted but limited to five refills within six months (or whichever occurs first).

34. **D**

    All original controlled substance prescriptions must be filed and stored for a minimum of two years.

35. **C**

    DEA 222 forms are used for ordering Schedule II substances and must be completed by a pharmacist.

36. **D**

    It is also more efficient, as it does not require time spent in the mail to the wholesaler, and instead is submitted electronically for more timely and accurate validation by the supplier. This also helps pharmacies maintain a smaller inventory because they can submit an electronic order and have the inventory replenished sometimes the next day. Records of electronic CSOS orders must also be maintained for two years.

37. **C**

    Ketamine is a Schedule III controlled substance, so it would have a CIII on the manufacturer labeling.

38. **B**

    A reverse distributor removes the expired inventory from a pharmacy and returns the drugs to the manufacturer. The manufacturer accepts the returns and may give credit back to the pharmacy.

39. **B**

    PPIs are developed by the manufacturer and are required to be dispensed with certain drug classes such as oral contraceptives or estrogen-containing products.

40. **B**

    A medication guide contains FDA-approved information for patients in an easy-to-read format to help inform patients about the potential for serious adverse events.

41. **D**

    Clozapine (Clozaril) is a medication used for the treatment of schizophrenia and has been associated with causing severe neutropenia.

42. **C**

    5 boxes. $21 \times 30 = 630$mg in each box. Total allowed in a one-day sale of pseudoephedrine = 3.6g. $3.6g \times 1,000 = 3,600$mg. $\frac{3,600\text{mg}}{630\text{mg}} = 5.7$ or 5 boxes.

43. **B**

    Requirements and restrictions of the CMEA include:

    - Daily sales not to exceed 3.6 grams
    - 30-day purchase limit of no more than 9 grams
    - Photo ID or proof of identity of any purchaser
    - Retrievable records of all purchases to be kept for a minimum of two years
    - Limit access to customers by selling behind the counter

44. **D**

    A drug that is genotoxic causes damage to genetic information in a cell, which can cause mutations and lead to cancer.

45. **D**

    The Resource and Conservation Recovery Act (RCRA) gives the EPA the authority to control hazardous waste.

46. **A**

    Used IV tubing and other infectious waste or blood products should be disposed of in the biohazard container.

47. **C**

    Lorazpam (Ativan) is a Schedule IV controlled substance.

48. **A**

    Marijuana is considered by the DEA to be a Schedule I substance.

49. **D**

    Schedule V substances have a low potential for abuse and are often used for antitussive, anticonvulsant, or antidiarrheal purposes.

50. **D**

    A Schedule II drug can be partially filled in an emergency only, and the patient must receive the full prescription within 72 hours.

CHAPTER 4

Patient Safety and Quality Assurance

PTCE Knowledge Domain: Patient Safety and Quality Assurance   26.25% of Exam

Knowledge Areas

- High-alert/risk medications and look-alike/sound-alike (LASA) medications

- Error prevention strategies (e.g., prescription or medication order to correct patient, tall man lettering, separating inventory, leading and trailing zeros, bar code usage, limit use of error-prone abbreviations)

- Issues that require pharmacist intervention (e.g., drug utilization review [DUR], adverse drug event [ADE], OTC recommendation, therapeutic substitution, misuse, adherence, post-immunization follow-up, allergies, drug interactions)

- Event reporting procedures (e.g., medication errors, adverse effects, product integrity, MedWatch, near miss, root-cause analysis [RCA])

- Types of prescription errors (e.g., abnormal doses, early refill, incorrect quantity, incorrect patient, incorrect drug)

- Hygiene and cleaning standards (e.g., handwashing; personal protective equipment [PPE]; cleaning counting trays, countertop, and equipment)

After reading Chapter 4 you will be able to:

- Identify high-alert/high risk and look-alike/sound-alike (LASA) medications

- Understand the importance of error prevention strategies, including tall man lettering and bar codes

- Explain error-prone abbreviations and the importance in eliminating use

- Differentiate between prescription errors and the impact of each on patient safety

- Describe the process of medication error reporting, including MedWatch and conducting a root cause analysis

- Identify types of pharmacist interventions and the importance of each

- Understand the importance of pharmacy technician support in adherence and how to calculate adherence percentage

- Describe quality control in a pharmacy, including hygiene and cleaning standards

As a pharmacy technician, you will play a vital role preventing medication errors and maintaining patient safety. There are several safety strategies and measures that can be taken to help prevent medication errors. This chapter reviews these strategies, as well as pharmacist interventions and reporting for medication errors.

ISMP Safe Medication Practices

The Institute for Safe Medication Practices (ISMP) is an organization devoted to preventing medication errors. ISMP publishes real-time medication error information in newsletters and offers educational tools and guidelines for healthcare facilities and pharmacies.

High-Alert/Risk Medications

To help prevent errors, ISMP has developed a list of **high-alert medications**, which are drugs that may cause greater harm if used in error. These drugs do not have a higher rate of error, but can be more devastating if used in error. ISMP publishes this high-alert list to help organizations identify which medications should have special strategies for error prevention, such as limiting access, using auxiliary labels, and standardizing ordering and preparation of these medications. Each pharmacy should also use the ISMP list to develop its own internal list of high-alert/high-risk medications.

The ISMP List of High-Alert Medications in Acute Care Settings follows.

CLASSES/CATEGORIES OF MEDICATIONS

adrenergic agonists, IV (e.g., **EPINEPH**rine, phenylephrine, norepinephrine)

adrenergic antagonists, IV (e.g., propranolol, metoprolol, labetalol)

anesthetic agents, general, inhaled and IV (e.g., propofol, ketamine)

antiarrhythmics, IV (e.g., lidocaine, amiodarone)

antithrombotic agents, including:
- anticoagulants (e.g., warfarin, low molecular weight heparin, IV unfractionated heparin)
- Factor Xa inhibitors (e.g., fondaparinux, apixaban, rivaroxaban)
- direct thrombin inhibitors (e.g., argatroban, bivalirudin, dabigatran etexilate) thrombolytics (e.g., alteplase, reteplase, tenecteplase)
- glycoprotein IIb/IIIa inhibitors (e.g., eptifibatide)

cardioplegic solutions

chemotherapeutic agents, parenteral and oral

dextrose, hypertonic, 20% or greater

dialysis solutions, peritoneal and hemodialysis

epidural or intrathecal medications

hypoglycemics, oral

inotropic medications, IV (e.g., digoxin, milrinone)

insulin, subcutaneous and IV

liposomal forms of drugs (e.g., liposomal amphotericin B) and conventional counter- parts (e.g., amphotericin B desoxycholate)

moderate sedation agents, IV (e.g., dexmedetomidine, midazolam)

moderate sedation agents, oral, for children (e.g., chloral hydrate)

narcotics/opioids
- IV
- transdermal
- oral (including liquid concentrates, immediate and sustained-release formulations)

neuromuscular blocking agents (e.g., succinylcholine, rocuronium, vecuronium)

parenteral nutrition preparations

radiocontrast agents, IV

sterile water for injection, inhalation, and irrigation (excluding pour bottles) in containers of 100 mL or more

sodium chloride for injection, hypertonic, greater than 0.9% concentration

SPECIFIC MEDICATIONS

EPINEPHrine, subcutaneous

epoprostenol (Flolan), IV

insulin U-500 (special emphasis)*

magnesium sulfate injection

methotrexate, oral, non-oncologic use

opium tincture

oxytocin, IV

nitroprusside sodium for injection

potassium chloride for injection concentrate

potassium phosphates injection

promethazine, IV

vasopressin, IV or intraosseous

*All forms of insulin, subcutaneous and IV, are considered a class of high-alert medications. Insulin U-500 has been singled out for special emphasis to bring attention to the need for distinct strategies to prevent the types of errors that occur with this concentrated form of insulin.

Look-Alike/Sound-Alike (LASA) Medications

The ISMP also compiles a list of confused drug names, which includes **look-alike and sound-alike (LASA)** name pairs of medications. Pharmacies and healthcare facilities can use this list to develop their own list of LASA drugs and strategies to prevent mix-ups. This could include using both the brand and generic names on prescriptions or labels, including the medication purpose on prescriptions, and configuring ordering solutions to prevent LASA names from appearing next to each other.

The FDA and the ISMP have a list of confused drug names. The following is the FDA and ISMP list of confused drug names:

DRUG NAME	CONFUSED DRUG NAME
Abelcet	*amphotericin B*
Accupril	Aciphex
acetaminophen	*aceta**ZOLAMIDE***
*aceta**ZOLAMIDE***	*acetaminophen*
*aceta**ZOLAMIDE***	*aceto**HEXAMIDE***
acetic acid for irrigation	*glacial acetic acid*
*aceto**HEXAMIDE***	*aceta**ZOLAMIDE***
Aciphex	Accupril
Aciphex	Aricept
Activase	Cathfo Activase
Activase	TNKase
Actonel	Actos
Actos	Actonel
Adacel (*Tdap*)	Daptacel (*DTaP*)
Adderall	Adderall XR
Adderall	Inderal
Adderall XR	Adderall
ado-trastuzumab emtansine	*trastuzumab*
Advair	Advicor
Advicor	Advair
Advicor	Altocor
Afrin (*oxymetazoline*)	Afrin (*saline*)
Afrin (*saline*)	Afrin (*oxymetazoline*)
Aggrastat	*argatroban*
Aldara	Alora
Alkeran	Leukeran
Alkeran	Myleran

DRUG NAME	CONFUSED DRUG NAME
Allegra (*fexofenadine*)	Allegra Anti-Itch Cream (*diphenhydr**AMINE**/allantoin*)
Allegra	Viagra
Allegra Anti-Itch Cream (*diphenhydr**AMINE**/allantoin*)	Allegra (*fexofenadine*)
Alora	Aldara
ALPRAZolam	clonaze**PAM**
ALPRAZolam	**LOR**azepam
Altocor	Advicor
amantadine	*amiodarone*
Amaryl	Reminyl
Ambisome	*amphotericin B*
Amicar	Omacor
Amikin	Kineret
a**MIL**oride	am**LODIP**ine
amiodarone	*amantadine*
am**LODIP**ine	a**MIL**oride
amphotericin B	Abelcet
amphotericin B	Ambisome
amphotericin B	*amphotericin B liposomal*
amphotericin B liposomal	*amphotericin B*
Anacin	Anacin-3
Anacin-3	Anacin
antacid	Atacand
anticoagulant citrate dextrose solution formula A	*anticoagulant sodium citrate solution*
anticoagulant sodium citrate solution	*anticoagulant citrate dextrose solution formula A*

DRUG NAME	CONFUSED DRUG NAME
Antivert	Axert
Anzemet	Avandamet
Apidra	Spiriva
Apresoline	Priscoline
argatroban	Aggrastat
argatroban	Orgaran
Aricept	Aciphex
Aricept	Azilect
ARIPiprazole	*proton pump inhibitors*
ARIPiprazole	**RABE**prazole
Arista AH (*absorbable hemostatic agent*)	Arixtra
Arixtra	Arista AH (*absorbable hemostatic agent*)
Asacol	Os-Cal
Atacand	*antacid*
atomoxetine	*atorvastatin*
atorvastatin	*atomoxetine*
Atrovent	Natru-Vent
Avandamet	Anzemet
Avandia	Coumadin
Avandia	Prandin
AVINza	Evista
AVINza	**INV**anz
Axert	Antivert
*aza***CITID***ine*	*aza***THIO***prine*
*aza***THIO***prine*	*aza***CITID***ine*
Azilect	Aricept
B & O (*belladonna and opium*)	Beano
BabyBIG	HBIG (*hepatitis B immune globulin*)
Bayhep-B	Bayrab
Bayhep-B	Bayrho-D
Bayrab	Bayhep-B
Bayrab	Bayrho-D
Bayrho-D	Bayhep-B
Bayrho-D	Bayrab

DRUG NAME	CONFUSED DRUG NAME
Beano	B & O (*belladonna and opium*)
Benadryl	*benazepril*
benazepril	Benadryl
Benicar	Mevacor
ARIPiprazole	*proton pump inhibitors*
ARIPiprazole	**RABE**prazole
Arista AH (*absorbable hemostatic agent*)	Arixtra
Arixtra	Arista AH (*absorbable hemostatic agent*)
Asacol	Os-Cal
Atacand	*antacid*
atomoxetine	*atorvastatin*
atorvastatin	*atomoxetine*
Atrovent	Natru-Vent
Avandamet	Anzemet
Avandia	Coumadin
Avandia	Prandin
AVINza	Evista
AVINza	**INV**anz
Axert	Antivert
*aza***CITID***ine*	*aza***THIO***prine*
*aza***THIO***prine*	*aza***CITID***ine*
Azilect	Aricept
B & O (*belladonna and opium*)	Beano
BabyBIG	HBIG (*hepatitis B immune globulin*)
Bayhep-B	Bayrab
Bayhep-B	Bayrho-D
Bayrab	Bayhep-B
Bayrab	Bayrho-D
Bayrho-D	Bayhep-B
Bayrho-D	Bayrab
Beano	B & O (*belladonna and opium*)
Benadryl	*benazepril*
benazepril	Benadryl

(continued)

DRUG NAME	CONFUSED DRUG NAME
Benicar	Mevacor
Betadine (with povidone-iodine)	Betadine (without povidone-iodine)
Betadine (without povidone-iodine)	Betadine (with povidone-iodine)
betaine (anhydrous form)	*betaine HCl*
betaine HCl	*betaine* (anhydrous form)
Bextra	Zetia
Bicillin C-R	Bicillin L-A
Bicillin L-A	Bicillin C-R
Bicitra	Polycitra
Bidex	Videx
Brethine	Methergine
Bio-T-Gel	T-Gel
Brevibloc	Brevital
Brevital	Brevibloc
Brilinta	Brintellix
Brintellix	Brilinta
buprenorphine	**HYDRO***morphone*
*bu***PROP***ion*	*bus***PIR***one*
*bus***PIR***one*	*bu***PROP***ion*
Capadex [non-US product]	Kapidex
Capex	Kapidex
Carac	Kuric
captopril	*carvedilol*
*car***BAM***azepine*	**OX***carbazepine*
CARBO*platin*	**CIS***platin*
Cardene	Cardizem
Cardizem	Cardene
Cardura	Coumadin
carvedilol	*captopril*
Casodex	Kapidex
Cathfo Activase	Activase
Cedax	Cidex
*ce***FAZ***olin*	*cef***TRIAX***one*
*cef***TRIAX***one*	*ce***FAZ***olin*
cefuroxime	*sulfa***SALA***zine*
Cele**BREX**	Cele**XA**

DRUG NAME	CONFUSED DRUG NAME
Cele**BREX**	Cerebyx
Cele**XA**	Cele**BREX**
Cele**XA**	Cerebyx
Cele**XA**	Zy**PREXA**
Cerebyx	Cele**BREX**
Cerebyx	Cele**XA**
cetirizine	*sertraline*
cetirizine	*stavudine*
*chlordiaze***POXIDE**	*chlorpro***MAZINE**
*chlorpro***MAZINE**	*chlordiaze***POXIDE**
*chlorpro***MAZINE**	*chlorpro***PAMIDE**
*chlorpro***PAMIDE**	*chlorpro***MAZINE**
Cidex	Cedax
CIS*platin*	**CARBO***platin*
Clarispray (*fluticasone propionate*)	Claritin (*loratadine*)
Claritin (*loratadine*)	Claritin Eye (*ketotifen fumarate*)
Claritin (*loratadine*)	Clarispray (*fluticasone propionate*)
Claritin-D	Claritin-D 24
Claritin-D 24	Claritin-D
Claritin Eye (*ketotifen fumarate*)	Claritin (*loratadine*)
Clindesse	Clindets
Clindets	Clindesse
*clo***BAZ***am*	*clonaze***PAM**
*clomi***PHENE**	*clomi***PRAMINE**
*clomi***PRAMINE**	*clomi***PHENE**
*clonaze***PAM**	**ALPRAZ***olam*
*clonaze***PAM**	*clo***BAZ***am*
*clonaze***PAM**	*clo***NID***ine*
*clonaze***PAM**	*clo***ZAP***ine*
*clonaze***PAM**	**LOR***azepam*
*clo***NID***ine*	*clonaze***PAM**
*clo***NID***ine*	*clo***ZAP***ine*
*clo***NID***ine*	Klono**PIN**
*clo***ZAP***ine*	*clonaze***PAM**

DRUG NAME	CONFUSED DRUG NAME	DRUG NAME	CONFUSED DRUG NAME
cloZAPine	*cloNIDine*	Depakote	Depakote ER
Clozaril	Colazal	Depakote ER	Depakote
coagulation factor IX (recombinant)	*factor IX complex, vapor heated*	**DEPO**-Medrol	**SOLU**-Medrol
codeine	Lodine	Depo-Provera	Depo-subQ provera 104
Colace	Cozaar	Depo-subQ provera 104	Depo-Provera
Colazal	Clozaril	*desipramine*	*disopyramide*
colchicine	Cortrosyn	*desmopressin*	*vasopressin*
Comvax	Recombivax HB	Desyrel	**SERO**quel
Cortrosyn	*colchicine*	*dexamethasone*	*dexmedetomidine*
Coumadin	Avandia	Dexilant	**DUL**oxetine
Coumadin	Cardura	*dexmedetomidine*	*dexamethasone*
Covaryx HS	Covera HS	*dexmethylphenidate*	*dexmethylphenidate mixed salts*
Covera HS	Covaryx HS	*dexmethylphenidate*	*methadone*
Cozaar	Colace	*dexmethylphenidate mixed salts*	*dexmethylphenidate*
Cozaar	Zocor	Diabenese	Diamox
Cubicin	Cubicin RF	Diabeta	Zebeta
Cubicin RF	Cubicin	Diamox	Diabenese
cyclophosphamide	*cycloSPORINE*	*diazePAM*	*dilTIAZem*
cycloSERINE	*cycloSPORINE*	Difucan	Diprivan
cycloSPORINE	*cyclophosphamide*	Dilacor XR	Pilocar
cycloSPORINE	*cycloSERINE*	Dilaudid	Dilaudid-5
cycloSPORINE	*cycloSPORINE modiied*	Dilaudid-5	Dilaudid
cycloSPORINE modiied	*cycloSPORINE*	*dilTIAZem*	*diazePAM*
Cymbalta	Symbyax	*dimenhyDRINATE*	*diphenhydrAMINE*
dabigatran	*vigabatrin*	*diphenhydrAMINE*	*dimenhyDRINATE*
DACTINomycin	**DAPTO**mycin	Dioval	Diovan
Daptacel (*DTaP*)	Adacel (*Tdap*)	Diovan	Darvon
DAPTOmycin	**DACTIN**omycin	Diovan	Dioval
Darvocet	Percocet	Diovan	Zyban
Darvon	Diovan	Diprivan	Difucan
DAUNOrubicin	**DAUNO**rubicin citrate liposomal	Diprivan	Ditropan
DAUNOrubicin	**DOXO**rubicin	*disopyramide*	*desipramine*
DAUNOrubicin	**IDA**rubicin	Ditropan	Diprivan
DAUNOrubicin citrate liposomal	**DAUNO**rubicin	**DOBUT**amine	**DOP**amine
Denavir	*indinavir*	**DOCE**taxel	**PACL**itaxel
		DOPamine	**DOBUT**amine

(continued)

DRUG NAME	CONFUSED DRUG NAME
Doribax	Zovirax
Doxil	Paxil
DOXOrubicin	**DAUNO**rubicin
DOXOrubicin	**DOXO**rubicin liposomal
DOXOrubicin	**IDA**rubicin
DOXOrubicin liposomal	**DOXO**rubicin
Dramamine (*dimenhy***DRINATE**)	Dramamine (*ginger root*)
Dramamine (*dimenhy***DRINATE**)	Dramamine (*meclizine*)
Dramamine (*ginger root*)	Dramamine (*dimenhy***DRINATE**)
Dramamine (*ginger root*)	Dramamine (*meclizine*)
Dramamine (*meclizine*)	Dramamine (*dimenhy***DRINATE**)
Dramamine (*meclizine*)	Dramamine (*ginger root*)
Dulcolax (*bisacodyl*)	Dulcolax (*docusate sodium*)
Dulcolax (*docusate sodium*)	Dulcolax (*bisacodyl*)
DULoxetine	Dexilant
DULoxetine	**FLU**oxetine
DULoxetine	**PAR**oxetine
Durasal	Durezol
Durezol	Durasal
Duricef	Ultracet
Dynacin	Dynacirc
Dynacirc	Dynacin
edetate calcium disodium	*edetate disodium*
edetate disodium	*edetate calcium disodium*
Effexor	Effexor XR
Effexor XR	Effexor
Effexor XR	Enablex
elvitegravir, cobicistat, emtricitabine, and tenofovir alafenamide	*elvitegravir, cobicistat, emtricitabine, and tenofovir disoproxil fumarate*
elvitegravir, cobicistat, emtricitabine, and tenofovir disoproxil fumarate	*elvitegravir, cobicistat, emtricitabine, and tenofovir alafenamide*
Enablex	Effexor XR
Enbrel	Levbid

DRUG NAME	CONFUSED DRUG NAME
Engerix-B adult	Engerix-B pediatric/adolescent
Engerix-B pediatric/adolescent	Engerix-B adult
En uvia	Januvia
e**PHED**rine	**EPINEPH**rine
EPINEPHrine	e**PHED**rine
epi**RUB**icin	eri**BUL**in
eri**BUL**in	epi**RUB**icin
Estratest	Estratest HS
Estratest HS	Estratest
ethambutol	Ethmozine
ethaverine [non-US name]	*etravirine*
Ethmozine	*ethambutol*
etravirine	*ethaverine [non-US name]*
Evista	**AVIN**za
factor IX complex, vapor heated	*coagulation factor IX (recombinant)*
Fanapt	Xanax
Farxiga	Fetzima
Fastin (*phentermine*)	Fastin (dietary supplement)
Fastin (dietary supplement)	Fastin (*phentermine*)
Femara	Femhrt
Femhrt	Femara
*fenta***NYL**	**SUF**entanil
Fetzima	Farxiga
Fioricet	Fiorinal
Fiorinal	Fioricet
*flavox***ATE**	*fluvoxa***MINE**
Flonase	Flovent
Floranex	Florinef
Florastor	Florinef
Florinef	Floranex
Florinef	Florastor
Flovent	Flonase
*flu***PHENAZ***ine*	*fluvoxa***MINE**
flumazenil	*influenza virus vaccine*
FLUoxetine	**DUL**oxetine

DRUG NAME	CONFUSED DRUG NAME
FLUoxetine	Loxitane
FLUoxetine	**PAR**oxetine
fluvoxa**MINE**	flavox**ATE**
fluvoxa**MINE**	flu**PHENAZ**ine
Focalgin B	Focalin
Focalin	Focalgin B
Folex	Foltx
folic acid	folinic acid (leucovorin calcium)
folinic acid (leucovorin calcium)	folic acid
Foltx	Folex
fomepizole	omeprazole
Foradil	Fortical
Foradil	Toradol
Fortical	Foradil
gabapentin	gemibrozil
gemibrozil	gabapentin
gentamicin	gentian violet
gentian violet	gentamicin
glacial acetic acid	acetic acid for irrigation
glipi**ZIDE**	gly**BURIDE**
Glucotrol	Glycotrol
gly**BURIDE**	glipi**ZIDE**
Glycotrol	Glucotrol
Granulex	Regranex
guai**FEN**esin	guan**FACINE**
guan**FACINE**	guai**FEN**esin
HBIG (hepatitis B immune globulin)	BabyBIG
Healon	Hyalgan
heparin	Hespan
Hespan	heparin
HMG-CoA reductase inhibitors ("statins")	nystatin
Huma**LOG**	Humu**LIN**
Huma**LOG**	Novo**LOG**
Huma**LOG** Mix 75/25	Humu**LIN** 70/30

DRUG NAME	CONFUSED DRUG NAME
Humapen Memoir (for use with Huma**LOG**)	Humira Pen
Humira Pen	Humapen Memoir (for use with Huma**LOG**)
Humu**LIN**	Novo**LIN**
Humu**LIN**	Huma**LOG**
Humu**LIN** 70/30	Huma**LOG** Mix 75/25
Humu**LIN** R U-100	Humu**LIN** R U-500
Humu**LIN** R U-500	Humu**LIN** R U-100
Hyalgan	Healon
hydr**ALAZINE**	hydro**CHLORO**thiazide
hydr**ALAZINE**	hydr**OXY**zine
Hydrea	Lyrica
hydro**CHLORO**thiazide	hydr**ALAZINE**
hydro**CHLORO**thiazide	hydr**OXY**zine
HYDROcodone	oxy**CODONE**
Hydrogesic	hydr**OXY**zine
HYDROmorphone	buprenorphine
HYDROmorphone	morphine
HYDROmorphone	oxy**MOR**phone
hydroxychloroquine	hydroxyurea
HYDROXYprogesterone	medroxy**PROGESTER**one
hydroxyurea	hydroxychloroquine
hydroxyurea	hydr**OXY**zine
hydr**OXY**zine	hydr**ALAZINE**
hydr**OXY**zine	hydro**CHLORO**thiazide
hydr**OXY**zine	Hydrogesic
hydr**OXY**zine	hydroxyurea
IDArubicin	**DAUNO**rubicin
IDArubicin	**DOXO**rubicin
IDArubicin	idaru**CIZU**mab
idaru**CIZU**mab	**IDA**rubicin
Inderal	Adderall
indinavir	Denavir
in**FLIX**imab	ri**TUX**imab
influenza virus vaccine	flumazenil
influenza virus vaccine	perflutren lipid microspheres

(continued)

DRUG NAME	CONFUSED DRUG NAME		DRUG NAME	CONFUSED DRUG NAME
influenza virus vaccine	*tuberculin puriied protein derivative* (PPD)		Kuric	Carac
Inspra	Spiriva		Kwell	Qwell
Intuniv	Invega		*labetalol*	La**MIC**tal
INVanz	**AVIN**za		*labetalol*	*lamo**TRI**gine*
Invega	Intuniv		La**MIC**tal	*labetalol*
iodine	Lodine		La**MIC**tal	Lam**ISIL**
Isordil	Plendil		Lam**ISIL**	La**MIC**tal
ISOtretinoin	*tretinoin*		*lami**VUD**ine*	*lamo**TRI**gine*
Jantoven	Janumet		*lamo**TRI**gine*	*labetalol*
Jantoven	Januvia		*lamo**TRI**gine*	*lami**VUD**ine*
Janumet	Jantoven		*lamo**TRI**gine*	*lev**ETIRA**cetam*
Janumet	Januvia		*lamo**TRI**gine*	*levothyroxine*
Janumet	Sinemet		Lanoxin	*levothyroxine*
Januvia	En uvia		Lanoxin	*naloxone*
Januvia	Jantoven		*lanthanum carbonate*	*lithium carbonate*
Januvia	Janumet		Lantus	Latuda
K-Phos Neutral	Neutra-Phos-K		Lantus	Lente
Kaopectate (*bismuth subsalicylate*)	Kaopectate (*docusate calcium*)		Lariam	Levaquin
			Lasix	Luvox
Kaopectate (*docusate calcium*)	Kaopectate (*bismuth subsalicylate*)		Latuda	Lantus
			Lente	Lantus
Kadian	Kapidex		Letairis	Letaris [non-US product]
Kaletra	Keppra		Letaris [non-US product]	Letairis
Kapidex	Capadex [non-US product]		*leucovorin calcium*	Leukeran
Kapidex	Capex		*leucovorin calcium*	**LEVO**leucovorin
Kapidex	Casodex		Leukeran	Alkeran
Kapidex	Kadian		Leukeran	leucovorin calcium
Kay Ciel	Kayexalate		Leukeran	Myleran
Kayexalate	Kay Ciel		Levaquin	Lariam
Kefex	Keppra		Levbid	Enbrel
Keppra	Kaletra		Levemir	Lovenox
Keppra	Kefex		*lev**ETIRA**cetam*	*lamo**TRI**gine*
Ketalar	*ketorolac*		*lev**ETIRA**cetam*	*lev**OCARN**itine*
ketorolac	Ketalar		*lev**ETIRA**cetam*	*levo**FLOX**acin*
ketorolac	*methadone*		*lev**OCARN**itine*	*lev**ETIRA**cetam*
Kineret	Amikin		*levo**FLOX**acin*	*lev**ETIRA**cetam*
Klono**PIN**	*clo**NID**ine*		**LEVO**leucovorin	*leucovorin calcium*

DRUG NAME	CONFUSED DRUG NAME
levothyroxine	lamoTRIgine
levothyroxine	Lanoxin
levothyroxine	liothyronine
Lexapro	Loxitane
Lexiva	Pexeva
linaCLOtide	linaGLIPtin
linaGLIPtin	linaCLOtide
liothyronine	levothyroxine
Lipitor	Loniten
Lipitor	ZyrTEC
lithium	Ultram
lithium carbonate	lanthanum carbonate
Lodine	codeine
Lodine	iodine
Loniten	Lipitor
Lopressor	Lyrica
LORazepam	ALPRAZolam
LORazepam	clonazePAM
LORazepam	Lovaza
Lotronex	Protonix
Lovaza	LORazepam
Lovenox	Levemir
Loxitane	FLUoxetine
Loxitane	Lexapro
Loxitane	Soriatane
Lunesta	Neulasta
Lupron Depot–3 Month	Lupron Depot–Ped
Lupron Depot–Ped	Lupron Depot–3 Month
Luvox	Lasix
Lyrica	Hydrea
Lyrica	Lopressor
Maalox	Maalox Total Stomach Relief
Maalox Total Stomach Relief	Maalox
Malarone	mefloquine
Matulane	Materna
Materna	Matulane
Maxzide	Microzide

DRUG NAME	CONFUSED DRUG NAME
medroxyPROGESTERone	HYDROXYprogesterone
medroxyPROGESTERone	methylPREDNISolone
medroxyPROGESTERone	methylTESTOSTERone
mefloquine	Malarone
memantine	methadone
Menactra	Menomune
Menomune	Menactra
Mephyton	methadone
Metadate	methadone
Metadate CD	Metadate ER
Metadate ER	Metadate CD
Metadate ER	methadone
metFORMIN	metroNIDAZOLE
methadone	dexmethylphenidate
methadone	ketorolac
methadone	memantine
methadone	Mephyton
methadone	Metadate
methadone	Metadate ER
methadone	methylphenidate
methadone	metOLazone
Methergine	Brethine
methazolAMIDE	methIMAzole
methazolAMIDE	metOLazone
methIMAzole	methazolAMIDE
methIMAzole	metOLazone
methotrexate	metOLazone
methotrexate	MTX Patch (lidocaine and menthol)
methylene blue	VisionBlue
methylphenidate	methadone
methylPREDNISolone	medroxyPROGESTERone
methylPREDNISolone	methylTESTOSTERone
methylTESTOSTERone	medroxyPROGESTERone
methylTESTOSTERone	methylPREDNISolone
metyraPONE	metyroSINE
metyroSINE	metyraPONE

(continued)

DRUG NAME	CONFUSED DRUG NAME	DRUG NAME	CONFUSED DRUG NAME
*met**OL**azone*	*methadone*	Mucinex D	Mucinex DM
*met**OL**azone*	*methazol**AMIDE***	Mucinex DM	Mucinex D
*met**OL**azone*	*meth**IMA**zole*	Mucomyst	Mucinex
*met**OL**azone*	*methotrexate*	Myleran	Alkeran
metoprolol succinate	*metoprolol tartrate*	Myleran	Leukeran
metoprolol tartrate	*metoprolol succinate*	*nalbuphine*	*naloxone*
*metro**NIDAZOLE***	*met**FORMIN***	*naloxone*	Lanoxin
Mevacor	Benicar	*naloxone*	*nalbuphine*
Micronase	Microzide	Narcan	Norcuron
Microzide	Maxzide	Natru-Vent	Atrovent
Microzide	Micronase	Navane	Norvasc
midodrine	Midrin	Neo-Synephrine (*oxymetazoline*)	Neo-Synephrine (*phenylephrine*)
Midrin	*midodrine*	Neo-Synephrine (*phenylephrine*)	Neo-Synephrine (*oxymetazoline*)
*mi**FEPRIS**tone*	*mi**SOPROS**tol*	*neratinib*	*nilotinib*
migalastat	*miglustat*	*neratinib*	*niraparib*
miglustat	*migalastat*	Neulasta	Lunesta
Miralax	Mirapex	Neulasta	Nuedexta
Mirapex	Miralax	Neulasta	Neumega
*mi**SOPROS**tol*	*mi**FEPRIS**tone*	Neumega	Neulasta
*mito**MY**cin*	*mito**XANTRONE***	Neumega	Neupogen
*mito**XANTRONE***	*mito**MY**cin*	Neupogen	Neumega
*mito**XANTRONE***	MTX Patch (*lidocaine and menthol*)	Neurontin	Motrin
morphine	***HYDRO**morphone*	Neurontin	Noroxin
morphine–non-concentrated oral liquid	*morphine – oral liquid concentrate*	Neutra-Phos-K	K-Phos Neutral
morphine – oral liquid concentrate	*morphine–non-concentrated oral liquid*	Nex**AVAR**	Nex**IUM**
Motrin	Neurontin	Nex**IUM**	Nex**AVAR**
MS Contin	Oxy**CONTIN**	*ni**CAR**dipine*	***NIFE**dipine*
MTX Patch (*lidocaine and menthol*)	*methotrexate*	*ni**CAR**dipine*	*ni**MOD**ipine*
MTX Patch (*lidocaine and menthol*)	*mito**XANTRONE***	***NIFE**dipine*	*ni**CAR**dipine*
Mucinex (*guai**FEN**esin*)	Mucinex Allergy (*fexofenadine*)	***NIFE**dipine*	*ni**MOD**ipine*
Mucinex	Mucomyst	*nilotinib*	*neratinib*
Mucinex Allergy (*fexofenadine*)	Mucinex (*guai**FEN**esin*)	*nilotinib*	*niraparib*
		*ni**MOD**ipine*	*ni**CAR**dipine*
		*ni**MOD**ipine*	***NIFE**dipine*
		niraparib	*neratinib*
		niraparib	*nilotinib*

DRUG NAME	CONFUSED DRUG NAME	DRUG NAME	CONFUSED DRUG NAME
Norcuron	Narcan	OxyCONTIN	oxyCODONE
Normodyne	Norpramin	OxyCONTIN	oxyMORphone
Noroxin	Neurontin	oxyMORphone	HYDROmorphone
Norpramin	Normodyne	oxyMORphone	oxyCODONE
Norvasc	Navane	oxyMORphone	OxyCONTIN
NovoLIN	HumuLIN	PACLitaxel	DOCEtaxel
NovoLIN	NovoLOG	PACLitaxel	PACLitaxel protein-bound particles
NovoLIN 70/30	NovoLOG Mix 70/30	PACLitaxel protein-bound particles	PACLitaxel
NovoLOG	HumaLOG	Pamelor	Panlor DC
NovoLOG	NovoLIN	Pamelor	Tambocor
NovoLOG Flexpen	NovoLOG Mix 70/30 Flexpen	Panlor DC	Pamelor
NovoLOG Mix 70/30 Flexpen	NovoLOG Flexpen	paregoric (camphorated tincture of opium)	opium tincture
NovoLOG Mix 70/30	NovoLIN 70/30	PARoxetine	DULoxetine
Nuedexta	Neulasta	PARoxetine	FLUoxetine
nystatin	HMG-CoA reductase inhibitors ("statins")	PARoxetine	piroxicam
Occlusal-HP	Ocufox	Patanol	Platinol
Ocufox	Occlusal-HP	Pavulon	Peptavlon
OLANZapine	QUEtiapine	Paxil	Doxil
Omacor	Amicar	Paxil	Plavix
omeprazole	fomepizole	Paxil	Taxol
opium tincture	paregoric (camphorated tincture of opium)	PAZOPanib	PONATinib
Oracea	Orencia	PEMEtrexed	PRALAtrexate
Orencia	Oracea	penicillin	penicillAMINE
Orgaran	argatroban	penicillAMINE	penicillin
Ortho Tri-Cyclen	Ortho Tri-Cyclen LO	Peptavlon	Pavulon
Ortho Tri-Cyclen LO	Ortho Tri-Cyclen	Percocet	Darvocet
Os-Cal	Asacol	Percocet	Procet
oxaprozin	OXcarbazepine	perflutren lipid microspheres	influenza virus vaccine
OXcarbazepine	oxaprozin	Pexeva	Lexiva
OXcarbazepine	carBAMazepine	PENTobarbital	PHENobarbital
oxybutynin	oxyCODONE	PHENobarbital	PENTobarbital
oxyCODONE	HYDROcodone	Pilocar	Dilacor XR
oxyCODONE	oxybutynin	piroxicam	PARoxetine
oxyCODONE	OxyCONTIN	Platinol	Patanol
oxyCODONE	oxyMORphone		
OxyCONTIN	MS Contin		

(continued)

DRUG NAME	CONFUSED DRUG NAME
Plavix	Paxil
Plavix	Pradax [non-US product]
Plavix	Pradaxa
Plendil	Isordil
pneumococcal 7-valent vaccine	pneumococcal polyvalent vaccine
pneumococcal polyvalent vaccine	pneumococcal 7-valent vaccine
Polycitra	Bicitra
polyethylene glycol	propylene glycol
PONATinib	**PAZOP**anib
potassium acetate	sodium acetate
PRALAtrexate	**PEME**trexed
Pradax [non-US product]	Plavix
Pradaxa	Plavix
Prandin	Avandia
Precare	Precose
Precose	Precare
predniso**LONE**	predni**SONE**
predni**SONE**	predniso**LONE**
Prenexa	Ranexa
Pri**LOSEC**	Pristiq
Pri**LOSEC**	**PRO**zac
Priscoline	Apresoline
Pristiq	Pri**LOSEC**
probenecid	Procanbid
Procan SR	Procanbid
Procanbid	probenecid
Procanbid	Procan SR
Procardia XL	Protain XL
Procet	Percocet
Prograf	Proscar
Prograf	**PRO**zac
propylene glycol	polyethylene glycol
propylthiouracil	Purinethol
Proscar	Prograf
Proscar	Provera
Protain XL	Procardia XL

DRUG NAME	CONFUSED DRUG NAME
protamine	Protonix
proton pump inhibitors	**ARIP**iprazole
Protonix	Lotronex
Protonix	protamine
Provera	Proscar
Provera	**PRO**zac
PROzac	Prograf
PROzac	Pri**LOSEC**
PROzac	Provera
Purinethol	propylthiouracil
Pyridium	pyridoxine
pyridoxine	Pyridium
QUEtiapine	**OLANZ**apine
qui**NID**ine	qui**NINE**
qui**NINE**	qui**NID**ine
Qwell	Kwell
RABEprazole	**ARIP**iprazole
Ranexa	Prenexa
ra**NITI**dine	ri**MANTA**dine
Rapafo	Rapamune
Rapamune	Rapafo
rasageline	repaglinide
Razadyne	Rozerem
Recombivax HB	Comvax
Regranex	Granulex
Reminyl	Amaryl
Reminyl	Robinul
Renagel	Renvela
Renvela	Renagel
repaglinide	rasageline
Reprexain	Zy**PREXA**
Restoril	Risper**DAL**
Retrovir	ritonavir
ribavirin	riboflavin
riboflavin	ribavirin
rifabutin	rifapentine
Rifadin	Rifater

DRUG NAME	CONFUSED DRUG NAME	DRUG NAME	CONFUSED DRUG NAME
Rifamate	*rifAMPin*	Serophene	Sarafem
rifAMPin	Rifamate	**SERO**quel	Desyrel
rifAMPin	*rifAXIMin*	**SERO**quel	**SERO**quel XR
rifapentine	*rifabutin*	**SERO**quel	Serzone
Rifater	Rifadin	**SERO**quel	**SINE**quan
rifAXIMin	*rifAMPin*	**SERO**quel XR	**SERO**quel
riMANTAdine	*raNITIdine*	*sertraline*	*cetirizine*
Risper**DAL**	Restoril	*sertraline*	Soriatane
Risper**DAL**	*rOPINIRole*	Serzone	**SERO**quel
risperiDONE	*rOPINIRole*	*silodosin*	*sirolimus*
Ritalin	*ritodrine*	Sinemet	Janumet
Ritalin LA	Ritalin SR	**SINE**quan	*saquinavir*
Ritalin SR	Ritalin LA	**SINE**quan	**SERO**quel
ritodrine	Ritalin	**SINE**quan	Singulair
ritonavir	Retrovir	**SINE**quan	Zeniquin [veterinary drug]
Rituxan	Rituxan Hycela	**SINE**quan	Zonegran
Rituxan Hycela	Rituxan	Singulair	**SINE**quan
riTUXimab	*inFLIXimab*	*sirolimus*	*silodosin*
Robinul	Reminyl	**SIT**agliptin	*sAXagliptin*
romiDEPsin	*romiPLOStim*	**SIT**agliptin	**SUMA**triptan
romiPLOStim	*romiDEPsin*	*sodium acetate*	*potassium acetate*
rOPINIRole	Risper**DAL**	Solu-**CORTEF**	**SOLU**-Medrol
rOPINIRole	*risperiDONE*	**SOLU**-Medrol	**DEPO**-Medrol
Roxanol	Roxicet	**SOLU**-Medrol	Solu-**CORTEF**
Roxanol	Roxicodone Intensol	Sonata	Soriatane
Roxicet	Roxanol	**SORA**fenib	**SUNI**tinib
Roxicodone Intensol	Roxanol	Soriatane	Loxitane
Rozerem	Razadyne	Soriatane	*sertraline*
Salagen	*selegiline*	Soriatane	Sonata
Sand**IMMUNE**	Sando**STATIN**	*sotalol*	Sudafed
Sando**STATIN**	Sand**IMMUNE**	Spiriva	Apidra
saquinavir	**SINE**quan	Spiriva	Inspra
saquinavir (free base)	*saquinavir mesylate*	*stavudine*	*cetirizine*
saquinavir mesylate	*saquinavir (free base)*	Sudafed	*sotalol*
Sarafem	Serophene	Sudafed	Sudafed PE
sAXagliptin	**SIT**agliptin	Sudafed 12 Hour	Sudafed 12 Hour Pressure + Pain
selegiline	Salagen		

(continued)

DRUG NAME	CONFUSED DRUG NAME
Sudafed 12 Hour Pressure + Pain	Sudafed 12 Hour
Sudafed PE	Sudafed
SUFentanil	*fenta**NYL***
*sulf**ADIAZINE***	*sulfa**SALA**zine*
*sulf**ADIAZINE***	*suli**SOXAZOLE***
*sulfa**SALA**zine*	*cefuroxime*
*sulfa**SALA**zine*	*sulf**ADIAZINE***
*suli**SOXAZOLE***	*sulf**ADIAZINE***
SUMAtriptan	**SIT**agliptin
SUMAtriptan	**ZOLM**itriptan
SUNItinib	**SORA**fenib
Symbyax	Cymbalta
T-Gel	Bio-T-Gel
tacrolimus	*tamsulosin*
Tambocor	Pamelor
tamsulosin	*tacrolimus*
Tanzeum	Tou eo
Tanzeum	Trad enta
Tanzeum	Tresiba
Tanzeum	Trulicity
Tarceva	Tresiba
Taxol	Paxil
Taxol	Taxotere
Taxotere	Taxol
TEGretol	**TEG**retol XR
TEGretol	Tequin
TEGretol	**TREN**tal
TEGretol XR	**TEG**retol
Tenex	Xanax
Tequin	**TEG**retol
Tequin	Ticlid
Testoderm	Testoderm TTS
Testoderm	Testoderm with Adhesive
Testoderm TTS	Testoderm
Testoderm TTS	Testoderm with Adhesive
Testoderm with Adhesive	Testoderm

DRUG NAME	CONFUSED DRUG NAME
Testoderm with Adhesive	Testoderm TTS
tetanus diptheria toxoid (Td)	*tuberculin puriied protein derivative (PPD)*
Thalomid	Thiamine
Thiamine	Thalomid
*tia**GAB**ine*	*ti**ZAN**idine*
Tiazac	Ziac
Ticlid	Tequin
*ti**ZAN**idine*	*tia**GAB**ine*
TNKase	Activase
TNKase	*t-PA (Activase)*
Tobradex	Tobrex
Tobrex	Tobradex
TOLAZamide	**TOLBUT**amide
TOLBUTamide	**TOLAZ**amide
Topamax	Toprol-XL
Toprol-XL	Topamax
Toradol	Foradil
Tou eo	Tanzeum
Tou eo	Trad enta
Tou eo	Tresiba
Tou eo	Trulicity
t-PA (Activase)	**TNK**ase
Tracleer	Tricor
Trad enta	Tanzeum
Trad enta	Tou eo
Trad enta	Tresiba
Trad enta	Trulicity
*tra**MAD**ol*	*tra**ZOD**one*
trastuzumab	*ado-trastuzumab emtansine*
*tra**ZOD**one*	*tra**MAD**ol*
TRENtal	**TEG**retol
Tresiba	Tanzeum
Tresiba	Tarceva
Tresiba	Tou eo
Tresiba	Trad enta
Tresiba	Trulicity

DRUG NAME	CONFUSED DRUG NAME
tretinoin	**ISO**tretinoin
Tricor	Tracleer
tromethamine	Trophamine
Trophamine	*tromethamine*
Trulicity	Tanzeum
Trulicity	Tou eo
Trulicity	Trad enta
Trulicity	Tresiba
tuberculin puriied protein derivative (PPD)	influenza virus vaccine
tuberculin puriied protein derivative (PPD)	tetanus diptheria toxoid (Td)
Tylenol	Tylenol PM
Tylenol PM	Tylenol
Ultracet	Duricef
Ultram	*lithium*
val**ACY**clovir	val**GAN**ciclovir
Valcyte	Valtrex
val**GAN**ciclovir	val**ACY**clovir
Valtrex	Valcyte
Varivax	VZIG (*varicella-zoster immune globulin*)
vasopressin	*desmopressin*
Venofer	Vfend
Venofer	Vimpat
Vesanoid	Vesicare
Vesicare	Vesanoid
Vesicare	Vessel Care (nutritional supplement)
Vessel Care (nutritional supplement)	Vesicare
Vexol	Vosol
Vfend	Venofer
Vfend	Vimpat
Viagra	Allegra
Vicodin	Visicol
Videx	Bidex
vigabatrin	*dabigatran*
Vimpat	Venofer

DRUG NAME	CONFUSED DRUG NAME
Vimpat	Vfend
*vin**BLAS**tine*	*vin**CRIS**tine*
*vin**CRIS**tine*	*vin**BLAS**tine*
Viokase	Viokase 8
Viokase 8	Viokase
Vioxx	Zyvox
Viracept	Viramune
Viramune	Viracept
Viramune (*nevairapine*)	Viramune (herbal product)
Viramune (herbal product)	Viramune (*nevairapine*)
Visicol	Vicodin
VisionBlue	*methylene blue*
Volumen	Voluven
Voluven	Volumen
Vosol	Vexol
VZIG (*varicella-zoster immune globulin*)	Varivax
Wellbutrin SR	Wellbutrin XL
Wellbutrin XL	Wellbutrin SR
Xanax	Fanapt
Xanax	Tenex
Xanax	Zantac
Xeloda	Xenical
Xenical	Xeloda
Yasmin	Yaz
Yaz	Yasmin
Zantac	Xanax
Zantac	Zyr**TEC**
Zavesca (*escitalopram*) [non-US product]	Zavesca (*miglustat*)
Zavesca (*miglustat*)	Zavesca (*escitalopram*) [non-US product]
Zebeta	Diabeta
Zebeta	Zetia
Zegerid	Zestril
Zelapar (Zydis formulation)	Zy**PREXA** Zydis
Zeniquin [veterinary drug]	**SINE**quan
Zerit	Zyr**TEC**

(continued)

DRUG NAME	CONFUSED DRUG NAME		DRUG NAME	CONFUSED DRUG NAME
Zestril	Zegerid		Zy**PREXA**	Cele**XA**
Zestril	Zetia		Zy**PREXA**	Reprexain
Zestril	Zy**PREXA**		Zy**PREXA**	Zestril
Zetia	Bextra		Zy**PREXA**	Zyr**TEC**
Zetia	Zebeta		Zy**PREXA** Zydis	Zelapar (Zydis formulation)
Zetia	Zestril		Zyr**TEC**	Lipitor
Ziac	Tiazac		Zyr**TEC**	Zantac
Zocor	Cozaar		Zyr**TEC**	Zerit
Zocor	Zyr**TEC**		Zyr**TEC**	Zocor
ZOLMitriptan	**SUMA**triptan		Zyr**TEC**	Zy**PREXA**
zolpidem	Zyloprim		Zyr**TEC**	Zyr**TEC**-D
Zonegran	**SINE**quan		Zyr**TEC** (cetirizine)	Zyr**TEC** Itchy Eye Drops (ketotifen fumarate)
Zostrix	Zovirax			
Zovirax	Doribax		Zyr**TEC**-D	Zyr**TEC**
Zovirax	Zostrix		Zyr**TEC** Itchy Eye Drops (ketotifen fumarate)	Zyr**TEC** (cetirizine)
Zovirax	Zyvox			
Zyban	Diovan		Zyvox	Vioxx
Zyloprim	zolpidem		Zyvox	Zovirax

Error Prevention Strategies

A **medication error** is an event that leads to patient harm or inappropriate medication use that was preventable. Medication errors can be caused by many factors, though some common causes can be communication failures, failure in procedure, and human error.

There are several strategies to reduce or prevent medication errors.

Tall Man Lettering

Medications on the confused drug list contain uppercase and bolded letters that are used to draw attention to the differences in each drug name. This is known as **tall man lettering**, and it helps distinguish between two drugs that look or sound similar. Pharmacies can also use tall man lettering in computerized ordering systems to allow prescribers to differentiate between LASA drugs safely.

The following examples are from the ISMP list for confused drug names with tall man lettering.

DRUG NAME WITH TALL MAN LETTERS	CONFUSED WITH
ALPRAZolam	**LOR**azepam, clonaze**PAM**
am**LODIP**ine	a**MIL**oride
Cele**BREX**	Cele**XA**
Diaze**PAM**	dil**TIAZ**em
Met**FORMIN**	Metro**NIDAZOLE**
Pri**LOSEC**	**PRO**zac

Leading and Trailing Zeros

Incorrect or misread doses can be a cause of medication errors. Leading zeros help minimize errors and should always be used. The leading zero comes before the decimal point, such as $\underline{0}$.7. If a leading zero is not used, .7 can be misread as 7 and a tenfold error could occur. Trailing zeros are after decimal points, such as 7.$\underline{0}$. Trailing zeros should never be used, as they can cause confusion if the decimal point is missed. This could also lead to a tenfold error. 7.0 can be misread as 70.

Selecting Correct Patient

When entering prescriptions, verifying orders, or administering medications, selecting the correct patient is crucial for medication safety. By following the five rights of medication safety, pharmacy technicians, pharmacists, nurses, and other healthcare providers can verify all appropriate information for each patient. The five rights are:

1. Right patient

2. Right drug

3. Right dose

4. Right route

5. Right time

Using the five rights can help prevent medication errors, but sometimes even valid attempts at verifying the five rights can fall short. This can be due to trailing zeros, misreading orders that are handwritten, and communication or procedural failure. Five rights remain a basic foundation to medication safety, but accomplishing this may require additional support from other error prevention strategies.

Bar Coding

Bar codes can also be used as an added level of medication error prevention when administering medications. Bar code medication administration (BCMA) is completed by a nurse or other healthcare professional prior to giving a patient medication. The patient's wristband is scanned, confirming the correct patient is receiving the medication. The patient's medications can then be scanned and documented in the medication administration record (MAR). The bar code of the manufacturer label or pharmacy label is scanned to confirm correct product selection. If the wrong medication is scanned, an alert will notify the nurse that there is a problem. BCMA should not take the place of the five rights, but help support medication safety.

Additional use of bar codes occurs in the pharmacy and nursing units. During the filling of prescriptions in a pharmacy, the bar code of the correct national drug code (NDC) is scanned to confirm product selection. The pharmacist may also scan the bar code when verifying the prescription prior to dispensing. Scanning the bar code may also deduct that stock from inventory, if a pharmacy uses perpetual inventory. This helps maintain drug replenishment and inventory levels.

In a hospital pharmacy, medications are scanned prior to loading in automated dispensing cabinets to confirm the correct product was selected. The medication is scanned when loading stock, and after the nurse dispenses, the medication is scanned again prior to patient administration. This offers additional safety measures for error prevention.

Error-Prone Abbreviations

Through the collection of data from reported medication events, the ISMP has identified error-prone abbreviations, symbols, and doses. These should never be used when communicating and always avoided whenever possible.

The ISMP has published a list of error-prone abbreviations, doses, and symbols, and The Joint Commission uses a similar list as a standard for safety within a hospital. Hospitals accredited by The Joint Commission are expected to use the dangerous abbreviations list from The Joint Commission as a "minimum list" of dangerous abbreviations, and follow this policy in practice as well as in the electronic medical record (EMR). When The Joint Commission surveys organizations, it reviews this list and ensures safety practices are being followed to prevent medication errors.

The ISMP List of Error-Prone Abbreviations, Symbols, and Dose Designations follows. Indicated with ** within this chart are those abbreviations included on The Joint Commission's minimum list that must be used on an organization's "Do Not Use" list.

ABBREVIATIONS	INTENDED MEANING	MISINTERPRETATION	CORRECTION
μg	Microgram	Mistaken as "mg"	Use "mcg"
AD, AS, AU	Right ear, left ear, each ear	Mistaken as OD, OS, OU (right eye, left eye, each eye)	Use "right ear," "left ear," or "each ear"
OD, OS, OU	Right eye, left eye, each eye	Mistaken as AD, AS, AU (right ear, left ear, each ear)	Use "right eye," "left eye," or "each eye"
BT	Bedtime	Mistaken as "BID" (twice daily)	Use "bedtime"
cc	Cubic centimeters	Mistaken as "u" (units)	Use "mL"
D/C	Discharge or discontinue	Premature discontinuation of medications if D/C (intended to mean "discharge") has been misinterpreted as "discontinued" when followed by a list of discharge medications	Use "discharge" and "discontinue"
IJ	Injection	Mistaken as "IV" or "intrajugular"	Use "injection"
IN	Intranasal	Mistaken as "IM" or "IV"	Use "intranasal" or "NAS"
HS	Half-strength	Mistaken as bedtime	Use "half-strength" or "bedtime"
hs	At bedtime, hours of sleep	Mistaken as half-strength	Use "half-strength" or "bedtime"
IU**	International unit	Mistaken as IV (intravenous) or 10 (ten)	Use "units"
o.d. or OD	Once daily	Mistaken as "right eye" (OD-oculus dexter), leading to oral liquid medications administered in the eye	Use "daily"
OJ	Orange juice	Mistaken as OD or OS (right or left eye); drugs meant to be diluted in orange juice may be given in the eye	Use "orange juice"
Per os	By mouth, orally	The "os" can be mistaken as "left eye" (OS-oculus sinister)	Use "PO," "by mouth," or "orally"
q.d. or QD**	Every day	Mistaken as q.i.d., especially if the period after the "q" or the tail of the "q" is misunderstood as an "i"	Use "daily"
qhs	Nightly at bedtime	Mistaken as "qhr" or every hour	Use "nightly"
qn	Nightly or at bedtime	Mistaken as "qh" (every hour)	Use "nightly" or "at bedtime"
q.o.d. or QOD**	Every other day	Mistaken as "q.d." (daily) or "q.i.d. (four times daily) if the "o" is poorly written	Use "every other day"
q1d	Daily	Mistaken as q.i.d. (four times daily)	Use "daily"
q6PM, etc	Every evening at 6 PM	Mistaken as every 6 hours	Use "daily at 6 PM" or "6 PM daily"
SC, SQ, sub q	Subcutaneous	SC mistaken as SL (sublingual); SQ mistaken as "5 every;" the "q" in "sub q" has been mistaken as "every" (e.g., a heparin dose ordered "sub q 2 hours before surgery" misunderstood as every 2 hours before surgery)	Use "subcut" or "subcutaneously"
ss	Sliding scale (insulin) or ½ (apothecary)	Mistaken as "55"	Spell out "sliding scale;" use "one-half" or "½"
SSRI	Sliding scale regular insulin	Mistaken as selective-serotonin reuptake inhibitor	Spell out "sliding scale (insulin)"
SSI	Sliding scale insulin	Mistaken as Strong Solution of Iodine (Lugol's)	Spell out "sliding scale (insulin)"

(continued)

ABBREVIATIONS	INTENDED MEANING	MISINTERPRETATION	CORRECTION
i/d	One daily	Mistaken as "tid"	Use "1 daily"
TIW or tiw	3 times a week	Mistaken as "3 times a day" or "twice in a week"	Use "3 times weekly"
U or u**	Unit	Mistaken as the number 0 or 4, causing a 10-fold overdose or greater (e.g., 4U seen as "40" or 4u seen as "44"); mistaken as "cc" so dose given in volume instead of units (e.g., 4u seen as 4cc)	Use "unit"
UD	As directed ("ut dictum")	Mistaken as unit dose (e.g., diltiazem 125 mg IV infusion "UD" misinterpreted as meaning to give the entire infusion as a unit [bolus] dose)	Use "as directed"

DOSE DESIGNATIONS AND OTHER INFORMATION	INTENDED MEANING	MISINTERPRETATION	CORRECTION
Trailing zero after decimal point (e.g., 1.0 mg)**	1 mg	Mistaken as 10 mg if the decimal point is not seen	Do not use trailing zeros for doses expressed in whole numbers
"Naked" decimal point (e.g., .5 mg)**	0.5 mg	Mistaken as 5 mg if the decimal point is not seen	Use zero before a decimal point when the dose is less than a whole unit
Abbreviations such as mg. or mL. with a period following the abbreviation	mg mL	The period is unnecessary and could be mistaken as the number 1 if written poorly	Use mg, mL, etc. without a terminal period
Drug name and dose run together (especially problematic for drug names that end in "l" such as Inderal40 mg; Tegretol300 mg)	Inderal 40 mg Tegretol 300 mg	Mistaken as Inderal 140 mg Mistaken as Tegretol 1300 mg	Place adequate space between the drug name, dose, and unit of measure
Numerical dose and unit of measure run together (e.g., 10mg, 100mL)	10 mg 100 mL	The "m" is sometimes mistaken as a zero or two zeros, risking a 10- to 100-fold overdose	Place adequate space between the dose and unit of measure
Large doses without properly placed commas (e.g., 100000 units; 1000000 units)	100,000 units 1,000,000 units	100000 has been mistaken as 10,000 or 1,000,000; 1000000 has been mistaken as 100,000	Use commas for dosing units at or above 1,000, or use words such as 100 "thousand" or 1 "million" to improve readability

DRUG NAME ABBREVIATIONS	INTENDED MEANING	MISINTERPRETATION	CORRECTION
To avoid confusion, do not abbreviate drug names when communicating medical information. Examples of drug name abbreviations involved in medication errors include:			
APAP	acetaminophen	Not recognized as acetaminophen	Use complete drug name
ARA A	vidarabine	Mistaken as cytarabine (ARA C)	Use complete drug name
AZT	zidovudine (Retrovir)	Mistaken as azathioprine or aztreonam	Use complete drug name
CPZ	Compazine (prochlorperazine)	Mistaken as chlorpromazine	Use complete drug name
DPT	Demerol-Phenergan-Thorazine	Mistaken as diphtheria-pertussis-tetanus (vaccine)	Use complete drug name
DTO	Diluted tincture of opium, or deodorized tincture of opium (Paregoric)	Mistaken as tincture of opium	Use complete drug name
HCl	hydrochloric acid or hydrochloride	Mistaken as potassium chloride (The "H" is misinterpreted as "K")	Use complete drug name unless expressed as a salt of a drug
HCT	hydrocortisone	Mistaken as hydrochlorothiazide	Use complete drug name
HCTZ	hydrochlorothiazide	Mistaken as hydrocortisone (seen as HCT250 mg)	Use complete drug name
$MgSO_4$**	magnesium sulfate	Mistaken as morphine sulfate	Use complete drug name
MS, MSO_4**	morphine sulfate	Mistaken as magnesium sulfate	Use complete drug name
MTX	methotrexate	Mistaken as mitoxantrone	Use complete drug name
NoAC	novel/new oral anticoagulant	No anticoagulant	Use complete drug name
PCA	procainamide	Mistaken as patient controlled analgesia	Use complete drug name
PTU	propylthiouracil	Mistaken as mercaptopurine	Use complete drug name
T3	Tylenol with codeine No. 3	Mistaken as liothyronine	Use complete drug name
TAC	triamcinolone	Mistaken as tetracaine, Adrenalin, cocaine	Use complete drug name
TNK	TNKase	Mistaken as "TPA"	Use complete drug name
TPA or tPA	tissue plasminogen activator, Activase (alteplase)	Mistaken as TNKase (tenecteplase), or less often as another tissue plasminogen activator, Retavase (retaplase)	Use complete drug name
$ZnSO_4$	zinc sulfate	Mistaken as morphine sulfate	Use complete drug name

STEMMED DRUG NAMES	INTENDED MEANING	MISINTERPRETATION	CORRECTION
"Nitro" drip	nitroglycerin infusion	Mistaken as sodium nitroprusside infusion	Use complete drug name
"Norflox"	norfloxacin	Mistaken as Norflex	Use complete drug name
"IV Vanc"	intravenous vancomycin	Mistaken as Invanz	Use complete drug name

SYMBOLS	INTENDED MEANING	MISINTERPRETATION	CORRECTION
ʒ	Dram	Symbol for dram mistaken as "3"	Use the metric system
♏	Minim	Symbol for minim mistaken as "mL"	Use the metric system
x3d	For three days	Mistaken as "3 doses"	Use "for three days"
> and <	More than and less than	Mistaken as opposite of intended; mistakenly use incorrect symbol; "< 10" mistaken as "40"	Use "more than" or "less than"
/ (slash mark)	Separates two doses or indicates "per"	Mistaken as the number 1 (e.g., "25 units/10 units" misread as "25 units and 110" units)	Use "per" rather than a slash mark to separate doses
@	At	Mistaken as "2"	Use "at"
&	And	Mistaken as "2"	Use "and"
+	Plus or and	Mistaken as "4"	Use "and"
°	Hour	Mistaken as a zero (e.g., q2° seen as q 20)	Use "hr," "h," or "hour"
Φ or ⊘	zero, null sign	Mistaken as numerals 4, 6, 8, and 9	Use 0 or zero, or describe intent using whole words

**These abbreviations are included on The Joint Commission's "minimum list" of dangerous abbreviations, acronyms, and symbols that must be included on an organization's "Do Not Use" list, effective January 1, 2004.

Separating Inventory

Another way to help prevent medication errors is by segregating inventory that may be more prone to errors or have a more adverse event if an error occurred. ISMP has published guidance on standardization of drugs, storage, and distribution as a way to help reduce the risk of a medication event. Some of the identified strategies from ISMP include:

- Use signing programs that draw attention to LASA drugs and high-risk/alert medications, such as stickers or separate inventory
- Avoid stocking LASA drugs in "fast mover" sections
- Do not store nondrug supplies, such as isopropyl alcohol, near diluents needed for reconstitution
- Immediately remove outdated, recalled, or discontinued drug products from inventory
- Store refrigerated medications in separate bins, such as insulins or other similar items
- Maintain a pickup/will-call area in a retail pharmacy free from clutter that has enough space to prevent spillage into another bin or basket
- Use dividers on crowded shelves to separate inventory
- All stock, including vials returned to stock, must be labeled with drug name, strength, expiration date, NDC number, and bar code if possible

Additionally, there are some specific medications that must be identified or separated from inventory:

TYPE OF MEDICATION	DESCRIPTION
Expired drugs	Segregated from in-dated inventory to prevent dispensing expired drug to patient
Recalled	Quarantined and removed from stock and sent back to manufacturer
High-alert	Require a method of distinction to identify, such as a high-alert sticker or be stored in a segregated area in the pharmacy
Hazardous drugs	Must be stored in a segregated area of the pharmacy to prevent hazardous drug contamination

Medication Error Reporting

A medication error is a preventable event that may lead to patient harm. Medication errors can occur at prescribing, filling and dispensing, administering, and even patient monitoring. If an error occurred and does not harm the patient, it is still deemed an error. A **near miss**, on the other hand, is a potential medication error that was caught before it reached the patient.

Adverse drug events (ADE) occur when a medication causes harm to a patient. ADEs consist of medication errors, adverse drug reactions, allergic reactions, or overdose. An **adverse drug reaction (ADR)** is an unwanted and undesirable effect of a medication that occurs during the standard clinical use or dose. An allergic reaction occurs when there is an abnormal immune response to a normal dose. An overdose occurs when an excessive or dangerous dose of drug is taken.

For all ADEs, documentation and reporting are the key to preventing future patient injuries. A near miss is just as crucial as an actual event to report, as this can help identify protocol failures, dangerous trends, or workflow issues prior to patient harm. Though the FDA requires extensive research and clinical trials for new drug approval, there are often adverse events that occur post-approval when the drug is on the market. Reporting these events is important for patient safety.

Types of Prescription Errors

Understanding how, where, and when prescription errors might occur can help mitigate potential issues before they happen. Prescription errors can be broken down into four main categories:

- Prescribing
- Dispensing
- Administration
- Monitoring

Prescribing errors occur from the written order of a provider, either a prescription or a medication order. This includes errors in prescribed dosage or drug strength, quantity (excessive or insufficient) needed for drug therapy, route or dosage form, rate of infusion, or drug ordered. A prescribing error can also include omitting necessary refills or approving early refills that may alter appropriate therapy. Incorrect patient errors can also occur during prescribing, including writing an order for a medication to a patient with a known allergy or contraindication.

Prescribing errors are often caused by communication failures, such as misinterpretation of handwritten or verbal orders. This can often be the result of using a confusing or dangerous abbreviation. Clarifying these orders is essential for patient safety. Computerized provider order entry (CPOE) can help prevent errors by removing the potential for misreading handwriting.

A **dispensing error** is a difference in what was prescribed and what is dispensed to a patient. Dispensing errors can be caused by anyone involved in this process—including both pharmacists and pharmacy technicians. It can result from a wrong product selection—including wrong strength or dosage form. Storing LASA drugs away from each other can help prevent these errors from occurring. Expired medications must also be removed from stock prior to expiration, as dispensing an expired medication would also be considered a dispensing error. Dispensing errors can also include the wrong quantity, such as giving only 30 tablets in a 60-tablet prescription. Omission of a drug can be considered a dispensing error. Using bar-coding to confirm the correct product, strength, and dosage form can help prevent dispensing errors.

An **administration error** occurs when there is a difference in what the patient is administered and what was prescribed. This includes administering the wrong drug, wrong dose, or at the wrong time. If a medication is given at the wrong time, it can exacerbate a disease. This could be the case when a patient has Parkinson's disease and the medications are given late. The patient's symptoms could worsen.

An administration error can also occur if a medication is given via the wrong route. For example, a patient is prescribed a subcutaneous dose of heparin. The nurse administers the dose IV push instead of subcutaneous. An omission error is also considered an administration error and occurs if a patient does not receive a medication at all. Errors in IV infusion rate can be prevented through the use of IV smart pumps. IV pumps have a built-in drug library, and some even have bidirectional capability, which allows the order from the MAR to flow to the pump and prevent overriding or incorrect infusion rates.

Using BCMA can help prevent administration errors. By scanning the drug prior to administering, a nurse can identify incorrect doses, routes, dosage form, or if the drug itself is incorrect. BCMA will also identify if the time is wrong—such as a too-early dose. Patient wrist bands are scanned to help prevent wrong patient errors as well. The five rights should also be used to prevent administration errors.

A **monitoring error** is when a drug treatment plan for a patient is not evaluated for appropriate prescribing. It can occur when a patient's response to therapy is not monitored appropriately, such as through lab results or signs of drug toxicity. Monitoring errors include a lack of response if a patient requires a modification to the prescribed dosing.

Preventing monitoring errors starts with proper training of providers on the potential negative effects of medications, which may indicate toxicity. Providers must also be trained in understanding monitoring methods, such as through vital signs and evaluating lab results—this includes pharmacists. Pharmacists often review lab results prior to initiating drug therapy, such as chemotherapy.

Prescribing errors	Prescription or medication order written incorrectly: ■ Abnormal dose ■ Incorrect quantity for therapy ■ Wrong route or dosage form ■ Incorrect dosing frequency ■ Wrong infusion rate ■ Incorrect drug ■ Incorrect patient Prescribing medication inappropriate based on patient—allergies or contraindication Error in drug selection for proper indication
Dispensing errors	Selecting or filling wrong drug Dispensing expired medication Dispensing wrong quantity Omitting drug from patient's medications
Administration errors	Administration of medication that was not prescribed ■ Wrong drug ■ Wrong dose ■ Wrong time (early or too late) ■ Wrong route ■ Wrong infusion rate ■ Omission of drug
Monitoring errors	Patient's response to therapy is not monitored appropriately ■ Lab results are not monitored for potential need for dosing adjustment ■ Signs of drug toxicity are missed ■ No response when patient requires modified dosage

Event Reporting Procedures

Most pharmacies and healthcare facilities have an internal mechanism to report medication errors. This may be online or on paper, but regardless of the process, reporting errors is essential to patient safety. Online reporting programs offer the capability of trending data, which helps plan investigations or create task forces to reduce the potential for errors.

The FDA uses a voluntary reporting system known as **MedWatch** for adverse and safety events. Healthcare professionals, consumers, or patients can all report through this online program. MedWatch reporting can include drugs, biologics, medical devices, dietary supplements, or cosmetics. This can also include suspected counterfeit medications.

The FDA uses the information from MedWatch to initiate recalls, investigate manufacturers, or make recommendations on medications. Reporting is therefore crucial for patient safety. While there is no legal requirement to report adverse events, MedWatch should be used in each the following situations:

1. Unexpected side effect or adverse event

2. Product quality issue

3. Potential medication errors that can be avoided, such as labeling or packaging

4. Therapeutic failure

When completing a MedWatch form online, the following information is required:

- Name of drug (and if medical device, model and serial number)
- Description of the adverse event
- Any concomitant medication use or disease history
- Date event occurred and when medication was started or stopped
- Dosage and directions for use
- The outcome of the event—for example, did the adverse event stop after the medication was discontinued?

ISMP also has a reporting database known as the Medication Error Reporting Program, or MERP. The goal of the ISMP and compiling data from MERP is to identify potential causes of errors and create information for pharmacies and healthcare organizations to follow. These safety practices can then be used by accrediting bodies, such as The Joint Commission, to review for patient safety.

When reporting a medication error in MERP, the following information is required:

- What went wrong or could go wrong
- Causes and contributing factors
- How the event was discovered or intercepted
- Actual or potential outcome of the involved patient(s)
- Your recommendations for error prevention
- Product names, dosage forms, and strength/dose
- Specific information regarding the model, build, and manufacturer of involved healthcare information technology and medication-related devices
- Any associated materials that help support the report being submitted (e.g., images of devices, display screens, products, containers, labels, de-identified prescription orders)

Root Cause Analysis

When a medication error occurs, it may require a more thorough investigation, or root cause analysis (RCA), to identify any underlying issues that could result in additional errors. An RCA is a process to find the "root cause" of a problem through a comprehensive review of all workflows and systems in place. This will then not only identify the problem, but help develop a way to prevent it from occurring again. Not all errors have one root cause, and an RCA can help identify additional causes if there are more than one.

An RCA should be conducted in a team approach. It is typically more beneficial to have the team be comprised of those who were not involved in the original error itself, but familiar with the workflows, processes, and procedures in the area it occurred.

The first step in an RCA is collecting data and reconstructing the error through a review of records and interviews of anyone involved. The RCA team then analyzes the events leading to the error, with the goal of understanding how and why the event occurred. The end result of an RCA is to prevent future adverse events from occurring.

A team conducting an RCA recognizes that human error can be a factor for all errors, but will instead focus on potential systematic issues that may have contributed to the event. Review the following medication error and think about how human error can play a role in this medication event.

> A nurse has an infusion of lipids to administer to a patient on TPN. The nurse is to program the pump to infuse over 12 hours, but instead programs the pump to infuse over 12 minutes. The patient receives the entire infusion in 12 minutes.

This example can be considered human error—the nurse did not enter the infusion rate correctly. However, an RCA identifies factors that may enhance the possibility of an error occurring. These are called contributing factors and can include circumstances or conditions that may increase the probability of an adverse event. Contributing factors to the preceding error were as follows: this unit was short staffed so no other nurse was available as a double-check on the infusion rate; this nurse was working her seventh straight day because of staffing issues; this nurse had four patients over a typical max patient load for one nurse.

While the error that occurred can be considered human failure, an RCA can identify the contributing factors and the root cause of the medication event. This medication error can be analyzed to be caused by an organizational failure—staffing was not at an appropriate or safe level for a nurse to care for patients. RCA can help prevent punitive responses to human error, and instead investigate the organizational or systemic failure behind the mistake to help prevent the same error from occurring in the future.

Product Integrity

MedWatch can also be used to report issues with product integrity. Integrity issues could include early degradation of a medication (after proper storage) and physical appearance that may suggest a medication is counterfeit. A counterfeit medication may contain no active ingredient, or a drug different than what is specified. It could also contain the wrong dose and has the potential to be harmful if taken. As a pharmacy technician, it is important to be on the lookout for counterfeit drugs. A visual inspection is the first step in identifying any potential integrity issues.

The drug package should be examined for tampering of the security seal, unusual fonts or print colors, and spelling errors, and the manufacturer address should be traceable. The dosage form itself can also be inspected for excessive powder or broken tablets in the bottom or discoloration of the tablet or capsule.

The Drug Supply Chain Security Act (DSCSA) was enacted in 2013 to help detect and remove counterfeit, stolen, or contaminated drugs from the US supply chain. Under the DSCSA, pharmacies must verify licensing of wholesalers and registration of manufacturers. All drugs must be accompanied by transaction information (TI), transaction history (TH), and a transaction statement (TS), and these must be stored for six years to provide tracking information. This information can be stored electronically.

TRANSACTION	DESCRIPTION
TI	Name, strength, dosage form, NDC, container size, number of containers purchased, lot number, date of purchase, business name, and address of purchaser
TH	Includes all transaction information dating back to the original manufacturing of the product
TS	Statement that the manufacturer follows the standards related to DSCSA

Pharmacist Intervention

Pharmacist interventions are an important part of patient safety and daily medication review. Pharmacy technicians can help identify the need for interventions by alerting pharmacists in the event a clinical review or consult is needed. Some potential issues requiring pharmacist intervention include drug utilization review (DUR), recommendation of OTC, therapeutic substitution, misuse or adherence issues, immunization follow-up, allergies, or drug interactions.

Drug Utilization Review (DUR)

A pharmacist completes a DUR by reviewing a prescription for potential drug interactions, allergies, contraindications, and compliance issues. A DUR provides a comprehensive review of prescriptions and medication data before and after dispensing to ensure a positive outcome.

The Omnibus Budget Reconciliation Act of 1990 (OBRA90) required a DUR to be completed for all Medicaid patients, though now a DUR is conducted on most claims submitted through insurance adjudication. Medicaid DUR is an ongoing program that reviews data submitted for patterns of drug use in Medicaid programs. A DUR can be considered prospective (screening of medication before it is dispensed) or retrospective (ongoing review of claims data).

Prospective DUR identifies issues such as:

- Therapeutic duplication
- Drug–disease interaction
- Drug–drug interaction
- Inappropriate prescribing, such as incorrect dosage, frequency, or duration
- Recommendations for substitutions and therapeutic interchange
- Allergies
- Misuse or abuse of a medication
- Appropriateness of medication for patient
- Pregnancy alert

Medicaid periodically completes retrospective DUR reviews claims data to identify patterns such as:

- Adverse events
- Therapeutic appropriateness
- Use of generic products
- Incorrect duration
- Abuse or fraud
- Unnecessary medical care

A DUR will notify the pharmacist if an intervention is necessary. The pharmacist may choose to proceed with the prescription as is (override the DUR), contact the provider for clarification or modification, or contact the insurance for approval or clarification.

Over-the-Counter Recommendations

Self-medicating with over-the-counter (OTC) products is very common in pharmacy practice. Pharmacy technicians can assist in selection of OTC products by helping patients locate specific products and answering any nonclinical questions. For instance, if a patient asks if the box of diphenhydramine on the shelf is the generic for Benadryl, a pharmacy technician can answer that question. If the patient asks what is recommended for allergies, a pharmacy technician must have the pharmacist answer for a clinical recommendation. The pharmacist must consider additional factors such as potential contraindications, concurrent medications, or disease state.

Therapeutic Substitution

A therapeutic substitution occurs when a medication is substituted with a drug that has a different active ingredient but with the same intended clinical effect. These drugs are typically in the same drug class. The intent of therapeutic substitution is to use the lowest-cost medication for drug therapy. In hospitals, therapeutic substitution is a method of reducing inventory. For example, if a patient is admitted to the hospital and typically takes lisinopril at home, but the hospital only stocks enalapril, a therapeutic substitution would occur so the patient could continue taking an ACE inhibitor while in the hospital, but a different medication than what was originally prescribed. The hospital can then stock only one ACE inhibitor, instead of many different drugs in the same class.

In retail pharmacy, insurance companies often dictate therapeutic substitution rules by requiring a step therapy or rejecting claims for more expensive drugs that have a cheaper or generic option in the same drug class. Patients may have to try the cheaper option first before getting an authorization for the more expensive option if there is treatment failure associated with the substitution. There are certain drug classes that must be careful about substituting, such as antidepressants, anticonvulsants, or hormone therapy. Patients often respond uniquely to these medications, and an alternate brand, generic, or different drug can have a negative impact on outcomes.

Misuse

Misuse of a prescription is when a patient intentionally or unintentionally takes a medication outside of the prescribed directions. This could include taking a prescription that is not prescribed to you, or using a medication for a high or euphoric feeling. Prescription drug abuse and misuse is a continued problem in the United States. It is often driven by the misperception that abusing prescription drugs is safer than abusing illicit substances. This has led to an increase in emergency room visits due to overdose and overdose deaths.

There are three classes of drugs that are most frequently abused:

1. Opioid analgesics used for pain

2. Sedatives, such as benzodiazepines or hypnotics used for anxiety and sleep

3. Stimulants used for ADHD

Adherence

Medication adherence is defined as the extent to which a patient takes a medication as prescribed. Adherence is a change in a patient's behavior by following prescribed regimen. Nonadherence can be caused by many issues such as cost of medication, side effects resulting in adherence issues, or cognitive deficits in understanding instructions or forgetting to take the drug. Pharmacy technicians can help identify these issues with patients and alert the pharmacist for potential adherence problems. If a patient is consistently late refilling a medication or asks for help with treatment of side effects, a pharmacist should intervene to provide clinical support. If a patient is forgetting to take their medication, recommending a pillbox reminder is a good tool to help improve adherence.

Adherence can be calculated as a percentage by dividing the total days' supply a patient filled by the total number of days and multiplying by 100.

$$\text{Adherence Percentage} = \frac{\text{Total Days' Supply of Patient Fills}}{\text{Total Days}} \times 100$$

For example, if a patient filled a medication for a 90-day supply, one time in 6 months, this would be 90 days of total therapy divided by 180 days of total time.

$$90\text{-day supply} = 90\text{-days' supply of patient fills}$$

$$6 \text{ months} \times 30\frac{\text{days}}{\text{month}} = 180 \text{ total days}$$

$$\frac{90 \text{ total days' supply}}{180 \text{ total days}} \times 100 = 50\%$$

This patient would have a 50% adherence rate.

Immunization

Depending on the state in which you live, pharmacists (and even pharmacy technicians in some states!) are able to give immunizations, though which specific vaccines depend on state law. Some states allow pharmacists to administer all vaccines to patients of all ages, while other states restrict which vaccines have a protocol for pharmacists and a minimum age for administration. Regardless of the state you're in, pharmacy technicians can assist the pharmacist for patients requesting vaccines by completing documentation for the patient, including informed consent for the vaccine risks and supplying a vaccine information statement (VIS). The VIS provides information on the vaccine, including risks of a reaction, reporting procedures for post-immunization follow-up, who should get vaccinated, and information that patients should tell their healthcare provider.

After an administration of a vaccine, pharmacists must provide post-immunization follow-up with the patient to detect possible safety concerns. Any concerns reported by patients for vaccines should be reported to the Vaccine Adverse Event Reporting System (VAERS). This system is designed to detect possible problems with US vaccines.

The objectives of VAERS include:

- Detecting new and unusual adverse vaccine events
- Monitoring increases in known adverse events
- Indentifying risk factors for patients for specific adverse events
- Assess new vaccines for safety
- Determine if reporting clusters exist, indicating potential geographic or lot issues
- Recognize administration issues
- Provide a monitoring system for large-scale program

Adverse Drug Events (ADEs) and Allergies

An adverse drug event occurs when medication use results in an injury to a patient. The ADE can be caused by an error or an ADR. A contributing factor to ADEs can be **polypharmacy**, or when a patient is taking multiple drugs, often for the same disease. Pharmacist intervention may be required if a patient's provider should be notified for a change in the drug therapy. This can help prevent a potential ADE.

Age may also be a risk factor for ADEs. Elderly patients are susceptible to disease–drug interactions due to chronic diseases requiring dose modifications. The Beers Criteria Medication List is published by the American Geriatrics Society and is a list of medications and drug classes that may be inappropriate for geriatric use. The Beers list provides recommendations on prescribing these drug classes to prevent ADEs for geriatric patients.

ADEs can also be caused by an allergic reaction. Pharmacy technicians can help prevent allergic reactions by documenting patient allergies each time a patient fills a prescription, to verify no changes have occurred. If a patient says they have no known allergies, it is important to identify if this refers to all medications only, or no allergies including other substances. This distinguishes NKA (no known allergies) from NKDA (no known drug allergies). If a patient has no known allergies, including all substances and drugs, this is NKA. If a patient has no known allergies to medications only, this is NKDA. This pharmacist intervention is caught through DUR.

Quality Control

Quality control (QC) in the pharmacy is required for Medicare Part D and for many accrediting bodies. Typically, pharmacies accomplish this through implementing a continuous quality improvement program (CQI). This helps find and assess issues, implement change, and measure progress. Reporting of medication errors often drives the processes to be reviewed in a CQI. If a trend is identified through error reporting, it can be targeted as a measure to evaluate improvement after a CQI is implemented.

Hygiene and Cleaning Standards

Quality control is also important for cleaning and hygiene standards. To prevent contamination of sterile compounds, USP has outlined standards for sterile compounding in USP chapter <797>. Compliance with these standards helps minimize sterility issues.

USP<797> provides standards and requirements on the following:

- Engineering controls for compounding equipment
- Training and competencies
- Certification requirements for hoods
- Beyond-use-dating
- Layout of facility
- Clean room design
- Environmental monitoring for potential contaminants

Handwashing and Personal Protection Equipment

Personal protection equipment (PPE) is required for all compounding procedures. PPE and hand hygiene help minimize microbials from entering a sterile environment needed to compound. PPE includes hair and beard cover, face mask, gloves, gown, and shoe covers. Donning, or putting on, PPE must follow a specific process to ensure proper protection. It should be completed "dirtiest" to "cleanest," such as putting on shoe covers before putting on gloves.

Proper hand hygiene and handwashing is an important part of sterile compounding and an overall obligation of a pharmacy technician. Good handwashing prevents the spread of illness and also helps maintain cleanliness within a pharmacy. The first step in handwashing for sterile compounding begins in the ante room, which is located adjacent to the compounding (buffer) room. Jewelry must be removed and no nail polish or artificial nails can be worn. Dirt and microbials can gather under artificial nails and nail polish can chip off and contaminate a sterile area. Hands should be washed with an antimicrobial soap up to the elbows with hot water for a minimum of 30 seconds. A nail pick should be used to clean under the fingernails and remove any debris. After cleaning, hands should be dried with a lint-free paper towel.

Below is the proper order of PPE donning, or garbing, for sterile compounding:

1. Start by removing any jewelry, makeup, artificial nails or polish before donning PPE.

2. Put on shoe covers.

3. Don hair cover—including beard cover if needed.

4. Put on a face mask or shield. A face shield or goggles are typically required only when compounding hazardous drugs.

5. Perform hand hygiene.

6. Don nonshedding gown over clean scrubs.

7. Use surgical (alcohol-based) hand scrub prior to putting on gloves. Allow to dry.

8. Don sterile gloves. Two pairs of chemotherapy gloves should be used if compounding a hazardous drug.

After completion of sterile compounding, doffing, or removing garb, should be in the reverse order of the preceding steps—starting with removal of sterile gloves and ending with removing shoe covers.

Cleaning the Pharmacy

Keeping a pharmacy clean is not just limited to areas where sterile compounding is performed. Areas in a pharmacy where nonsterile compounding must also be kept clean and the pharmacy must be kept free from clutter for patient safety. Part of this cleaning includes counting trays, which are used for counting patient prescriptions. There is often a residue that remains after the medication has been counted. Trays should be cleaned with 70% isopropyl alcohol (IPA). Cleaning counting trays regularly helps prevent cross-contamination, which is the contamination of another medication due to residual residue left on a counting tray. Drugs that leave a powder on the tray can contaminate the next prescription if the tray is not cleaned in between prescriptions. This is especially true for medications that have allergy implications. For example, if a counting tray is not cleaned following the counting of amoxicillin, and a patient has a penicillin allergy, this could result in an allergic reaction if the residue remains on the tray when counting the next prescription.

Countertops should also be cleaned regularly in all pharmacies. Hospital pharmacies, or those with a clean room, follow standards in USP<797>, which require monthly cleaning of walls, ceilings, and shelves that are in the buffer or ante room. This cleaning must be documented on a log each month.

Cleaning equipment in the pharmacy is typically completed in the clean room with the primary engineering control (PEC) used for sterile compounding. The ISO level in the pharmacy determines how clean the air is. If the ISO level is higher, the air is dirtier. In the ante area outside the buffer area, the air should be no higher than ISO class 8. The buffer room must have a level no higher than ISO class 7, and within the PEC, the ISO level cannot be greater than ISO class 5.

If the PEC has been shut off at any time, it should be turned on and left to run for 30 minutes prior to use. If a laminar airflow hood is being used for compounding, air is pulled into the HEPA filter and blown out horizontally toward the employee. This is why hazardous drug compounding should not be done in a laminar airflow hood. To clean, use sterile 70% IPA and start with the bar used for hanging IV bags. Next, clean the sides of the hood using a bottom to top motion. Finally, the surface should be cleaned using a side to side motion, starting in the back and working toward the front. Avoid any sprays as this could result in damage to the HEPA filter. Cleaning of the hood should be done at the beginning of every shift, every 30 minutes or before every batch, and if a spill occurs. Cleaning for all PECs must be documented on a log. The HEPA filter must be certified every six months. In addition, during this certification, surface and air samples are taken to verify proper cleaning and airflow is occuring.

For hazardous drug compounding, a vertical flow hood or biological safety cabinet is used, which provides a vertical flow of air down after HEPA filtration. This negative pressure helps prevent air exposure to an employee working. Cleaning of the vertical flow hood is done in the same manner as the horizontal flow hood. In addition to 70% IPA, a sporicidal cleaner is recommended to prevent hazardous drug contamination.

Review Questions

The following questions help you review the chapter. Test your knowledge by working through the next 50 questions to test yourself and identify any areas you may need to review.

1. The ISMP has a published list of medications that may cause greater harm if used in error. These are known as
   A. LASA
   B. high-alert/high-risk
   C. tall man
   D. confused abbreviations

2. Which drugs should not be stocked next to each other on the shelf?
   A. high alert
   B. generic
   C. fast movers
   D. LASA

3. Uppercase and bolded letters used to draw attention to differences in drug names are known as
   A. tall man lettering
   B. LASA
   C. confused drug list
   D. leading zeros

4. Which of the following should never be used as it could cause a tenfold error?
   A. trailing zero
   B. leading zero
   C. bar coding
   D. five rights

5. AD, AS, and AU are all on the ISMP List of Error-Prone Abbreviations, Symbols, and Dose Designations for being potentially confused with
   A. subcutaneous, intramuscular, and intradermal
   B. before lunch, with meals, and after lunch
   C. right eye, left eye, each eye
   D. once daily, twice daily, three times daily

6. A medication error that was caught before it reached the patient is known as a(n)

    A. near miss
    B. adverse drug reaction
    C. high alert
    D. recalled

7. A medication error that includes an incorrect strength, quantity, or dosage written would be which type of error?

    A. prescribing
    B. dispensing
    C. administration
    D. monitoring

8. A voluntary reporting system for adverse and safety events managed by the FDA is

    A. MERP
    B. CQI
    C. RCA
    D. MedWatch

9. Counting trays in a pharmacy should be cleaned with

    A. soap and water
    B. distilled water
    C. 70% IPA
    D. bleach

10. An unwanted and undesirable effect of a medication that occurs during a normal dose is a(n)

    A. near miss
    B. medication error
    C. recall
    D. adverse drug reaction

11. Which of the following ISO levels represents the cleanest air?

    A. ISO class 5
    B. ISO class 6
    C. ISO class 7
    D. ISO class 8

12. Which process helps identify the origin of a problem instead of focusing on the human error?

    A. CQI
    B. MERP
    C. RCA
    D. ISMP

13. Which of the following could be a therapeutic substitution for Vasotec?

    A. lisinopril
    B. olmesartan
    C. propranolol
    D. lansoprazole

14. The best way to prevent the spread of illness and germs is through

    A. donning shoe covers
    B. handwashing
    C. changing scrubs hourly
    D. wearing a mask

15. Implementing a plan for improvement measures in a pharmacy, including responding to medication error reporting, is known as

    A. ADR
    B. RCA
    C. CQI
    D. PPE

16. Counting trays should be cleaned regularly, especially after a powder residue, to prevent

    A. cross-contamination
    B. monitoring errors
    C. BCMA
    D. microbial infection

17. Taking multiple drugs, often for the same disease, is known as

    A. Beers list
    B. ADE
    C. polypharmacy
    D. DUR

18. A medication event caused by a vaccine should be reported to

    A. MedWatch
    B. MERP
    C. VAERS
    D. ISMP

19. Which medication is most likely to be misused?

    A. levothyroxine
    B. alprazolam
    C. spironolactone
    D. pantoprazole

20. Which of the following is used to help identify drugs that may be inappropriate for geriatric use?

    A. polypharmacy
    B. LASA list
    C. BCMA
    D. Beers list

21. Which medication could be a therapeutic substitution for Protonix?

    A. Pepcid
    B. Prilosec
    C. Tagamet
    D. Carafate

22. Which of the following questions could a pharmacy technician answer?

    A. Where can I find the loratadine?
    B. What should I take for my cough?
    C. I'm having drowsiness with my medication, is this normal?
    D. Can I take ibuprofen though I have a stomach ulcer?

23. Which of the following would flag on a prospective DUR?

    A. patient change in address
    B. interaction with other concurrent medication
    C. declined credit card
    D. expired driver's license

24. Which of the following is a review for potential drug interactions, allergies, contraindications, or compliance issues?

    A. OBRA

    B. BCMA

    C. OTC

    D. DUR

25. The Drug Supply Chain and Security Act was passed to help prevent

    A. drug shortages

    B. product integrity issues

    C. sterile compounding errors

    D. insurance rejections

26. When a drug treatment plan for a patient is not evaluated appropriately, this would be considered a

    A. prescribing error

    B. dispensing error

    C. administration error

    D. monitoring error

27. A patient has a prescription for 10 tablets to take 1 tab q12h PRN. The patient requests a refill after 3 days. How many days early is the patient requesting the refill?

    A. 1 day

    B. 2 days

    C. 4 days

    D. 6 days

28. Which chapter of USP outlines standards for sterile compounding?

    A. 795

    B. 797

    C. 800

    D. 826

29. How often must the HEPA filter be certified?

    A. 30 days

    B. 6 months

    C. 1 year

    D. 2 years

30. When doffing PPE, what should be removed first?

    A. shoe covers

    B. face mask

    C. gown

    D. gloves

31. A patient has a 30-day supply of a medication with 4 refills. The patient fills this prescription a total of 3 times in 5 months. What is the adherence percentage?

    A. 50%

    B. 60%

    C. 70%

    D. 80%

32. A nurse accidentally misses giving a patient their morning medications. Which type of error would this be?

    A. prescribing error

    B. dispensing error

    C. administration error

    D. monitoring error

33. USP<797> provides standards on which of the following?

    A. cleaning guidelines for nonsterile compounding

    B. handling of hazardous drugs

    C. compounding of radiopharmaceuticals

    D. competencies for sterile compounding

34. Which of the following medications is considered high risk?

    A. Lantus

    B. Mobic

    C. Zyrtec

    D. Prevacid

35. A pharmacist checking a prescription notices there are only 30 tablets in a bottle for a prescription written for 60. The pharmacist has caught a potential

    A. prescribing error

    B. dispensing error

    C. administration error

    D. monitoring error

36. When a nurse scans a medication prior to administering to a patient, this is known as

    A. five rights
    B. tall man lettering
    C. MAR
    D. BCMA

37. A patient fills a 30-day supply of a medication 6 times in 9 months. What is the adherence percentage during this 9-month period?

    A. 33%
    B. 45%
    C. 55%
    D. 67%

38. When cleaning a laminar airflow hood, which should be cleaned first?

    A. top of hood
    B. bottom of hood
    C. IV hanging bar
    D. sides of hood

39. A vertical flow hood should be used when compounding

    A. all IVs
    B. antibiotics only
    C. hazardous drugs
    D. ampules only

40. Which of the following is considered a high-alert medication?

    A. esomeprazole
    B. warfarin
    C. doxycycline
    D. folic acid

41. How should three milligrams be written on a prescription?

    A. 0.3mg
    B. 3.0mg
    C. 3 mg
    D. three milligrams

42. Which of the following should be avoided and never used when communicating?

    A. bar codes

    B. tall man lettering

    C. error-prone abbreviations

    D. MAR

43. A medication is written for a patient that is contraindicated with a patient's disease state. This would be what type of error?

    A. prescribing

    B. dispensing

    C. administration

    D. monitoring

44. ISMP has a medication error reporting database known as

    A. MedWatch

    B. MERP

    C. RCA

    D. CQI

45. Which of the following could be a therapeutic substitution for Coreg?

    A. lisinopril

    B. metoprolol

    C. valsartan

    D. hydrochlorothiazide

46. When donning for sterile compounding, which PPE should be put on first?

    A. face mask

    B. gown

    C. gloves

    D. shoe covers

47. Which medication has the highest chance of being misused?

    A. Adderall

    B. Lipitor

    C. Aldactone

    D. Bactrim

48. When a medication causes an injury to a patient, this is known as a(n)
    A. ADE
    B. EMR
    C. VAERS
    D. LASA

49. A patient has filled a 30-day supply of a prescription 6 times in the last 180 days. What is the patient's adherence percentage?
    A. 25%
    B. 50%
    C. 75%
    D. 100%

50. HS should never be used to abbreviate "half-strength," as this could be confused with
    A. every day
    B. units
    C. discharge or discontinue
    D. at bedtime

Answer Key

1. **B**
   To help prevent errors, ISMP has developed a list of high-alert medications, which are drugs that may cause greater harm if used in error.

2. **D**
   LASA (look-alike and sound-alike) drugs should not be stored next to each other to avoid a potential mix-up.

3. **A**
   Medications on the confused drug list contain uppercase and bolded letters that are used to draw attention to the differences in each drug name. This is known as tall man lettering and helps distinguish between two drugs that look or sound similar.

4. **A**
   Trailing zeros are after decimal points, such as 7.0. Trailing zeros should never be used, as they can cause confusion if the decimal point is missed. This could also lead to a tenfold error.

5. **C**
   The intended meaning of AD, AS, and AU is right ear, left ear, and both ears. It is often confused with right eye, left eye, and each eye.

6. **A**
   A near miss is a potential medication error that was caught before it reached the patient.

7. **A**
   Prescribing errors occur from the written order of a provider, either a prescription or a medication order. This includes errors in prescribed dosage or drug strength, quantity (excessive or insufficient) needed for drug therapy, route or dosage form, rate of infusion, or drug ordered.

8. **D**
   The FDA uses a voluntary reporting system known as MedWatch for adverse and safety events.

9. **C**
   Counting trays should be cleaned with 70% isopropyl alcohol (IPA).

10. **D**
    An adverse drug reaction (ADR) is an unwanted and undesirable effect of a medication that occurs during the standard clinical use or dose.

11. **A**
    The ISO level in the pharmacy determines how clean the air is. If the ISO level is higher, the air is dirtier.

12. **C**

An RCA is a process to find the "root cause" of a problem through a comprehensive review of all workflows and systems in place.

13. **A**

Vasotec (enalapril) is an ACE inhibitor and so is lisinopril.

14. **B**

Good handwashing prevents the spread of illness and also helps maintain cleanliness within a pharmacy.

15. **C**

Pharmacies accomplish quality control through implementing a continuous quality improvement program (CQI). This helps find and assess issues, implement change, and measure progress.

16. **A**

Cleaning counting trays regularly helps prevent cross-contamination, which is the contamination of another medication due to residual residue left on a counting tray.

17. **C**

Polypharmacy is when a patient is taking multiple drugs, often for the same disease.

18. **C**

Any concerns reported by patients for vaccines should be reported to the Vaccine Adverse Event Reporting System (VAERS). This system is designed to detect possible problems with US vaccines.

19. **B**

Alprazolam is a benzodiazepine. Opioid analgesics, sedatives such as benzodiazepines, and stimulants are all drugs that are more frequently abused than other medications.

20. **D**

The Beers list is published by the American Geriatrics Society and is a list of medications and drug classes that may be inappropriate for geriatric use. The Beers list provides recommendations on prescribing these drug classes to prevent ADEs for geriatric patients.

21. **B**

Prilosec is the name brand for omeprazole. Protonix is a proton pump inhibitor and the generic is pantoprazole. Omeprazole would be the only suitable substitution for pantoprazole.

22. **A**

A pharmacy technician can instruct a patient where to find an OTC medication, but cannot give clinical guidance.

23. **B**

    Prospective DUR identify issues such as drug–drug interaction, therapeutic duplication, and drug–disease interaction.

24. **D**

    A pharmacist completes a DUR by reviewing a prescription for potential drug interactions, allergies, contraindications, and compliance issues. A DUR provides a comprehensive review of prescriptions and medication data before and after dispensing to ensure a positive outcome.

25. **B**

    The Drug Supply Chain Security Act (DSCSA) was enacted in 2013 to help detect and remove counterfeit, stolen, or contaminated drugs from the US supply chain.

26. **D**

    A monitoring error is when a drug treatment plan for a patient is not evaluated for appropriate prescribing. It can occur when a patient's response to therapy is not monitored appropriately, such as through lab results or signs of drug toxicity.

27. **B**

    2 days. The patient is prescribed to take 2 tablets daily as needed. This is a max of 2 tablets daily. Since the patient has 10 tablets, this should last the patient 5 days.

28. **B**

    USP<797> provides standards for sterile compounding.

29. **B**

    The HEPA filter must be certified every 6 months.

30. **D**

    After completion of sterile compounding, doffing or removing garb should start with removal of sterile gloves and end with removing shoe covers.

31. **B**

    The patient fills a 30-day supply 3 times in 5 months. $3 \times 30 = 90$. 5 months = 150 days.

    $$\text{adherence percentage} = \frac{90}{150} \times 100 = 60\%$$

32. **C**

    An administration error occurs when there is a difference in what the patient is administered and what was prescribed. This includes administering the wrong drug, wrong dose, or at the wrong time. An omission error is also considered an administration error and occurs if a patient does not receive a medication at all.

33. **D**

    USP<797> includes standards related to sterile compounding such as competency and training requirements, facility layout, cleanroom design, and environmental monitoring.

34. **A**

    Lantus is an insulin, and all insulins are considered a high-risk medication.

35. **B**

    A dispensing error is a difference in what was prescribed and what is dispensed to a patient. Dispensing errors can also include the wrong quantity, such as giving only 30 tablets in a 60-tablet prescription.

36. **D**

    Bar code medication administration (BCMA) is completed by a nurse or other healthcare professional prior to giving a patient medication.

37. **D**

    67%. Start by determining the total days of patient fills. $30 \times 6 = 180$. Next, calculate the amount of days in 9 months. $9 \times 30 = 270$.

    $$\text{adherence percentage} = \frac{180}{270} \times 100 = 67\%$$

38. **C**

    To clean, use sterile 70% IPA and start with the bar used for hanging IV bags.

39. **C**

    For hazardous drug compounding, a vertical flow hood or biological safety cabinet is used, which provides a vertical flow of air down after HEPA filtration.

40. **B**

    Warfarin is on the ISMP high-alert medication list.

41. **C**

    3 mg does not have a decimal point, so it does not need a leading zero and trailing zeros should never be used.

42. **C**

    Through the collection of data from reported medication events, the ISMP has identified error-prone abbreviations, symbols, and doses. These should never be used when communicating and always avoided whenever possible.

43. **A**

    Incorrect patient errors can occur during prescribing, including writing an order for a medication to a patient with a known allergy or contraindication.

44. **B**

    ISMP is also a reporting database known as the Medication Error Reporting Program (MERP).

45. **B**

Coreg (carvedilol) is a beta blocker and so is metoprolol.

46. **D**

PPE is donned dirtiest to clean, with shoe covers first and gloves last.

47. **A**

Adderall is a stimulant used for ADHD and has a more likely chance of being misused.

48. **A**

An adverse drug event (ADE) occurs when medication use results in an injury to a patient.

49. **D**

100%. Start by determining the total days of patient fills. $30 \times 6 = 180$.

$$\text{adherence percentage} = \frac{180}{180} \times 100 = 100\%$$

50. **D**

At bedtime. Every night at bedtime and half strength can both be abbreviated HS.

CHAPTER 5

Order Entry and Processing

PTCE Knowledge Domain: Order Entry and Processing   21.25% of Exam

Knowledge Areas:

- Procedures to compound nonsterile products (e.g., ointments, mixtures, liquids, emulsions, suppositories, enemas)

- Formulas, calculations, ratios, proportions, alligations, conversions, sig codes (e.g., b.i.d., t.i.d., Roman numerals), abbreviations, medical terminology, and symbols for days supply, quantity, dose, concentration, dilutions

- Equipment/supplies required for drug administration (e.g., package size, unit dose, diabetic supplies, spacers, oral and injectable syringes)

- Lot numbers, expiration dates, and National Drug Code (NDC) numbers

- Procedures for identifying and returning dispensable, nondispensable, and expired medications and supplies (e.g., credit return, return to stock, reverse distribution)

After reading Chapter 5 you will be able to:

- Use sig codes, pharmacy abbreviations, and medical terminology to process prescriptions

- Use ratio-proportion and dimensional analysis to solve dosage calculations

- Convert between metric, household, and temperature systems

- Explain how to calculate days' supply and concentrations and dilutions

- Demonstrate the steps of nonsterile compounding, including alligations and supplies needed

- Describe expiration dates, lot numbers, and NDC numbers

- Differentiate between credit returns, return to stock, and reverse distribution

Pharmacy technicians across many settings are an integral part of the order entry process. This includes both prescriptions in a retail setting and medication orders in the institutional setting. Pharmacy technicians accept new prescriptions and refills from patients, collect and maintain patient data and profiles, and may initiate calls to providers for refill authorizations. This chapter reviews procedures for prescription processing, including dosage calculations, nonsterile compounding, supplies needed for dispensing and administration medications, and the process for returning unused or expired drugs.

Pharmacy Calculations

To process prescriptions and medication orders efficiently, pharmacy technicians must have a good understanding of pharmacy calculations, abbreviations, and sig codes. This includes starting with basic math and applying it to pharmacy calculations.

Sig Codes

Abbreviations used on prescriptions and medication orders are known as sig codes. These codes are used by physicians and pharmacies to communicate prescription information such as dosing frequency and time, route of administration, and dosage form. Sig codes are not intended for patients to understand. It is the duty of the pharmacy to translate the code onto a label that can be understood by the patient.

The following is a guide to sig codes and their meaning. You should spend some time reviewing and practicing these codes to prepare for certification and reading prescriptions.

SIG CODE	MEANING
AAA	apply to affected area
ac	before meals
ad	right ear
am	morning
amp	ampule
APAP	acetaminophen
as	left ear
ASA	acetylsalicylic acid, aspirin
aq	water
ATC	around the clock
au	both ears
BID	twice daily
bucc	buccal (inside the cheek)
c	with
cap	capsule
cc	cubic centimeter (same as 1mL)
CMPD	compound
d	day
D5W	dextrose 5% in water
DAW	dispense as written
DC, D/C	discontinue
DS	double strength
DR	delayed release
EC	enteric coated
elix	elixir
fl oz	fluid ounce
gal	gallon
g, gm	gram
gr	grain
gtt	drop
hr	hour
HCTZ	hydrochlorothiazide
HS	at bedtime
ID	intradermal
IM	intramuscular
INH	inhalation
IR	immediate release
IV	intravenous
IVP	IV push
IVPB	IV piggyback
IU	international unit
mcg	microgram
MDI	metered dose inhaler

SIG CODE	MEANING
mEq	milliequivalent
MOM	milk of magnesia
NPO	nothing by mouth
NS	normal saline 0.9%
od	right eye
ODT	oral disintegrating tablet
oint, ung	ointment
ophth	ophthalmic
os	left eye
OTC	over-the-counter
ou	both eyes
pc	after meals
PCN	penicillin
pm	evening
PO	by mouth
post	after
post op	after surgery
PR	per rectum
PRN	as needed
q	each, every
Qam	every morning
qd	every day, daily
qhr	every hour
qhs	before bedtime
qid	four times daily
qod	every other day
qpm	every evening
qs	a sufficient quantity
qwk	every week
S	without
SC, subcut, subQ	subcutaneous
sl	sublingual
soln	solution
ss	one-half
STAT	at once, now
subling	sublingual
supp	suppository
susp	suspension
syr	syrup
tab	tablet
tbsp	tablespoon
tid	three times daily
tsp	teaspoon

Many prescriptions are written with pharmacy sig codes for abbreviations and Roman numerals indicating quantity.

The following is a Roman numeral conversion up to 1,000.

Roman Numeral	Number Value
ss	0.5
I or i	1
V or v	5
X or x	10
L or l	50
C or c	100
D or d	500
M or m	1,000

When reading Roman numerals, there are a few rules to remember to make sure you're calculating the accurate value.

1. If the value of the Roman numeral decreases from left to right, the total is the sum of all the numerals. Example: XV = 10 + 5 = 15.

2. If a Roman numeral is repeated three times in a row, these three numbers are added. It cannot be repeated more than three times. Example: XXX = 30.

3. If a smaller Roman numeral is written to the left of a larger value, you should subtract the smaller value from the larger. Example: IV = 5 – 1 = 4.

Self-Test: Define the following:

1. II tab PO BID ×7d

2. III cap PO TID PRN

3. 5mL PO QID ×5d

Answers:

1. Take 2 tablets by mouth twice daily for 7 days.

   II = 2

   tab = tablet

   PO = by mouth

   BID = twice daily

   ×7d = for 7 days

2. Take 3 capsules by mouth three times daily as needed.

> III = 3
>
> cap = capsule
>
> PO = by mouth
>
> TID = three times daily
>
> PRN = as needed

3. Take 5mL by mouth four times daily for 5 days.

> PO = by mouth
>
> QID = four times daily
>
> ×5d = for 5 days

Medical Abbreviations

Medical abbreviations for diseases are also used frequently in pharmacy practice. The following is a list of medical conditions and the corresponding abbreviation. You should spend some time familiarizing yourself with these abbreviations as they may show up in patients' charts or prescriptions when you are processing orders.

MEDICAL ABBREVIATION	DEFINITION
ADD	attention deficit disorder
ADHD	attention deficit hyperactivity disorder
BM	bowel movement
BP	blood pressure
BPH	benign prostatic hyperplasia
BS	blood sugar
CA	cancer
CAD	coronary artery disease
CHF	congestive heart failure
CNS	central nervous system
COPD	chronic obstructive pulmonary disorder
DOB	date of birth
Dx	diagnosis
ECG/EKG	electrocardiogram
ER/ED	emergency room/department
GERD	gastroesophageal reflux disease
GI	gastrointestinal
HA	headache

(continued)

MEDICAL ABBREVIATION	DEFINITION
HR	heart rate
HTN	hypertension
Hx	history
ID	infectious disease
MI	myocardial infarction
MRI	magnetic resonance imaging
N & V	nausea and vomiting
NKA	no known allergies
NKDA	no known drug allergies
NPO	nothing by mouth
OR	operating room
RA	rheumatoid arthritis
RBC	red blood cell or red blood count
SOB	shortness of breath
Sx	symptoms
TB	tuberculosis
Tx	treatment
UA	urinalysis
URI	upper respiratory tract infection
UTI	urinary tract infection
VS	vital signs
WBC	white blood cell or white blood count
WT	weight

Medical Terminology

In addition to abbreviations, pharmacy technicians frequently encounter medical terms that are composed of a prefix, root word, and suffix. Having an understanding of these parts of a word can help you describe many illnesses, body processes, procedures, and even pharmacology.

Prefix	Placed at the beginning of a word to modify the meaning
Root	Central part of the word
Suffix	Ending part of a word that modifies the meaning

Each of the following tables are frequently used prefixes, roots, and suffixes.

PREFIX	MEANING		ROOT WORD	MEANING
a-, an-	without, not		aden/o	gland
ab-	away from		aer/o	air
ad-	toward		andr/o	male
ante-	before		ather/o	plaque—fatty substance
anti-	against, opposed to		bacteri/o	bacteria
bi-	double, two		bas/o	base (opposite of acid)
brady-	slow		bucc/o	cheek
dys-	bad, difficult		carcin/o	cancer
hemi-	one half		cardi/o	heart
hyper-	above normal, excessive		cephal/o	head
hypo-	below normal, deficient		cyst/o	bladder
inter-	between		derm/o, dermat/o	skin
intra-	within		electr/o	electricity
macro-	large		erythr/o	red
micro-	small		ferr/o	iron
pre-	before		gastr/o	stomach
post-	after		gluc/o	sugar
retro-	behind, backward		gyn, gyn/o	woman
tachy-	fast		hemat/o	blood
tri-	three		hepat/o	liver
			home/o	sameness, unchanging
			hormon/o	hormone
			hyster/o	uterus
			leuk/o	white
			lith/o	stone
			mamm/o	breast
			mort/o	death
			necr/o	death
			nephr/o	kidney
			neur/o	nerve
			noct/o	night
			obstetr/o	pregnancy, birth
			ocul/o	eye
			oste/o	bone
			ot/o	ear
			phil/o	love, attraction to
			phleb/o	vein

(continued)

ROOT WORD	MEANING
pulm/o	lung
pyr/o	heat, fever
ren/o	kidney
sarc/o	flesh
sinus/o	sinus
ur/o	urine, urinary tract
valv/o	valve
ven/o	vein
vascul/o	vessel

SUFFIX	MEANING
-ac, -al, -tic	related or pertaining to
-algia	pain
-ase	enzyme
-centesis	surgical puncture
-cyte	cell
-ectomy	removal, excision
-emia	blood condition
-gen	production, origin
-gram	recording
-graph	instrument used to record
-ism	condition, disease
-itis	inflammation
-ologist	one who studies, specialist
-ology	study of
-oma	tumor
-pathy	disease
-scope	instrument used to visually examine
-scopy	process of visually examining

Medical terms can be used to build words or define them. For example, acetaminophen is an *antipyrogenic* medication. Define this word.

Anti—against

Pyr/o—fever, heat

Genic—to produce

So an antipyrogenic would be "against production of fever."

Self-Test: **Define or build words.**

1. sinusitis

2. cardiopathy

3. nerve pain

Answers

1. inflammation of the sinus

   sinus/o = sinus

   -itis = inflammation

2. disease of the heart

   cardi/o = heart

   pathy = disease

3. neuroalgia

   nerve = neur/o

   pain—algia

Fractions, Decimals, and Percents

A fraction is a value that is not a whole number. The top of the fraction is the numerator, and the bottom is the denominator. If a patient is to take 1/4 of a tablet daily, 1 is the numerator and 4 is the denominator. Fractions can be converted into a decimal by dividing the numerator by the denominator.

Example: Convert 1/4 into a decimal.

$$\frac{1}{4} = 0.25$$

The dose could then be written as 1/4 tablet or 0.25 tablet.

A decimal is a fraction written with a denominator as a power of 10. For example 4/10 would be written as 0.4. Numbers written to the rig of the decimal point are below 1, whereas numbers on the left of the decimal point are greater than 1. So 0.4 is less than 1.4. As you move the decimal point to the right or the left one space, the value either decreases or increases by a factor of 10. This is indicated by the following chart.

THOUSANDS	HUNDREDS	TENS	ONES	DECIMAL POINT	TENTHS	HUNDREDTHS	THOUSANDTHS	TEN THOUSANDTHS
4,000	400	40	4	0	0.4	0.04	0.004	0.0004

To convert a decimal into a fraction, remove the decimal point from the number for the numerator, and for the denominator, count the number of places to the right of the decimal point. Decimals can be converted into fractions by the following steps:

Example: Convert 0.75 to a fraction.

1. Rewrite the decimal as the numerator over 1, with 1 being the denominator.

$$\frac{0.75}{1}$$

2. Multiply both the numerator and denominator by 10 for every digit after the decimal. For example, 0.75, there are 2 places after the decimal = 100.

$$\frac{0.75 \times 100}{1 \times 100} = \frac{75}{100}$$

3. Reduce or simplify the fraction.

$$\frac{75}{100} = \frac{3}{4}$$

When completing pharmacy calculations, you often encounter decimals that need to be rounded appropriately for dosage calculations. Sometimes the tenth place is appropriate, but sometimes the hundredths or thousandths place is needed for accuracy. You should always consult the pharmacist if unsure which place to round. To round a decimal, look at the digit one space to the right on the desired place. If it is greater than 5, round the number up. If it is less than 5, the number remains the same.

Example: Round 8.426 to the hundredths place.

1. First, determine which is the hundredths place: 8.4<u>2</u>6

2. Look at the digit one space to the right of the hundredths. Is it greater than 5? 8.42<u>6</u>

3. Because 6 is greater than 5, this number would be rounded up.

4. Round up the hundredths place for the answer: 8.43

Remember that you *always* want a **leading zero**, and *never* want a **trailing zero**!

Percents are also used frequently in pharmacy calculations. A percent is a part per 100. So 70% solution means there are 70 parts of active ingredient in 100 total parts. Percentages can be converted into and from fractions and decimals easily.

Example: 30% is the same as saying $\frac{30}{100}$ as a fraction.

To convert into a decimal, you can either divide the percent by 100 or move the decimal point over two spaces to the left.

Dividing by 100: $\frac{30}{100} = 0.3$

To get a percent from a fraction or decimal, you can multiply the decimal by 100.

Example: If a patient needs to take 0.5 tablet, what percent of a tablet is this?

$$0.5 \times 100 = 50\%$$

If you are starting with a fraction, convert into a decimal first, and then follow the previous steps to convert into a percent.

Example: A patient is taking ½ tab. What percent of a tablet is this?

$$\frac{1}{2} = 0.5$$

Now use the decimal to convert into a percent by multiplying by 100.

$$0.5 \times 100 = 50\%$$

Conversion between fractions, decimals and percentages is an important skill to have as a baseline before moving on to dosage calculations. Test yourself with a few practice conversions to make sure you're ready for ratios and proportions.

Self-Test: **Round to the nearest tenth place**

1. Convert 1/3 into a decimal.

2. Convert 0.85 into a percentage.

3. Convert 68% into a fraction.

4. Convert 2/3 into a percentage.

5. Convert 0.25 into a fraction.

6. Convert 90% into a decimal.

Answers:

1. 0.3

2. 85%

3. 17/25

4. 66.7%

5. 1/4

6. 0.9

Ratios and Proportions

A ratio is a relationship between two quantities that can be used to solve dosage calculations in pharmacy practice. A ratio indicates how many times one number contains another. For example, if a medication is 20mg/mL, this means each mL contains 20mg. Mg/mL is a common ratio in both retail and inpatient pharmacies. Two equal ratios are known as a proportion, and this is helpful when determining an unknown quantity if three other values are known.

To solve a ratio-proportion calculation, write out the ratios with like units on the top and bottom. Then solve for the unknown.

Example: Using the previous example, calculate how many mL would be needed for a dose of 46mg if a medication is available as 20mg/1mL.

1. Start with setting up your two ratios, using x mL for the answer you're solving for. Keep mL together on one level and mg together on the other.

$$\frac{x \, mL}{46mg} = \frac{1mL}{20mg}$$

2. Once the proportion is set up, solve for x. Complete this through cross multiplying first.

$$(1)(46) = (x)(20)$$

3. Next, solve for x, by dividing both sides to get x by itself. In this equation, that would be 20.

$$\frac{(1)(46)}{20} = \frac{(x \, mL)(20)}{20}$$

4. Multiply and divide to solve for x. Divide both sides by 20 to get x by itself.

$$\frac{(1)(46)}{20} = \frac{(x \, mL)(20)}{20}$$

$$\frac{46}{20} = x \, mL$$

$$x = 2.3mL$$

Remember, you can estimate what the answer should be close to, so you have an idea if your calculations are correct. In this case, if you know your dose is 46mg and the medication is available in 20mg/mL, you can guess that the answer should be a little bit more than 2mL since 20mg can go into 46 twice. So if you get an answer like 20mL or 0.2mL, that should give you a clue that your answer is off.

Dimensional Analysis

Another method of calculating unknown variables in an equation is through dimensional analysis. This process uses the cancelation method of like units to determine the answer. Setting up dimensional analysis equations are different from ratio-proportion in that you want to keep the same units on the top and bottom so they can be cancelled.

Example: Using the previous example, calculate how many mL would be needed for a dose of 46mg if a medication is available as 20mg/1mL.

1. Start with setting up your equation so that the like units are on the top and bottom so they can be cancelled. In this case, we know that 46mg is 1 dose and there are 20mg in 1mL. We would want the mg to be on the top and bottom.

$$\frac{46mg}{1\ dose} \times \frac{1mL}{20mg}$$

2. Next, cancel your like units, and determine what you have remaining. With the units remaining, our answer will be mL/dose, which is what we are looking for.

$$\frac{46\cancel{mg}}{1\ dose} \times \frac{1mL}{20\cancel{mg}}$$

3. To solve, multiply the numbers across the top. Then multiply the numbers across the bottom.

$$46 \times 1 = 46$$

$$1 \times 20 = 20$$

Take the product of the numerators divided by the product of the denominators, and this will give you your answer.

$$\frac{46}{20} = 2.3$$

4. Be sure to include your units—in this case, we were solving for mL/dose, so the answer would be 2.3mL.

Self-Test: **Round to the nearest tenths place**

Use ratio-proportion or dimensional analysis to answer the following.

1. How many mg is in a dose of 7.5mL of a 250mg/5mL suspension?

2. What volume dose would be given for a patient who had a dose of 84mg of a 100mg/5mL solution?

3. A patient has a dose of 1,250mg. The medication is available as 500mg tablets. How many tablets are in each dose?

Answers:

1. 375mg

   Ratio-proportion:

   $$\frac{x\,\text{mg}}{7.5\text{mL}} = \frac{250\text{mg}}{5\text{mL}}$$

   $$(x)(5) = (7.5)(250)$$

   $$\frac{(7.5)(250)}{5} = 375\text{mg}$$

   Dimensional analysis:

   $$\frac{7.5\cancel{\text{mL}}}{1\,\text{dose}} \times \frac{250\text{mg}}{5\cancel{\text{mL}}}$$

   $$\frac{(7.5)(250)}{(1)(5)} = 375\text{mg}$$

2. 4.2mL

   Ratio-proportion:

   $$\frac{x\,\text{mL}}{84\text{mg}} = \frac{5\text{mL}}{100\text{mg}}$$

   $$(x)(100) = (84)(5)$$

   $$\frac{(84)(5)}{100} = 4.2\text{mL}$$

   Dimensional analysis:

   $$\frac{84\cancel{\text{mg}}}{1\,\text{dose}} \times \frac{5\text{mL}}{100\cancel{\text{mg}}}$$

   $$\frac{(84)(5)}{(1)(100)} = 4.2\text{mL}$$

3. 2.5 tabs

   Ratio-proportion:

   $$\frac{x\,\text{tab}}{1{,}250\text{mg}} = \frac{1\,\text{tab}}{500\text{mg}}$$

   $$(x)(500) = (1{,}250)(1)$$

   $$\frac{(1{,}250)(1)}{500} = 2.5\,\text{tabs}$$

Dimensional analysis:

$$\frac{1,250\cancel{mg}}{1\ \text{dose}} \times \frac{1\ \text{tab}}{500\cancel{mg}}$$

$$\frac{(1,250)(1)}{(1)(500)} = 2.5\,\text{tabs}$$

The Metric System

The metric system is a system of measurement used around the world and in hospitals, pharmacies, and healthcare systems. The metric system is based on a factor of 10, and conversion between units is an important part of dosage calculations.

For length, the base unit is a meter, but millimeter and kilometer are also common. Mass has a basic unit of gram, but in pharmacy practice, micrograms, milligrams, and kilograms are all used regularly. For volume, the liter is the base unit, but many pharmacy calculations and most liquid medications are dosed in milliliters.

The three most common prefixes you will use in pharmacy practice are *micro-*, *milli-*, and *kilo-*. These prefixes follow with their value and an example for each.

PREFIX	VALUE	SYMBOL	EXAMPLE
micro-	one-millionth or 0.000001 × base unit (10^{-6})	mc-	mcg (microgram)
milli-	one-thousandth or 0.001 × base unit (10^{-3})	m-	mL (milliliter)
kilo-	one thousand or 1,000 × base unit (10^{3})	k	kg (kilogram)

To convert between units in the metric system in pharmacy calculations, there are three methods you can use.

Move the Decimal Point

If you are converting from a smaller unit to a larger unit, move the decimal point to the left (the number gets smaller).

If you are converting from a larger unit to a smaller unit, move the decimal point to the right (the number gets bigger).

The following chart gives an idea of how many decimal points you would need to move. If converting between each unit, such as from micrograms to milligrams, you would move the decimal point three places. If you convert to the next unit, such as from micrograms to grams, you would move the decimal point six places. If you were to convert between micrograms and kilograms, you would move the decimal point nine places.

KILOGRAM	GRAM	MILLIGRAM	MICROGRAM
1 kg	1,000gm	1,000,000mg	1,000,000,000mcg
0.001 kg	1gm	1,000mg	1,000,000mcg
0.000001 kg	0.001gm	1mg	1,000mcg
0.000000001 kg	0.000001gm	0.001mg	1mcg

Example: Convert 458mg to g.

1. We are moving from mg to g, which is a smaller unit to a bigger unit, so the decimal point will go to the left and the number will get smaller.

2. Mg to g is 3 places.

   458. = 0.458g

Multiply or Divide

This method has the same theory as moving the decimal point. If you are converting from a smaller unit to a larger unit, you will divide (the number gets smaller).

If you are converting from a larger unit to a smaller unit, you will multiply (the number gets larger).

The amount to divide or multiply depends on the value of the unit conversions. Similar to moving the decimal point 3 spaces, if you are converting from one unit to another next to each other on the previous chart, you will multiply or divide by 1,000 (such as microgram to milligram). If you skip a unit, such as converting from milligram to kilogram, you will divide by 1,000,000. Converting from microgram to kilogram would be dividing by 1,000,000,000.

Example: Convert 458mg to g.

1. Moving from mg to g means a smaller unit to a larger unit, so you will divide.

2. Mg and g are next to each other on the unit table, so you will divide by 1,000.

$$\frac{458}{1,000} = 0.458g$$

Ratio-Proportion

The ratio-proportion method uses the conversion factors listed in the previous chart. The x should always be opposite of the number you are converting from. This ratio should equal the conversion factor, such as 1 g = 1,000mg or 1mg = 1,000mcg.

Example: Convert 458mg to g.

1. Set up your ratio-proportion, keeping like units on the top and bottom.

$$\frac{x \text{ g}}{458\text{mg}} = \frac{1\text{g}}{1,000\text{mg}}$$

2. Cross multiply and divide.

$$\frac{x \text{ g}}{458 \text{mg}} = \frac{1 \text{g}}{1{,}000 \text{mg}}$$

$$(x)(1{,}000) = (458)(1)$$

3. Solve for x.

$$(x) = \frac{(458)(1)}{(1{,}000)} = 0.458 \text{g}$$

The same conversion can be done for volume, using liter and milliliter. The conversions for volumes follow.

LITER	MILLILITER
1L	1,000mL

Example: A patient has an order for 2,500mL of fluid. How many L is this?

Converting from mL to L is converting from a smaller unit to a larger unit, so to solve, divide by 1,000, move the decimal point three places to the right, or set up using ratio-proportion.

$$\frac{x \text{ L}}{2{,}500 \text{mL}} = \frac{1 \text{L}}{1{,}000 \text{mL}}$$

$$(x)(1{,}000) = (2{,}500)(1)$$

$$\frac{(2{,}500)(1)}{1{,}000} = 2.5 \text{L}$$

Self-Test: **Complete the conversions**

1. Convert 2.2g to kg.

2. Convert 500mL to L.

3. Convert 0.125mg to mcg.

Answers:

1. 0.0022kg

    g to kg = smaller to bigger unit

    Divide by 1,000.

    Move the decimal point three places to the left.

    Set up ratio-proportion:

    $$\frac{x \text{ kg}}{2.2\text{g}} = \frac{1\text{kg}}{1,000\text{g}}$$

    $$(x)(1,000) = (2.2)(1) = 0.0022\text{kg}$$

2. 0.5L

    mL to L = smaller to bigger unit

    Divide by 1,000.

    Move the decimal point three places to the left.

    Set up ratio-proportion:

    $$\frac{x \text{ L}}{500\text{mL}} = \frac{1\text{L}}{1,000\text{mL}}$$

    $$(x)(1,000) = (500)(1) = 0.5\text{L}$$

3. 125mcg

    mg to mcg = bigger to smaller unit

    Multiply by 1,000.

    Move the decimal point three places to the right.

    Set up ratio-proportion:

    $$\frac{x \text{ mcg}}{0.125\text{mg}} = \frac{1,000\text{mg}}{1\text{mg}}$$

    $$(x)(1) = (0.125)(1,000) = 125\text{mcg}$$

The Household System

The household system of measurement is used in the United States and mainly in homes or kitchens. You may see prescriptions written for patients to take a teaspoon or tablespoon of a medication. This is an example of a household measurement. This system of measurement is less accurate than metric. Not everyone is going to measure one teaspoon in a measuring spoon or cup, and not all teaspoons are created equal. When completing the order entry process for prescriptions with household measurements, you should also include the metric equivalent for more precise dosing.

The household system measurements for volume and weight follow, along with their metric conversions.

HOUSEHOLD MEASUREMENT	ABBREVIATION	HOUSEHOLD EQUIVALENT	METRIC EQUIVALENT
1 teaspoon	tsp	–	5mL
1 tablespoon	tbsp.	3 teaspoons	15mL
1 fluid ounce	fl oz	2 tablespoons	30mL
1 cup	c	8 fluid ounces	240mL
1 pint	pt	2 cups	480mL
1 quart	qt	2 pints	960mL
1 gallon	gal	4 quarts	3,840mL
1 ounce	oz	–	30g
1 pound	lb	16 ounces	454g
2.2 pounds	lb	–	1kg

For example, a common calculation pharmacy technicians complete is conversion of a patient weight from lb to kg. This can be completed through the ratio-proportion method or by simply dividing the total pounds by 2.2. The opposite is true if needing to calculate from kg to lb. You would then multiply by 2.2 to get your answer. Remember that the kg value will always be less than the lb value.

Example: A patient weighs 96 lb. Determine how much she weighs in kg. Round your answer to the tenths place.

Ratio-proportion

$$\frac{x \text{ kg}}{96 \text{ lb}} = \frac{1\text{kg}}{2.2 \text{ lb}}$$

$$(x)(2.2) = (96)(1)$$

$$\frac{96}{2.2} = 43.6\text{kg}$$

The other option to solve is to remember that when converting from lb to kg, dividing by 2.2 will give you the same solution.

$$\frac{96 \text{ lb}}{2.2} = 43.6\text{kg}$$

Converting from fl oz to mL is also a common conversion pharmacy technicians will complete regularly. Knowing that 1 fl oz = 30mL is helpful when using the ratio-proportion method to solve. Another way to solve is to remember that when converting from fl oz to mL, you multiply the number of fl oz by 30 to get your total mL. Conversely, when converting from mL to fl oz, you divide by 30 to get your total fl oz.

The following is a chart of fl oz to mL conversion.

HOUSEHOLD MEASUREMENT	METRIC MEASUREMENT
1 fl oz	30mL
2 fl oz	60mL
3 fl oz	90mL
4 fl oz	120mL
5 fl oz	150mL
6 fl oz	180mL
8 fl oz	240mL
9 fl oz	270mL
10 fl oz	300mL
11 fl oz	330mL
12 fl oz	360mL

Example: A prescription is written for 3 fl oz. How many mL is this?

Ratio-proportion:

$$\frac{x \text{ mL}}{3 \text{ fl oz}} = \frac{30 \text{ mL}}{1 \text{ fl oz}}$$

$$(x)(1) = (3)(30) = 90\text{mL}$$

This can also be solved by remembering that converting from fl oz to mL means you should multiply your total fl oz by 30 to get your total mL.

$$(3 \text{ fl oz})(30) = 90\text{mL}$$

Self-Test: **Complete the conversions**

1. Convert 180mL to fl oz.

2. Convert 45mL to tablespoons.

3. Convert 24kg to lb.

Answers:

1. 6 fl oz

    Ratio-proportion:

    $$\frac{x \text{ fl oz}}{180 \text{mL}} = \frac{1 \text{ fl oz}}{30 \text{mL}}$$

    $$(x)(30) = (180)(1)$$

    $$\frac{180}{30} = 6 \text{ fl oz}$$

    Converting from mL to fl oz = divide by 30

    $$\frac{180}{30} = 6 \text{ fl oz}$$

2. 3 Tbsp

    Ratio-proportion:

    $$\frac{x \text{ tbsp}}{45 \text{mL}} = \frac{1 \text{ tbsp}}{15 \text{mL}}$$

    $$(x)(15) = (45)(1) = \frac{45}{15} = 3 \text{ tbsp}$$

    Converting from mL to tbsp: there are 15mL in 1 tbsp so you can simply divide by 15.

    $$\frac{45}{15} = 3 \text{ tbsp}$$

3. 55 lb

    Ratio-proportion:

    $$\frac{x \text{ lb}}{25 \text{kg}} = \frac{2.2 \text{ lb}}{1 \text{ kg}}$$

    $$(x)(1) = (25)(2.2) = 55 \text{ lb}$$

    Converting from kg to lb = multiply by 2.2

    $$(25)(2.2) = 55 \text{ lb}$$

The Apothecary System

The apothecary system is a very old measurement system that has minimal use in pharmacy practice today. Though there are some medications that may still use the apothecary system as a form of measurement, it has overall been replaced with the metric system. Apothecary symbols are considered dangerous abbreviations and should not be used.

The following are a few apothecary measurements and the corresponding metric conversions.

APOTHECARY MEASUREMENT	METRIC EQUIVALENT
1 grain	60mg or 65mg
1 ounce	30g

Aspirin, thyroid medication, and phenobarbital may still use grains as a form of measurement. Also, medication vials used in the pharmacy may be measured as drams—an apothecary unit of measurement for weight.

Temperature Conversions

Understanding temperature measurement systems is an important skill for pharmacy technicians. Part of the metric system is the Celsius scale. In the Celsius scale, water freezes at 0°C and boils at 100°C. The United States uses the Fahrenheit scale. In this scale, water freezes at 32°F and boils at 212°F. Converting between Fahrenheit and Celsius scales may be necessary for proper inventory management and storage. As a pharmacy technician, you may be responsible for logging daily temperatures of refrigerators, freezers, and room temperature for drug storage units. If a refrigerator or freezer contains a vaccine, the temperatures must be logged twice a day.

When converting between temperature measurement systems, use the following equations and plug in the known temperature to calculate the solution.

To convert from Celsius to Fahrenheit:

$$°F = (1.8 \times °C) + 32$$

To convert from Fahrenheit to Celsius:

$$°C = \frac{(°F - 32)}{1.8}$$

Example: Convert 76°F to Celsius. Round to the tenths place.

$$°C = \frac{(76 - 32)}{1.8}$$

$$°C = \frac{(44)}{1.8}$$

$$°C = 24.4\,°C$$

Pharmacy Dosage Calculations

When solving dosage calculations, keep in mind that a dose is a specified amount of drug that is taken at a certain time. You may need to calculate how many doses there are in a quantity of medication, how long a medication will last, or using known variables to solve for the unknown amount. Ratio-proportion and dimensional analysis are both used to solve dosage calculations.

Example: How many mL are in a 250mg dose of a medication available as 125mg/5mL?

You can use ratio-proportion or dimensional analysis to solve.

Ratio-proportion:

$$\frac{x \text{ mL}}{250\text{mg}} = \frac{5\text{mL}}{125\text{mg}}$$

$$(x)(125) = (250)(5)$$

$$\frac{1,250}{125} = 10\text{mL}$$

Dimensional analysis:

$$\frac{250\cancel{\text{mg}}}{1 \text{ dose}} \times \frac{5\text{mL}}{125\cancel{\text{mg}}}$$

$$\frac{(250)(5)}{(1)(125)} = 10\text{mL}$$

Dosage calculations often include weight-based dosing, in which you must determine the dose for a patient with a specified weight.

Example: A prescriber orders trastuzumab 4mg/kg to be infused over 90 minutes. The patient weighs 175 lb. What will the dose be?

1. The order is written for mg/kg and the patient's weight is given in lb. First convert the lb to kg.

$$\frac{175 \text{ lb}}{2.2} = 79.5\text{kg}$$

2. The patient is getting 4mg for every 1 kg. To solve for the dose, multiply the 4mg by the total patient kg. This can be set up as ratio-proportion as well.

$$\frac{x \text{ mg}}{79.5\text{kg}} = \frac{4\text{mg}}{1\text{kg}}$$

$$(x)(1) = (79.5)(4)$$

$$(4\text{mg})(79.5\text{kg}) = 318\text{mg}$$

In addition to weight, some orders, such as chemotherapy or pediatric, may use **body surface area (BSA)** as a precise method of dosing. BSA is a dosing based on the patient's height and weight and is measured in m².

Example: A patient has an order for vincristine 2mg/m². The patient's BSA is 1.4 m². Calculate the dose for this patient.

Use ratio-proportion and solve for x.

$$\frac{x \text{ mg}}{1.4 \text{m2}} = \frac{2 \text{mg}}{1 \text{m2}}$$

$$(x)(1) = (1.4)(2)$$

$$x = 2.8 \text{mg}$$

Milliequivalents (mEq) and **units** are other measurements used for specific medications. MEq may be used when calculating orders for potassium, especially if preparing to compound total parenteral nutrition (TPN).

Example: A patient is prescribed 100mEq total daily in four divided doses. How many mEq are in each dose?

To determine each dose, divide the total daily amount by the number of doses given each. You can also set up a ratio-proportion.

$$\frac{x \text{ mEq}}{1 \text{ dose}} = \frac{100 \text{mEq}}{4 \text{ dose}}$$

$$(x)(4) = (1)(100)$$

$$\frac{100}{4} = 25 \text{mEq}$$

Units are used for dosing in medications such as heparin, penicillin, and insulin and for certain vitamins. Standard insulin vials contain 1,000units/10mL, though there are also 300units/3mL vials, insulin pens with varied dosing, and concentrated U-500 insulin, at 500units/mL.

Example: A patient is prescribed 36 total units of insulin per dose. How many mL from a 1,000unit/10mL vial will the patient inject for one dose?

Set up a ratio proportion.

$$\frac{x \text{ mL}}{36 \text{ units}} = \frac{10 \text{mL}}{1,000 \text{ units}}$$

$$(x)(1,000) = (36)(10)$$

$$x \text{ mL} = \frac{(36)(10)}{1,000}$$

$$x = 0.36 \text{mL}$$

Self-Test: **Complete the dosage calculations**

1. How many mL are needed for a 64mg dose of a 100mg/10mL solution?

2. How many 0.8g tablets are needed for a dose of 4,000mg?

3. How many grams are in 2,000mL of a 500mg/50mL solution?

Answers:

1. 6.4mL

$$\frac{x \text{ mL}}{64\text{mg}} = \frac{10\text{mL}}{100\text{mg}}$$

$$(x)(100) = (64)(10)$$

$$\frac{640}{100} = 6.4\text{mL}$$

If you want to do a quick check that your answer makes sense, think about 64mg and that this is over half of 100mg. That means our answer needs to be greater than 5mL (half of 10mL).

2. 5 tablets

First we need to convert g to mg.

$$0.8\text{g} \times 1,000 = 800\text{mg}$$

$$\frac{x \text{ tab}}{4,000\text{mg}} = \frac{1\text{tab}}{800\text{mg}}$$

$$(x)(800) = (4,000)(1)$$

$$\frac{4,000}{800} = 5\text{ tabs}$$

3. 20g

$$\frac{x \text{ mg}}{2,000\text{mL}} = \frac{500\text{mg}}{50\text{mL}}$$

$$(x)(50) = (2,000)(500)$$

$$\frac{1,000,000}{50} = 20,000\text{mg}$$

Now convert the mg to g.

$$\frac{20,000\text{mg}}{1,000} = 20\text{g}$$

Days' Supply and Quantity

Pharmacy technicians often complete calculations needed for a total days' supply for prescriptions. This calculation is important for insurance billing if patients have a specified day limit on medications. If the total drug dispensed is incorrect for the days' supply billed to the patient's insurance, it could result in the patient not having sufficient supply for the time frame billed.

Example: A patient is prescribed Norco 1–2 tabs PO Q6–8h PRN pain dispense 40 tabs. Calculate the total days' supply for this order.

1. Start by determining how many tablets the patient will take in 1 day. For range orders, such as 1–2 tablets and 6–8hr, assume the maximum amount a patient could take. In this example, 2 tablets every 6 hours is the most the patient should take.

$$\frac{x \text{ tabs}}{24\text{hr}} = \frac{2 \text{ tabs}}{6\text{hr}}$$

$$(x)(6) = (24)(2)$$

$$\frac{48}{6} = 8 \text{ tabs in 24 hr}$$

2. After finding how many tablets the patient will take in 24 hours, divide the total tablets prescribed by the total needed for 24 hours.

$$\frac{x \text{ days}}{40 \text{ tabs}} = \frac{1 \text{ day}}{8 \text{ tabs}}$$

$$\frac{40 \text{ tab}}{8 \text{ tab}} = 5 \text{ days}$$

This prescription would be billed for 40 tablets = 5-day supply. It's important to assume the patient will take the maximum amount for range orders. If this was calculated as 1 tablet every 6 hours, that would only be a total of 4 tablets per day, which would equal a 10-day supply for 40 tablets. If the patient needed a refill after 5 days, it could be flagged as too early to refill. Calculating days' supply accurately is important not only for clinical safety but also for patient compliance and insurance processing.

Other days' supply orders include calculating the quantity needed for a total days' supply. For example, if a patient is taking 1 tab BID for 30 days, how many tablets are needed to fill this prescription?

To solve, calculate how many tablets are needed for 24 hours, then multiply by the total days' prescribed. For this example, BID = 2 tablets taken daily. 30 days × 2 tabs daily = 60 total tabs.

Example: A patient is taking 2 tab PO QID for 14 days. How many tablets are needed to fill this order?

1. Calculate 24 hr supply. Assume QID = 4 times daily or Q6H.

$$\frac{x \text{ tab}}{24\text{hr}} = \frac{2 \text{ tab}}{6\text{hr}}$$

$$(x)(6) = (24)(2)$$

$$\frac{48}{6} = 8 \text{ tabs in 24 hr}$$

2. Next, multiply the 24hr quantity by the total days' supply needed.

$$\frac{x \text{ tab}}{14 \text{ days}} = \frac{8 \text{ tab}}{1 \text{ day}}$$

$$(x)(1) = (14)(8) = 112 \text{ tabs}$$

You may also encounter calculations in which the answer is not an even number. Always round down for days' supply calculations. Even if your answer is 7.8 days, that is not 8 and by rounding up, a patient wouldn't have enough for the total days.

Example: A patient takes Lantus 15 units subQ TID. How long will one vial of insulin last? Assume 1 vial = 1,000 units/10mL.

1. Calculate how much is taken in 24 hours. You can use ratio-proportion or multiply 15 units by 3 (TID = three times daily).

$$\frac{x \text{ unit}}{24\text{hr}} = \frac{15 \text{ units}}{8\text{hr}}$$

$$(x)(8) = (24)(15)$$

$$\frac{360}{8} = 45 \text{ units}$$

2. Use the total vial contents to determine how many mL is needed for 45 units per day dose.

$$\frac{x \text{ day}}{1,000 \text{ units}} = \frac{1 \text{ day}}{45 \text{ units}}$$

$$(x)(45) = (1,000)(1)$$

$$\frac{1,000}{45} = 22.2 \text{ days} = 22 \text{ days}$$

Self-Test: **Calculating days' supply**

1. A prescriber orders prednisone 20mg 5 tabs QD × 5 days, then 4 tab QD × 3 days, then 2 tabs QD × 3 days, then 1 tab QD × 3 days. Calculate the total amount of prednisone tablets needed to fill this order.

2. A patient is prescribed 200mg of a 250mg/5mL suspension PO QID × 7 days. How many mL is needed to fill the whole prescription?

3. A patient uses 17 units of insulin TID. How many vials of 1,000 units/10mL does he need for a 30-day supply?

4. A patient has a prescription for Lantus SoloSTAR insulin pen. Each pen contains 450 units of insulin in 1.5mL. There are 3 pens per box. A patient takes 30 units BID and must prime the pen with 2 units at each injection. Calculate how many days the box of pens will last the patient.

Answers:

1. 46 tabs

    Start by calculating the daily amount for each quantity. Remember that QD = daily.

    5 tabs QD × 5 days = 25 tabs

    4 tabs QD × 3 days = 12 tabs

    2 tabs QD × 3 days = 6 tabs

    1 tab QD × 3 days = 3 tabs

    25 + 12 + 6 + 3 = 46 tabs

2. 112mL

    First, determine how many mL are needed for 1 day.

    $$\frac{x \text{ mL}}{200\text{mg}} = \frac{5\text{ml}}{250\text{mg}}$$

    $$(x)(250) = (200)(5)$$

    $$\frac{1,000}{250} = 4\text{mL}$$

    QID = 4 times daily

    $4 \times 4\text{mL} = 16\text{mL}$ daily

Next, multiply the total days needed by the daily amount.

$$\frac{x \text{ mL}}{7 \text{ days}} = \frac{16 \text{mL}}{1 \text{ day}}$$

$$(x)(1) = (7)(16)$$

$$(7)(16) = 112 \text{mL}$$

3. 2 vials

First, calculate the daily amount of insulin total.

TID = 3 times daily

$$(17)(3) = 51 \text{ units daily}$$

Next, determine how many days 1 vial will last

$$\frac{x \text{ days}}{1,000 \text{ units}} = \frac{1 \text{ day}}{51 \text{ units}}$$

$$(x)(51) = (1,000)(1)$$

$$\frac{1,000}{51} = 19.6 \text{ days}$$

1 vial will last 19 days, so divide 30 (days in a month) by the total days per 1 vial to see how many vials are needed.

$$\frac{30}{19} = 1.5 = 2 \text{ vials}$$

4. 23 days

First, calculate how many insulin units the patient needs daily.

BID = 2 times daily

$$(30)(2) = 60 \text{ units daily}$$

$$(2 \text{ units to prime})(2) = 4 \text{ units}$$

$$(60) + (4) = 64 \text{ total units daily}$$

Next, calculate the total of units in one box of pens.

$$\frac{x \text{ units}}{3 \text{ pens}} = \frac{450 \text{ units}}{1 \text{ pen}}$$

$$(450)(3) = 1,500 \text{ units in 1 box}$$

$$\frac{x \text{ day}}{1,500 \text{ units}} = \frac{1 \text{ day}}{64 \text{ units}} = 23.4 \text{ days or round down to 23 days}$$

Percent Concentration

Percent concentrations are an expression of the ratio of active ingredient in total product. This is expressed as a solid in a liquid (w/v), solid in a solid (w/w), or liquid in a liquid (v/v). For example, a 5% solution of alcohol is 5mL alcohol in a 100mL solution.

See the following chart for a summary of each percent concentration.

w/v	Weight/volume	Solid in a liquid vehicle	g active ingredient per 100mL
w/w	Weight/weight	Solid in a solid vehicle	g active ingredient per 100g
v/v	Volume/volume	Liquid in a liquid vehicle	mL active ingredient per 100mL

Percent concentrations are used often to determine how much active ingredient is in a specified amount, in order to properly dose a medication.

Example: How much hydrocortisone is in a 2.5% tube of 45 grams?

This would be considered a w/w percent, as there is a solid (hydrocortisone) dissolved in 45g of cream base. To solve, set up a ratio-proportion. In this case, the unknown is how many grams hydrocortisone are in 45g. The ratio is 2.5g in every 100g (2.5%).

$$\frac{x \text{ g}}{45\text{g}} = \frac{2.5\text{g}}{100\text{g}}$$

Then solve for x.

$$(x)(100) = (45)(2.5)$$

$$\frac{112.5}{100} = 1.125\text{g}$$

Again, you can check your answer by looking at the problem and checking that it makes sense. If there are 2.5g in every 100g, and we are trying to find how many grams are in 45g, look at the relationship between 45 and 100. 45 is just about half of 100. This means the answer should be just about half of 2.5.

The same type of problem can be completed with a w/v.

Example: How many grams of sodium chloride are in a 500mL bag of 0.9% solution?

Set up your ratio-proportion. Remember w/v = g/100mL.

$$\frac{x \text{ g}}{500\text{mL}} = \frac{0.9\text{g}}{100\text{mL}} \qquad (x)(100) = (500)(0.9)$$

$$\frac{450}{100} = 4.5\text{g}$$

Last, in a volume/volume or v/v, you can calculate how many mL are in a solution.

Example: How many mL of IPA are in 15mL of a 60% solution?

$$\frac{x \text{ mL}}{15\text{mL}} = \frac{60\text{mL}}{100\text{mL}} \quad (x)(100) = (15)(60)$$

$$\frac{900}{100} = 9\text{mL}$$

Self-Test: **Percent concentration**

1. How many g ingredient are in 15g of a 5% cream?

2. How many mg are in 200mL of a 10% solution?

3. How many mL are in 500mL of a 3% solution?

Answers:

1. 0.75g

$$\frac{x \text{ g}}{15\text{g}} = \frac{5\text{g}}{100\text{g}}$$

$$(x)(100) = (15)(5)$$

$$\frac{75}{100} = 0.75\text{g}$$

2. 20,000mg

This question is asking for mg, but remember w/v is in g/100mL. You must first find the grams, then convert to milligrams.

$$\frac{x \text{ g}}{200\text{mL}} = \frac{10\text{g}}{100\text{mL}}$$

$$(x)(100) = (200)(10)$$

$$\frac{2,000}{100} = 20\text{g}$$

$$(20\text{g})(1,000) = 20,000\text{mg}$$

3. 15mL

$$\frac{x \text{ mL}}{500\text{mL}} = \frac{3\text{mL}}{100\text{mL}}$$

$$(x)(100) = (500)(3)$$

$$\frac{1,500}{100} = 15\text{mL}$$

Dilutions

A dilution is the process of decreasing the concentration of a solution. This is usually done through the addition of more solvent, or base solution. In the pharmacy, you may see more concentrated solutions that are then diluted to a less-concentrated form or larger volume.

Calculating a dilution can be completed using the following equation.

$$(C1)(V1)=(C2)(V2)$$

C1 = concentration of stock

V1 = volume of stock

C2 = final concentration of desired product

V2 = final volume of desired product

Example: An order is written for 100mL of a 10% solution. You have a 15% solution in stock. How much stock solution and how much diluent is needed to compound this order?

First, determine the values for the variables in the equation.

C1 = 15

V1 = x

C2 = 10

V2 = 100

Solve for x.

$$(15)(x)=(10)(100)$$

$$x=\frac{(10)(100)}{15}$$

x = 66.7mL of stock solution is needed

This question also asks for quantity of diluent needed with the stock solution. This can be found by taking the final volume and subtracting the stock volume needed.

100mL − 66.7mL = 33.3mI

33.3mL diluent is added to 66.7mL stock solution to get a final volume of 100mL.

***Self-Test:* Dilutions**

1. An order is written for 250mL of a 20% solution. You have a 40% solution in stock. How much stock solution and how much diluent are needed to compound this order?

2. An order is written for 500mL of a 50% solution. You have a 75% solution in stock. How much stock solution and how much diluent are needed to compound this order?

Answers:

1. 125mL stock, 125mL diluent

$$C1 = 40$$

$$V1 = x$$

$$C2 = 20$$

$$V2 = 250$$

$$(40)(x) = (20)(250)$$

$$\frac{5,000}{40} = 125\text{mL}$$

125mL of 40% solution is needed.

Now find the diluent by subtracting from the total desired volume.

$$250 - 125 = 125\text{mL}$$

2. 333.3mL stock, 166.7mL diluent

$$C1 = 75$$

$$V1 = x$$

$$C2 = 50$$

$$V2 = 500$$

$$(75)(x) = (50)(500)$$

$$\frac{25,000}{75} = 333.3\text{mL}$$

333.3mL of 75% solution is needed.

Now find the diluent by subtracting from the total desired volume.

$$500 - 333.3 = 166.7\text{mL}$$

Alligations

Alligations are another method of calculating dilutions. In this method, you have two stock concentrations and are calculating how much of each is needed to compound a final product. The final product will have a concentration between the two stock solutions used.

To solve an alligation, you set up a grid or tic-tac-toe board.

Next, place the higher concentration in the top left corner, the lower concentration in the bottom left, and the desired strength (what you are solving for) in the middle box.

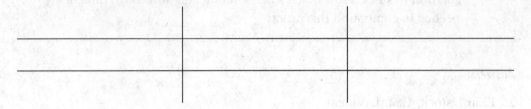

After the table is set up, subtract the desired concentration from the higher concentration and put this value in the bottom right corner. Do the same for the lower concentration, and put this number in the upper right hand corner (ignore the negative value).

These values reflect the number of parts needed for the higher strength and lower strengths, respectively.

These differences total the number of parts needed for each concentration. The top right is equivalent to the total parts needed for the higher strength and the bottom left is equal to the total parts needed for the lower strength. Adding these parts together will equal the total parts needed.

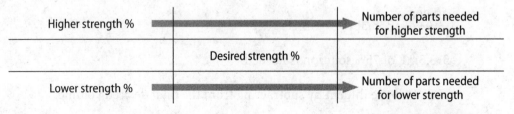

Now a ratio-proportion can be set up to determine the total parts that will be needed for each concentration. There are some diluents, such as water or petrolatum, that have no concentration, and therefore 0 will be used as the concentration percentage in the grid.

Example: Prepare 300 grams of 2.5% hydrocortisone cream using 5% and 1% hydrocortisone base. Determine how many grams of each are required to compound this order.

1. Set up the alligation putting the higher concentration in the top left, lower concentration in the bottom left, and desired concentration in the middle. You do not need to include the units (%).

5		
	2.5	
1		

2. Next, subtract the difference to find the total parts needed and place this into the top right and bottom right squares.

5		1.5
	2.5	
1		2.5

3. Looking at the differences of each diagonal subtraction, there are 1.5 parts of the 5% and 2.5 parts needed of the 1%. Now add together these parts to get the total parts needed.

$1.5 + 2.5 = 4$ total parts

4. Now you can set up a ratio-proportion to determine the quantity of each needed.

For the 5% hydrocortisone, we need 1.5 parts out of 4 total parts. We can compare this to the total amount to be compounded (300g).

$$\frac{x \text{ g}}{300\text{g}} = \frac{1.5 \text{ parts}}{4 \text{ parts}}$$

$$(x)(4) = (300)(1.5)$$

$$\frac{450}{4} = 112.5 \text{g of hydrocortisone 5\%}$$

5. The same process should be completed to determine how much 1% hydrocortisone is needed. For 1% hydrocortisone, 2.5 parts are needed out of 4 parts.

$$\frac{x\,g}{300g} = \frac{2.5 \text{parts}}{4 \text{parts}}$$

$$(x)(4) = (300)(2.5)$$

$$\frac{750}{4} = 187.5 \text{ g of hydrocortisone } 1\%$$

The answers would be 112.5g of hydrocortisone 5% and 187.5g of hydrocortisone 1%. To check your answer, be sure that the two totals from each concentration add up to the desired quantity. In this case 112.5 + 187.5 = 300.

> ### *Self-Test:* **Alligations**
> Round the answer to the nearest tenth place.
>
> 1. Prepare 100mL of 75% isopropyl alcohol using 90% and 20% IPA base. Determine how many mL of each are required to compound this order.
>
> 2. Prepare 45 g of 5% coal tar ointment using a 3% and 10% base. Determine how many grams are required to compound this order.

Answers:

1. 76.8mL of the 90% IPA and 21.4mL of the 20% IPA

    First set up your alligation grid.

90			55
		75	
20			15

    Add up your total parts: 55 + 15 = 70

    Set up a ratio-proportion. Remember the parts per each concentration are directly to the right of each concentration.

    For the 90% IPA:

    $$\frac{x \text{ mL}}{100mL} = \frac{55 \text{ parts}}{70 \text{ parts}}$$

    $$(x)(70) = (100)(55)$$

$$\frac{5,500}{70} = 78.6 \text{mL of the} 90\% \text{ IPA}$$

For the 20% IPA:

$$\frac{x \text{ mL}}{100 \text{mL}} = \frac{15 \text{ parts}}{70 \text{ parts}}$$

$$(x)(70) = (100)(15)$$

$$\frac{1,500}{70} = 21.4 \text{mL of the 20\% IPA}$$

Check your answers by adding your two quantities together:
78.6 + 21.4 = 100mL

2. 12.9g of 10% and 32.1g of the 3%

First set up your alligation grid.

10			2
		5	
3			5

Add up your total parts: 2 + 5 = 7

Set up a ratio-proportion. Remember the parts per each concentration are directly to the right of each concentration.

For the 10% coal tar:

$$\frac{x \text{ g}}{45 \text{g}} = \frac{2 \text{ parts}}{7 \text{ parts}}$$

$$(x)(7) = (45)(2)$$

$$\frac{90}{7} = 12.9 \text{g of the 10\%}$$

For the 3% coal tar:

$$\frac{x \text{ g}}{45 \text{g}} = \frac{5 \text{ parts}}{7 \text{ parts}}$$

$$(x)(7) = (45)(5)$$

$$\frac{225}{7} = 32.1 \text{g of the} 3\%$$

Check your answers by adding your two quantities together:
12.9 + 32.1 = 45g

Nonsterile Compounding Processes

Compounding is the process of mixing together two or more ingredients to create a medication specific to the needs of a patient. Compounded medications are those that are not available from a manufacturer and must be altered in some way for a patient order. Nonsterile compounding is often prescribed for patients to allow for a different dosing method or flavor, which in turn may help improve patient compliance. Compounding includes the addition of an active ingredient to an inert or inactive substance known as an **excipient**. The inactive substance could be a filler, flavor, binder, dye, or other component that does not alter the active ingredient, but assists the delivery of the medication.

Having the proper equipment is essential to following all standards and practices in nonsterile compounding. A clean area is required for compounding, and proper PPE must be worn. This may include just gloves, though it is recommended to don a hair cover, gown, and mask with a lab coat or clean scrubs. PPE is essential when compounding hazardous substances or aerosolizing particles.

When compounding nonsterile products, a balance is often used to weigh substances. Many states require pharmacies to have a Class A balance. This type of balance consists of a two-pan system, with the substance being weighed in one pan and the calibration weights in the other, measuring the weight of the substance. Weigh papers or weigh boats are used to keep the ingredients in place while weighing. After the weight of the paper or boat is found, it is zeroed from the scale so it will not be included in the final weight of the measured substance. An electronic or digital scale can also be used for measuring.

For liquids, measurement occurs in beakers and graduated or conical cylinders. A **beaker** (Figure 5.1) is a cylindrical container, usually glass, that has a flat bottom. It typically will have a spout to pour from and can also be used for mixing and heating liquids. A **graduated cylinder** (Figure 5.2) is a tall, narrow container which has straight sides. A **conical cylinder** (Figure 5.3) is similar to a graduated cylinder, except it is cone-shaped (wider at the bottom than the top). When you are measuring a liquid, it is important to read the measurement at the bottom of the curved fluid surface, which is known as the **meniscus** (Figure 5.4). This allows for a more accurate measurement, as reading the top of the meniscus would be an inaccurately high value and too much liquid would be used. **Glass stirring rods** can be used if any compound needs dissolved or to be mixed thoroughly.

Figure 5.1 Beaker

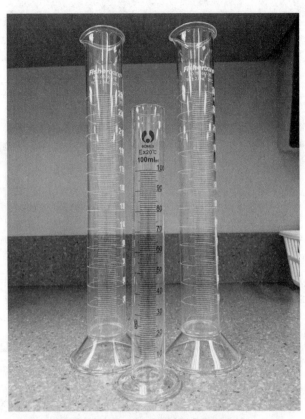

Figure 5.2 Graduated cylinders

Figure 5.3 Conical cylinders

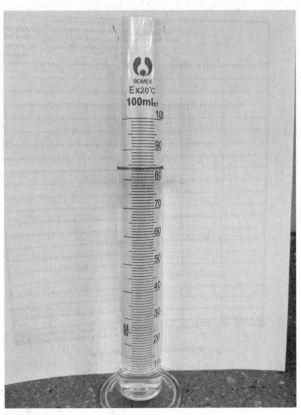

Figure 5.4 Graduated cylinder showing the meniscus

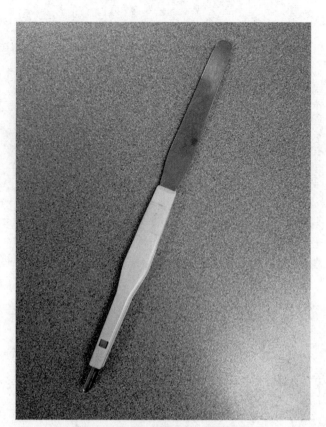

Figure 5.5 Glass mortar and pestle   **Figure 5.6 Stainless Steel Spatula**

If tablets or powders must be crushed or mixed, a **mortar and pestle** (Figure 5.5) may be used. A mortar is a bowl, and a pestle is a tool with a rounded end that is used for crushing and grinding. **Trituration** is the process of reducing a particle to a powder through grinding using a mortar and pestle.

When compounding pastes, gels, creams, or ointments, a **spatula** (Figure 5.6) may be used for mixing ingredients. A spatula has a handle and a flat blade on the end that is typically made of stainless steel, rubber, or plastic. **Spatulation** is the process of using a spatula to mix substances together. An **ointment slab** may be used for mixing, which is a large glass or porcelain slab that offers a hard, nonabsorbable surface for combining ingredients.

Levigation is also a technique used to mix substances together, specifically grinding powder (similar to tritruation) but with a small amount of liquid. The liquid used is known as a **levigating agent**, and this helps make a smoother compound.

When mixing together powders that are of unequal size, **geometric dilution** is the process that can be used to ensure a well-mixed compound. In this process, the smallest amount of powder is added first and mixed with an equal amount of the powder in the larger quantity. That mixture is then mixed with an equal amount of the larger quantity and repeated until the entire mixture is completed.

Compounding Record Keeping

Once you have the supplies needed for your compound, it is important to review the master formula record (MFR) or "recipe" for your compound you are preparing. USP<795> requires the MFR be followed for all compounds. The MFR contains:

- Drug name, strength, and dosage form
- Amount of all component needed
- Complete instructions for preparation, including equipment, supplies, and compounding steps
- Description of final product
- Assigned beyond-use-date (BUD) and requirements for storage (reference also required)
- Calculations if applicable
- Labeling requirements, such as "shake well"
- Quality control procedures, such as visual inspection or expected result

The MFR is the process to be followed for each compound to ensure standardization of the formula. A compounding record is also required for each compound. This is different from the MFR in that it is unique for each specific compound completed. The MFR is the recipe used each time, while the compounding record is a log of the actual compound that is made. A compounding record must include:

- Name, strength, and dosage form of final compound
- Date and time of preparation
- Assigned internal identification number (such as prescription number)
- Individuals involved in the compounding process
- Lot numbers, expiration dates, and manufacturer of each component used
- Weight or measurement of each component
- Total quantity compounded
- Assigned BUD and required storage
- Calculations if any were required
- Physical description of final product
- Results of final control procedures
- Copy of the MFR
- Copy of the patient label

Beyond-use-dates (BUDs) are calculated based on guidance from USP<795>. The final BUD of a compounded product cannot exceed the expiration date of any of the individual components. So if there are three ingredients in a compound, and one of them expires in 4 days, the BUD will have to be 4 days.

The required storage conditions and BUDs for compounded products follow.

COMPOUNDED PRODUCT	BUD	STORAGE CONDITIONS
Aqueous dosage forms with a preservative (emulsions, gels, creams, solutions, sprays, or suspensions)	30 days	Controlled room temperature
Aqueous dosage forms without a preservative (emulsions, gels, creams, solutions, sprays, or suspensions)	14 days	Refrigerated
Nonaqueous dosage forms (suppositories, ointments)	90 days	Controlled room temperature
Solid dosage forms (capsule, tablet, powder)	180 days	Controlled room temperature

Now you know the tools and documentation needed for nonsterile compounding. Let's discuss the different types of compounds you may encounter as a pharmacy technician.

Compounding Ointments

An ointment is a semisolid compound used topically on the skin. Ointments help protect the skin by providing a barrier against moisture and air. When compounding an ointment, the medication is added to a base. For example, hydrocortisone ointment is made by adding hydrocortisone to a semisolid base. Some examples of bases used in compounding ointments include:

- Petrolatum (Vaseline)
- Lanolin
- Paraffin
- Eucerin
- Polyethylene glycol (PEG)

Ointments are compounded through spatulation and geometric dilution to mix a semisolid base with the active ingredient. They may also require heat to melt the waxy base and dissolve all substances; once cooled, the compound will congeal into an ointment. After the ointment has been compounded, it is transferred into an ointment jar to be labeled and dispensed.

Compounding Mixtures and Emulsions

An emulsion is a mixture consisting of two liquids that do not normally mix together. There are two different types of emulsions—oil-in-water (o/w) *and* water-in-oil (w/o). Creams and lotions are emulsions and can be either o/w or w/o. If it is oil-in-water, it contains more water than oil and will leave a wet sensation on the skin. Water-in-oil has more oil content and leaves a greasier feel after being applied. Creams typically have a higher oil content than lotions, which makes them thicker. Lotions have a higher water content and are moisturizing. This allows lotions to be spread over large parts of the body, as thinner emulsions are easier to spread.

The active ingredient is first weighed, prior to compounding. If needed, a mortar and pestle can be used to crush it to a powder. A levigating agent can be added to wet the mixture. Following the formulation record closely is very important. The cream or lotion base can be added into the mixture. When compounding emulsions, it is important to make sure the emulsion is well-mixed to allow the active ingredient to be consistent in each dose. After compounding, the cream or lotion can be transferred to a container, similar to an ointment jar, and labeled to be dispensed.

Compounding Liquids

Oral liquid dosage forms can be compounded into elixirs, solutions, suspensions, or syrups. An elixir is a clear, sweet solution that contains alcohol. The amount of alcohol in elixirs varies depending on the compound—the concentration needed is the amount required to keep the drug in solution. Elixirs are used infrequently, and there are many patients who should avoid use of elixirs, including children, patients who take medications that may interact with alcohol, patients with a history of alcohol abuse, and patients who are pregnant.

Solutions are composed of a liquid with a completely dissolved active ingredient. A beaker and stirring rod may be used to help compound a solution with a liquid and powder. A solution may also be a dilution of a concentrate. This is compounded by adding a diluent to the concentrated liquid to reduce the concentration and increase the volume. Because a solution is completely dissolved, it does not require shaking after compounded.

Suspensions, on the other hand, must be shaken before administering each time to disperse the drug evenly. A suspension is a powder with a specified amount of diluent added. The powder never fully dissolves, and this is one of the disadvantages of suspensions, as there is potential for settling of the drug and nonuniformity throughout the bottle. Suspensions do allow for flavoring and the ability to mask unpleasant taste. When compounding a suspension, a compounding record and MFR is not required, as the instructions for mixing are supplied by the manufacturer.

Syrups are made of mostly sugar and water. They can be flavoring syrup, such as cherry syrup, or medicinal syrup, which has an active ingredient added, such as loratadine syrup. Syrups are sticky and become stickier with higher sugar content. They should be avoided in patients with diabetes.

Oral liquids are often compounded for flavoring to help with patient compliance. Pharmacy technicians may add flavoring agents to suspensions or solutions prior to dispensing. A specific formula is followed, depending on which flavor is used and which medication is being flavored. Flavoring does require a compounding record or modify the BUD of the suspension or solution.

Compounding Capsules

Capsules can be compounded for patients who may be unable to or have difficulty swallowing tablets. They can also be compounded for a patient if the prescribed dose is unavailable or if a patient has a sensitivity to one of the inactive ingredients in the manufactured product.

Capsules consist of a base known as a body, and a cap, known as the head. Sizes of capsules range from 5 being the smallest to 000 being the largest.

The following chart indicates the capsule size and the average mg amount contained.

CAPSULE SIZE	AVERAGE AMOUNT CONTAINED
5	50 mg
4	150 mg
3	200 mg
2	250 mg
1	300 mg
0	450 mg
00	750 mg
000	1,000 mg

To compound capsules, a capsule-filling machine or the punch method can be used. A filling machine is a device that can fill many capsules at one time. The punch method is used for a smaller quantity. In this method, the height of the active ingredient powder is the same height as the capsule base. The pharmacy technician compounding can then punch the capsule into this powder, which will fill the entire base. This method does create some difficulty in ensuring an even distribution of ingredient in each capsule.

Compounding Suppositories

Suppositories are solid dosage forms that are inserted into the body and melt at body temperature or dissolve into the mucous membranes. They are compounded using a mold depending on the type of suppository (they can be administered into the rectum, vagina, or urethra).

There are a few different types of bases used for suppositories. Cocoa butter is solid at room temperature, but around body temperature, it melts into an oil and can release medication into the surrounding membranes. Suppositories made of cocoa butter should be refrigerated in warmer climates.

Another base use is polyethylene glycol (PEG), which does not melt at body temperature but dissolves and provides a more prolonged release. These suppositories also do not require refrigeration, as they do not dissolve at elevated temperatures.

When compounding suppositories, the active ingredient is added to the base and melted into a liquid to be mixed thoroughly. This solution is poured into the suppository mold and cooled until the suppositories harden. They are then packaged and dispensed to a patient with proper storage instructions depending on the base used for compounding.

Compounding Enemas

Enemas are solutions that are administered rectally to help initiate a bowel evacuation. Because they are not administered into the bloodstream, they are safe to compound in a clean, nonsterile environment.

To compound an enema, the active ingredient is measured and weighed. This may require crushing of tablets into a fine powder to dissolve into the solution. For example, if a prescriber requests an antibiotic enema of 1,000mg, and the pharmacy stocks 500mg tablets, two tablets must be triturated with a mortar and pestle. This powder is then mixed into the vehicle base solution of enema and titrated to the desired quantity. This is then poured into an enema bag for patient administration.

Equipment and Supplies for Drug Administration

As a pharmacy technician, you will be filling different types of orders for patients. With each order, you will choose the best package type and size to dispense the medication. For safety and to prevent accidental poisoning of children, all medications must be dispensed in a child-resistant container. This is a result of the Poison Prevention Packaging Act of 1970 (PPPA), which requires most OTC and prescription drugs be packaged in containers that cannot be opened by 80% of children under five, but can be opened by 90% of adults. Patients who have difficulty opening containers may request a non-child-resistant container and sign a waiver or acknowledgment in the pharmacy computer system so future prescriptions are filled without the safety cap. There are exceptions to the PPPA and drugs that are exempt from child-resistant packaging. Some of these include sublingual nitroglycerin, oral contraceptives, or powdered aspirin.

Package Size

Pharmacy technicians in a retail pharmacy count prescriptions and dispense into amber vials (Figure 5.7). Many medications are sensitive to light, and the amber bottle helps protect from light degradation. Amber prescription vials are measured in drams. They typically range in size from a 6-dram vial (smallest) to a 60-dram vial (largest).

Figure 5.7 Amber vials

Figure 5.8 Capsules being counted on a counting tray

**Figure 5.9 Using the spout to pour into
the bottle of an appropriate size**

Figure 5.10 Amber bottles for liquids

Figure 5.11 Fluid oz markings for amber liquid bottle

After counting the prescription on a counting tray (Figure 5.8), use the spout to pour the medication into the vial (Figure 5.9). You should choose a vial that is a closest fit to the quantity dispensed, but careful to not overfill the bottle.

When dispensing liquid medications, you use amber bottles that are measured in fluid ounces. Remember the conversion for fluid ounces to mL (1 fl oz = 30mL). The same is true for liquids as solid doses—select the bottle size closest to the prescription without overfilling the bottle. You may need to do some quick math when selecting the bottle size for your prescription. For example, if a prescription is written for 115mL, which size bottle would you select?

Look at the bottles in Figure 5.10. You can choose between a 2, 3, 4, or 6 fl oz bottle. If you choose a 3 fl oz bottle, that would be 90mL—not enough. If you choose a 6 fl oz bottle, that would be 180mL—which seems like some wasted space. A 4 fl oz bottle gives you 120mL, which is the perfect size. If you ever aren't sure of the size of a bottle, you can look at the fl oz markings on the side. Figure 5.11 shows the fl oz markings on a 14 fl oz bottle in increments of 2 fl oz.

Many pharmacies stock a variety of different-size bottles for liquid medications, while some stick with the four most commonly used sizes, as shown previously. A conversion chart for fluid ounces to mL for a quick reference follows.

1 fl oz	30 mL
2 fl oz	60 mL
3 fl oz	90 mL
4 fl oz	120 mL
6 fl oz	180 mL
8 fl oz	240 mL
10 fl oz	300 mL
12 fl oz	360 mL

Unit Dose, Repackaging, and Unit-of-Use

A **unit dose** medication is a drug packaged for a single administration. They can be purchased from the manufacturer as a unit dose or repackaged on site from a bulk bottle into unit dose packages. Oral solid medications are the majority of unit dose products, such as tablets or capsules, though liquids can also be packaged in unit dose cups (Figure 5.12).

Unit doses are dispensed most commonly in the institutional setting, because it allows reuse of a medication if the package has not been opened. Unit dose also allows the nurse or caregiver administering the medication the ability to dispense without manipulation, and scan to the bar code prior to dispensing. This is safer for the patient and more efficient for the nurse.

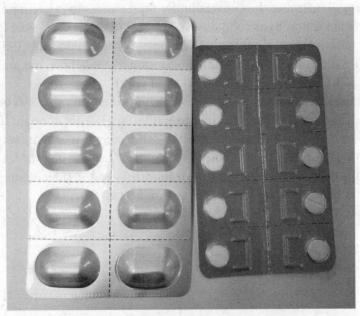

Figure 5.12 Unit dose capsules and tablets

In a hospital, much of the drug inventory stored outside of the main pharmacy is within an automated dispensing machine or cabinet (ADM or ADC). Unit dose medications must be used to stock the ADMs, as bar code scanning is required prior to loading the machine. The doses in dispensing cabinets are not patient specific, so if a nurse pulls five different medications for a patient and then the patient is discharged and unable to take those medications, they can be returned back to the machine to be redispensed to another patient (if unopened). This helps decrease costs of inventory and prevents wasting the drug. The packaging of the drug protects both the identification as well as the integrity (prevents breakdown) of the medication.

The FDA does have requirements for the labeling of each unit dose medication. This includes:

- Drug name and quantity of active ingredient per unit (e.g., 300mg in 5mL or 30mg tablet)
- Expiration date
- Lot number
- Name of manufacturer
- Special storage requirements, such as refrigerate or protect from light
- Special dosing characteristics, such as sustained release or enteric coated
- Statement: Warning may be habit forming, for controlled substances
- Bar code
- NDC number (not required but is recommended)

Although unit dose medications are safer and more efficient for hospitals, they are not always cheaper to purchase. A hospital may find that buying a bulk bottle of medication and repacking is more cost effective than purchasing the unit dose directly from the manufacturer. Or a medication may not yet be available in unit dose packaging. Regardless of the reason, hospitals must dispense unit dose medications to patients and ensure the labeling and bar coding is appropriate for administration. **Repackaging** is a common practice that allows hospitals to dispense unit dose medications and maintain safety and efficiency.

The FDA defines repackaging as "taking a finished drug product from the container in which it was distributed by the manufacturer and placing into a different container without further manipulation." In other words, a pharmacy technician removes the drug from a bulk bottle and packages into individual doses for distribution.

Labeling of repackaged medication is just as important as unit dose medications. Repackaged drugs act similarly to unit dose, though the BUD is typically shorter due to removal from original packaging. A pharmacy must keep a log of all repackaged medications. The log should include the information required on the label (a copy of the label will work), how much was repacked, and the signatures of the technician repacking and pharmacist verifying accuracy.

The label on a repackaged medication must include the following:

- "This drug was repackaged by [NAME OF FACILITY]"
- Address and phone number of facility repacking
- Drug name
- Lot number of drug being repackaged
- Dosage form and strength
- Date of drug repackaging
- BUD as the expiration date for the repackaged product
- Storage and handling instructions
- NDC of repackaged drug
- Manufacturer name and lot number

The BUD of the repackaged drug depends on the dosage form. These BUDs are for nonsterile repacking only, which follows USP<795> guidelines. For pharmacies completing sterile repacking, USP<797> standards must be followed.

FORMULATION	BUD
Nonaqueous formulations	6 months, or expiration date of drug being repacked if sooner
Water-containing oral formulations	14 days, or expiration date of drug being repacked if sooner
Water-containing topical/dermal liquid and semisolid formulations	30 days, or expiration date of drug being repacked if sooner

Unit-of-use packaging is packaging that allows for a medication to be dispensed directly to a patient without any manipulation except applying a label (Figure 5.13). Whereas unit dose delivers enough medication for one dose, or for 24 hours, unit-of-use is designed to deliver medication for the duration of therapy. For example, a blister pack of oral contraception for a 28-day supply is dispensed as a pack with a label applied. The tablets are not punched through the blister pack and put in a bottle for the patient. This is considered unit-of-use. Additional examples

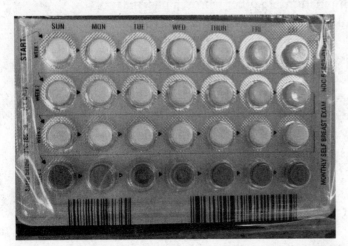 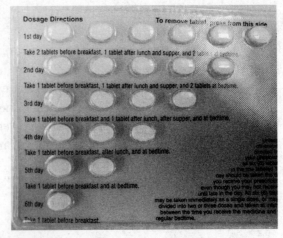

Figure 5.13 Unit-of-Use Medications

include 30-day starter packs or a steroid dose pack that is administered as a full course of treatment.

Oral and Injectable Syringes

Syringes are used for both oral administration and injection of medications. An injectable syringe should use a **Luer lock** so a needle can be screwed on the top, whereas an oral syringe has a flat or slip tip that a cap can slip on (Figure 5.14). Luer-lock syringes have a threading mechanism that allows a needle to screw on tight and prevent it from falling off.

Because of the similarity between oral and injectable syringes, the ISMP has developed safe practice recommendations to avoid inadvertent administration of an oral medication into an IV line. These may include using amber-colored oral syringes and implementing a quality assurance process when a patient has both an IV line and any kind of tube-feeding line. Oral syringes are labeled with "FOR ORAL USE ONLY" to help prevent errors (Figure 5.15).

Oral syringes are used for liquid medications, most commonly for pediatric patients. They are used without a needle, but are more precise than a dosing cup or household tool (such as a teaspoon or tablespoon). A syringe cap is attached to the tip of an oral syringe after drawing up the medication.

Injectable syringes are usually hypodermic and can hold anywhere from 3mL to 60mL. A needle is attached to a hypodermic syringe and can be used for sterile compounding or patient administration, such as IM or IV push. Selecting the smallest size syringe to fit the total volume is similar to selecting the smallest size vial to fit the tablets being counted. The closer to the total volume you can get without overfilling, the better. For example, you have a 3mL, 5mL, and 10mL syringe in stock and need to draw up 4.8mL. You would choose the 5mL syringe, as the 3mL would not be large enough, and the 10mL would be less accurate than the 5mL measurement.

Insulin syringes are also used for patients with diabetes when administering insulin. These syringes hold 1mL or less, and are measured in both mL and insulin

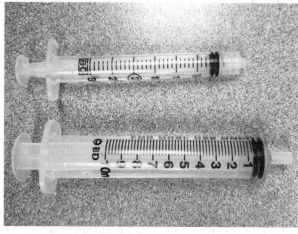

Figure 5.14 An injectable syringe with a Luer lock versus an oral syringe

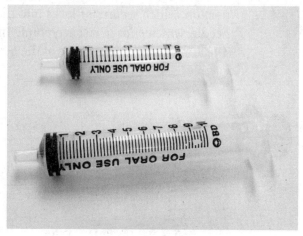

Figure 5.15 Oral syringe without Luer lock

units. Insulin syringes will indicate total units per mL. For example, a U-100 syringe contains 100 units/1mL.

Tuberculin syringes are also small syringes that are designed for 1mL intradermal administration of tuberculin purified protein derivative (PPD). This injection helps diagnosis tuberculosis in a patient. Tuberculin syringes often come prepackaged with the needle already attached.

Syringes are all made of the same components—a plunger and a barrel. The plunger is used to draw up the medication into the syringe. The barrel is a tube with the calibration lines used for measuring volume. The top of the plunger is black rubber within the syringe that is used to determine where to read the measurement. The top of the plunger is where the measurement should be read. (See Figure 5.16.)

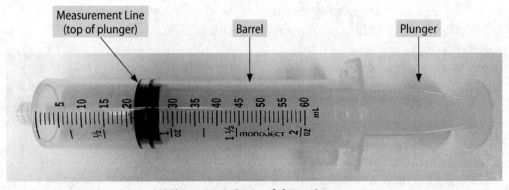

Figure 5.16 Parts of the syringe

Needles

A needle is attached to a syringe for sterile compounding and for medication administration. Pharmacy technicians use various size needles depending on the type of solution or suspension that is being drawn up. Needles used for medication administration are typically smaller to help minimize pain with injection.

There are three main parts to a needle. The hub of the needle is the bottom portion, which secures or locks into the syringe. The shaft is the long stem of the needle, which ends in a sharp point. The point of the needle is known as the bevel. The lumen is the hollow bore of the bevel.

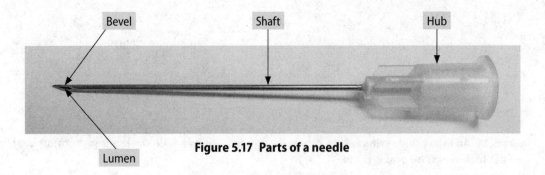

Figure 5.17 Parts of a needle

The size of the needle is determined by the gauge and length. The gauge of the needle ranges from 6G to 32G, with the most commonly used gauges between 15G and 32G. The size of the needle increases as the number of gauge decreases, so a 6G needle is the largest gauge and a 32G needle is the smallest. The size of gauge used depends on what procedure is being administered. Small gauge or large needles are used for viscous or thick liquids to help draw fluid into the syringe. Using this size for administration, however, would be painful, so larger gauge, or smaller, needles should be used.

The following chart shows the gauge of needle used for medication administration.

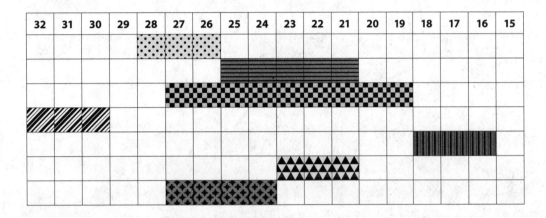

32	31	30	29	28	27	26	25	24	23	22	21	20	19	18	17	16	15

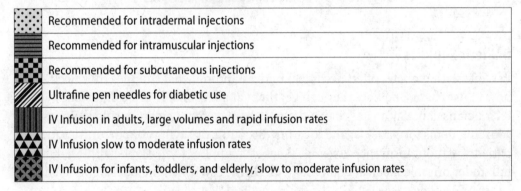

(dotted)	Recommended for intradermal injections
(horizontal lines)	Recommended for intramuscular injections
(checkerboard)	Recommended for subcutaneous injections
(diagonal lines)	Ultrafine pen needles for diabetic use
(vertical lines)	IV Infusion in adults, large volumes and rapid infusion rates
(triangles)	IV Infusion slow to moderate infusion rates
(cross-hatch)	IV Infusion for infants, toddlers, and elderly, slow to moderate infusion rates

The length of the needle is also important when selecting a size. Needle lengths range from 3/8 inch to 3 1/2 inch. Smaller length needles would be used for injections closer to the surface of the skin, such as intradermal injections. For intramuscular injections, the needle must inject under the muscle and must therefore be longer. Needle length and gauge are indicated on the needle packaging. For example, the following needle is a 22 gauge 1 1/2 inch needle (Figure 5.18).

Figure 5.18 Needle with cap indicating size

Injections are also given at specific angles depending on the injection type. The following chart and graphic (Figure 5.19) showing the location and angle of each injection. This can be helpful when understanding what size needle should be used for administration of medication.

INJECTION TYPE	ANGLE OF INSERTION
Intradermal	10°–15°
Subcutaneous	45°
Intramuscular	90°

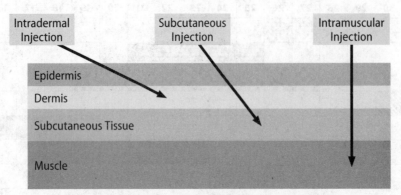

Figure 5.19 Location and angle of injections

Diabetic Supplies

Patients with diabetes often need help understanding what supplies they need, how to use them, and how they can get them at a reasonable price. Pharmacy technicians can play a vital role in diabetes management by procuring supplies, sourcing items for patients, and locating discounts or savings opportunities to patients without insurance coverage. Diabetic supplies for patients with Medicare fall under durable medical equipment, or **DME**. DME also includes items such as canes or crutches, wheelchairs, or other medical devices.

Patients with diabetes need to continuously monitor blood glucose levels. To do this at home, a **glucometer** is recommended. Glucometers are manufactured by many different vendors, and each has its own unique **test strips**. The test strip collects the blood from the patient and is inserted into the glucometer, which then reads the blood glucose levels. To draw blood, a patient may use a **lancet**, which is a device that quickly pricks the skin.

If patients are using insulin from a vial, they need insulin syringes and needles for administration. Newer forms of insulin are administered through an insulin pen, which is a prefilled cartridge that has a dial for measuring doses, instead of using a syringe and needle. Insulin pens use pen needles, which are smaller, often less painful, needles.

As a pharmacy technician, it is important you understand what each diabetic supply is used for and how to match test strips with glucometers. The following is a quick summary of the most often used supplies for diabetes.

DIABETIC SUPPLY

Glucometer	Meter that uses a test strip to identify blood glucose level
Test strip	Used with a glucometer to detect blood glucose level
Lancet	Pierces skin to draw blood for blood glucose monitoring
Insulin pen	Type of insulin that has doses that can be premeasured and dispensed without having to draw into a needle
Pen needles	Needles used with insulin pens

Respiratory Supplies

DME is also used for respiratory ailments. This includes nebulizers and spacers. A **nebulizer** is a machine that uses a nebule (vial of solution) and turns it into a mist to be inhaled. For example, a nebule of albuterol is opened and poured into the nebulizer. The machine then takes the liquid and turns it into fine droplets that can be inhaled. A patient wears a mask so the mist can be breathed in directly.

Another way to get medication into the lungs is through a metered dose inhaler (MDI). Sometimes when the inhaler is puffed, the medication does not get completely into the lungs. A **spacer** attaches to the end of the MDI so the aerosolized medication stays within the chamber, and then the patient breathes into the other end of the spacer to absorb more of the drug. Spacers can be a variety of sizes, depending on the size of the patient.

Lot Numbers, Expiration Dates, and National Drug Code (NDC) Numbers

A lot number is a number assigned to a batch of medication. It allows the manufacturer to trace potential adverse incidents in a particular group of drugs. If a recall is necessary, lot numbers are used to identify the specific drugs impacted. Pharmacies then use that information to pull from inventory. Lot numbers can also be used for supply chain security. The lot number is printed on each bottle or unit dose and is often next to the expiration date.

The expiration date of a drug is the last date at which the product is known to remain stable and able to retain strength, quality, and purity when stored in its labeled conditions. Expiration dates are different from BUDs in that the expiration date is assigned by the manufacturer and printed on the product. A BUD is assigned by the pharmacy and calculated based on risk level, stability, and sterility.

Expiration dates may be in a month/day/year format, or just month/year format. If a manufacturer indicates a month and year only, you can assume it is the last day of this month—meaning if an expiration date is 5/25, this product would be good until 5/31/2025. As a pharmacy technician, one of your jobs is to pull outdated medications each month and to look for expired drugs, including nursing units, floor stock dispensing cabinets, crash carts, and pharmacy inventory.

Along with a lot number and expiration date, each drug has a national drug code (NDC) that has been required by the FDA since the Drug Listing Act of 1972. An NDC is made up of 10 or 11 digits, grouped into three different segments. The FDA maintains a searchable database of all NDCs, including OTC drugs. Although 10-digits are required, 11 digits are used for billing purposes, so if a manufacturer uses a 10-digit NDC, the pharmacy will add a 0 in a specific location to bill correctly.

The first series of numbers is known as the labeler code and represents the manufacturer, repackager, or distributor. The labeler code is 5 numbers, but if the 10-digit format is used, it may be 4. To make it a 5-digit code, the pharmacy would add a 0 before the first number. So if the labeler code was 9876, the pharmacy would add a 0 to the beginning and the 5-digit code would then be 09876.

The second set of numbers is the product code. This identifies the product, including the drug strength and dosage form. For example, if the same manufacturer makes diphenhydramine in capsules and liquid, the first set of numbers (labeler code) would be the same, but the second set would remain different, even though they are both diphenhydramine. The product code is 4 numbers, unless the manufacturer uses a 10-digit format, then it could be 3 digits. In this case, if the digits are 543, the pharmacy would add the 0 to the beginning and use 0543 as the product code.

The last set of numbers is the package code. This describes the packages size and type. The package code is 2 digits, though if a manufacturer uses a 10-digit NDC, it may be only 1. The pharmacy will put a 0 before the last digit in this case.

Figure 5.20 is an example of an NDC number in the 5-4-2 (11-digit) format.

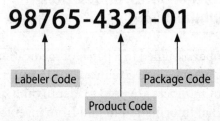

Figure 5.20   An NDC number in the 5-4-2 (11-digit) format

It may also be helpful to understand where to add a "0" when converting from a 10-digit NDC to an 11-digit NDC. The following are 10-digit formats and examples of each and where the 0 would be added to convert to 11-digits.

10-DIGIT FORMAT	EXAMPLE OF 10-DIGIT NDC FORMAT	11-DIGIT CONVERSION
4-4-2	5555-5555-55	**0**5555-5555-55
5-3-2	88888-888-88	88888-**0**888-88
5-4-1	11111-1111-1	11111-1111-**0**1

Procedures for Identifying and Returning Medications and Supplies

Pharmacy technicians have an important role in inventory management in the pharmacy. As a pharmacy technician, you will need to continuously monitor expired or soon-to-expire drugs for returns, returning to stock, or reviewing return with a reverse distributor.

Credit Returns

Managing excess inventory is important in controlling cost that is tied up in inventory. Excess inventory could be a result of errors in ordering, stocking for patient-specific medication who may have changed regimens, or overall change in prescribing. A credit return is a credit from the wholesaler to an invoice after sending back eligible drugs. Medications eligible for credit cannot have been opened or damaged or be close to expiration. Typically, drugs need to have at least 6 months out from the expiration to be returnable for credit.

Not all medications are eligible for credit from the wholesaler. Unless the medication arrived damaged or in error, the product must be able to be resold to be returned. Drugs that may not be returnable include frozen or refrigerated medications, some hazardous drugs, and special orders that a wholesaler may "drop ship" to a pharmacy. Prior approval is given from the wholesaler and paperwork to process the return. When the wholesaler has received the medications and approves the return, credit is issued back to the pharmacy account.

Return to Stock

Prescriptions that have not been picked up for a specific number of days in a pharmacy are able to be returned back to stock. Return to stock (RTS) drugs are put back into the pharmacy inventory and can be dispensed to another patient. It is important to note that prescriptions can only be returned to stock if they have not left the pharmacy. If a prescription leaves a pharmacy, it cannot be returned, as would be impossible to verify it was stored appropriately or not tampered with. Medications to be returned to stock must not be expired, and when they are returned to the shelf, they must remain in the original container in which they were filled. The label should not be removed, though the patient information should be blacked out if possible. Keeping the label on the bottle ensures the NDC and manufacturer can be matched to the inventory on the shelf. If the prescription was a unit-of-use or sealed manufacturer bottle, the label may be removed to be relabeled for another future patient. Contents of a RTS prescription must never be returned back into the manufacturer's stock bottle, as the original stock bottle may be a different lot number or have a different expiration date.

Each pharmacy has a unique timeline for how long a prescription can be available before returning to stock. This is typically between 7 to 10 days. As a pharmacy technician, you will help with the RTS process by running daily reports of prescriptions due to be returned to stock and notifying patients. If the prescription is still not picked up, a pharmacy technician can process the RTS and put the bottle back on the shelf with the other inventory. Insurance companies may also dictate the RTS time frame. Part of the RTS process is reversing the claim if it was processed through insurance. If the prescription was not reversed, the pharmacy would still claim payment on the prescription without the patient picking up the medication. This would be a form of insurance fraud.

Reverse Distribution

Credit returns and RTS are for medications that are not expired. Outdated medications cannot be returned to a wholesaler, so a reverse distributor can be used instead. A reverse distributor processes expired or damaged drugs from a pharmacy and removes them to be returned back to the manufacturers for credit. Pharmacies in return can then receive back partial credit for expired medications, and also benefit from not having to dispose of the expired medications themselves.

Not all expired drugs are eligible for credit. Medications that are compounded are not eligible for return to a manufacturer. Partially filled liquid bottles may not be eligible. A reverse distributor can remove expired or damaged drug from a pharmacy, return to manufacturers where appropriate, then give the pharmacy back the credit. Reverse distributors typically take part of the credit as their payment for service.

Review Questions

The following questions help you review the chapter. Test your knowledge by working through the next 50 questions to test yourself and identify any areas you may need to review.

1. A prescription filled for a patient that has not been picked up in a specified number of days is able to be
   A. sent with a reverse distributor for manufacturer credit
   B. sent back to the wholesaler for a refund
   C. returned to stock
   D. given back to the manufacturer for a refund

2. A credit from the wholesaler may be given for
   A. expired drugs
   B. damaged drugs
   C. all refrigerated drugs
   D. unopened drugs not close to expiration

3. A medication is available as 125mg/5mL. How many mL is a 112mg dose?
   A. 4.5mL
   B. 5.2mL
   C. 5.4mL
   D. 6.2mL

4. The last set of numbers in an NDC describes
   A. the drug
   B. the package size
   C. the manufacturer
   D. the expiration date

5. A medication is prescribed to a patient at 3.5mg/kg. The patient weighs 92 lb. How many mg is one dose for this patient?
   A. 122mg
   B. 146.3mg
   C. 163.5mg
   D. 322mg

6. An expiration date on a drug stock bottle of 12/26 would expire on
   A. December 26 of the current year
   B. December 31 of 2026
   C. December 1 of 2026
   D. December 26 of 2026

7. How much active ingredient (in mg) is in 5mL of a 35% solution?

   A. 1.75mg

   B. 204mg

   C. 1,750mg

   D. 1,895mg

8. Which of the following is a machine that turns a liquid into fine droplets able to be inhaled?

   A. spacer

   B. nebulizer

   C. MDI

   D. nebule

9. How many mL of active ingredient are in 150mL of a 5% solution?

   A. 1.5mL

   B. 5.4mL

   C. 6.2mL

   D. 7.5mL

10. Which device is used to draw blood for a point of care test?

   A. test strip

   B. glucometer

   C. lancet

   D. DME

11. How many mg of hydrocortisone is in a 15g tube of 1% ointment?

   A. 150mg

   B. 1.5mg

   C. 250mg

   D. 375mg

12. Which gauge needle would be most likely selected to draw up thick or viscous liquid?

   A. 32g

   B. 29g

   C. 27g

   D. 21g

13. How many mL are needed to fill a 7-day supply of a 500mg/5mL medication given TID?

    A. 22mL

    B. 64mL

    C. 105mL

    D. 115mL

14. A patient has a prescription for 4 fl oz. How many mL is this?

    A. 30mL

    B. 60mL

    C. 120mL

    D. 180mL

15. When reading a measurement for a liquid, such as in a graduated cylinder, you should read

    A. at the bottom of the meniscus

    B. at the top of the meniscus

    C. at the bottom of the bubble

    D. even with the top of the water line

16. Which of the following would be used to crush or mix powders?

    A. conical cylinder

    B. mortar and pestle

    C. beaker

    D. spatula

17. How many mg will a 64kg patient take per dose, if the order is written for 2.5mg/kg/day in 3 divided doses?

    A. 35.3mg

    B. 42.9m

    C. 53.3mg

    D. 160mg

18. The process of grinding a particle to a powder is known as

    A. spatulation

    B. geometric dilution

    C. trituration

    D. reconstitution

19. A liquid dosage form that is compounded so the active ingredient is completely dissolved is a

    A. cream
    B. suspension
    C. solution
    D. gel

20. A drug packaged for a single administration is a(n)

    A. BCMA
    B. ADC
    C. unit-of-use
    D. unit dose

21. How many mg are in a 150mL of a 12% solution?

    A. 12,000mg
    B. 13,000mg
    C. 16,000mg
    D. 18,000mg

22. A patient has a prescription for the following:

    Lantus insulin 1,000units/10mL vial

    Inject 30 units in the morning and 20 units in the evening subcutaneously.

    How many vials should be dispensed for a 30 day supply?

    A. 1.5 vials
    B. 2 vials
    C. 2.5 vials
    D. 3 vials

23. Define the following prescription:

    1 tab PO Q4–6H PRN HA

    A. 1 tablet dissolved under the tongue every 4 to 6 hours as needed for heartburn
    B. 1 tablet by mouth every 4 hours as needed for hypertension
    C. 1 tablet by mouth every 4 to 6 hours as needed for headache
    D. 1 tablet in the cheek every 4 to 6 hours as needed for heart rate

24. How many mg are in a dose of 15mL of a 250mg/5mL suspension?

    A. 250mg
    B. 500mg
    C. 750mg
    D. 1,000mg

25. A 189 lb patient is prescribed 5mg/kg Q8H. How many mg does the patient take in one day?

    A. 945mg

    B. 1,298mg

    C. 2,393mg

    D. 2,835mg

26. A patient has an order for 0.025 L of a medication PO QID. How many mL will the patient take daily?

    A. 0.1mL

    B. 75mL

    C. 100mL

    D. 1,000mL

27. A patient is prescribed a medication 2.3mg/m². The patient's BSA is 1.8 m². What is the dose for this patient?

    A. 0.78mg

    B. 1.28mg

    C. 4.14mg

    D. 5.9mg

28. An inactive or inert substance is known as a(n)

    A. active ingredient

    B. tritruation

    C. meniscus

    D. excipient

29. What is the process of mixing two substances together, sometimes on an ointment slab, using a spatula?

    A. spatulation

    B. trituration

    C. geometric dilution

    D. levigation

30. A hospitalized patient has an order for 16mEq of potassium injection 2mEq/mL in a 20mL vial. How many mL should be drawn up for one dose?

    A. 1.25mL

    B. 8mL

    C. 10mL

    D. 32mL

31. A technique used for mixing, in which a small amount of liquid is mixed with a powder, is known as

    A. tritruation
    B. levigation
    C. geometric dilution
    D. spatulation

32. Which of the following would require a mold when compounding?

    A. enema
    B. elixir
    C. suppository
    D. cream

33. An order is written for 50mL of a 10% solution. You have a 35% solution in stock. How much stock solution and how much diluent is needed to compound this order?

    A. 40mL of stock, and 10mL of diluent
    B. 49mL of stock and 1mL of diluent
    C. 42.9mL of stock and 7.1mL of diluent
    D. 38.4mL of stock and 11.6mL of diluent

34. A technician is preparing 30g of 2% hydrocortisone ointment using a 1% and 10% base. Determine how many grams of each base are required to compound this order.

    A. 28g of 10% and 2g of 1%
    B. 3.3g of 10% and 26.7g of 1%
    C. 4.8g of 10% and 25.2g of 1%
    D. 9.4g of 10% and 20.6g of 1%

35. A prescription for 160mL would best fit in which size bottle?

    A. 3 fl oz
    B. 4 fl oz
    C. 5 fl oz
    D. 6 fl oz

36. Which part of the syringe has the calibration lines to measure volume?

    A. barrel
    B. plunger
    C. hub
    D. bevel

37. A patient has an order for 100mg suspension to be taken every 6 hours. How many doses can the patient get from one 300mL bottle of 250mg/5mL?

    A. 15 doses

    B. 75 doses

    C. 100 doses

    D. 150 doses

38. A pharmacy must compound sodium bicarbonate into a syringe. How much active ingredient is needed to make 50mL of an 8.4% solution?

    A. 4.2g

    B. 0.4mg

    C. 8.4mg

    D. 0.08g

39. A device that measures blood glucose levels at home is known as a

    A. spacer

    B. nebulizer

    C. lancet

    D. glucometer

40. A pediatric patient is ordered 3.5mcg/kg PO BID. The child weighs 23 lb. What volume should be given per dose, if the medication is available as 125mcg/1mL?

    A. 0.29mL

    B. 3.675mL

    C. 2.93mL

    D. 36.75mL

41. A lot number is used for

    A. expiration dating

    B. recalls

    C. fast mover information

    D. LASA

42. An order for prednisone reads:

    Prednisone 10mg. Take 3 tabs TID × 3 days, then 2 tabs TID × 3 days, then 1 tab BID × 5 days, then 1 tab QD × 3 days.

    How many prednisone 10mg tablets are needed to fill this order?

    A. 47 tabs

    B. 52 tabs

    C. 57 tabs

    D. 58 tabs

43. The middle set of numbers in an NDC will tell the

    A. manufacturer

    B. drug

    C. package size

    D. wholesaler

44. How many clonidine patches are needed to fill a prescription for a patient applying 1 patch every 7 days for a 30-day supply?

    A. 3 patches

    B. 4 patches

    C. 5 patches

    D. 6 patches

45. A pharmacy technician is completing temperature checks and notes a temperature as 35.3°C. What temperature in °F is this?

    A. 70.2°F

    B. 79.6°F

    C. 86.8°F

    D. 95.4°F

46. A pharmacy technician is drawing up 34 units of insulin into an insulin syringe. If the vial holds 1,000units/10mL, how many mL will be drawn up into the syringe?

    A. 0.1mL

    B. 0.34mL

    C. 3.4mL

    D. 10mL

47. How many 25mg tablets are needed to compound 150mL of a 0.5mg/mL suspension?

    A. 1 tab

    B. 3 tabs

    C. 7 tabs

    D. 9 tabs

48. A pharmacy is compounding 200mL of a 10% dextrose solution. The pharmacy has 50% dextrose on hand and is mixing with sterile water. How much sterile water should be mixed with the dextrose to reach 10%?

    A. 40mL

    B. 74mL

    C. 140mL

    D. 160mL

49. How much volume of magnesium sulfate 50% would be needed for a dose of 32g?

    A. 18mL

    B. 36mL

    C. 64mL

    D. 97mL

50. A cephalexin suspension is available as 250mg/5mL. A patient is prescribed 7.5mL PO BID. How many mg will a patient take daily?

    A. 375mg

    B. 425mg

    C. 585mg

    D. 750mg

Answers

1. **C**

   Prescriptions that have not been picked up for a specific number of days in a pharmacy can be returned back to stock.

2. **D**

   A credit return is a credit from the wholesaler to an invoice after sending back eligible drugs. Medications eligible for credit cannot have been opened or damaged or be close to expiration. Typically, drugs need to be at least 6 months out from the expiration to be returnable for credit.

3. **A**

   4.5mL.

   $$\frac{x\,\text{mL}}{112\text{mg}} = \frac{5\text{mL}}{125\text{mg}}$$

   $$(x)(125) = (112)(5)$$

   $$\frac{560}{125} = 4.5\text{mL}$$

4. **B**

   The last set of numbers is the package code. This describes the package's size and type.

5. **B**

   146.3mg.

   $$\frac{92}{2.2} = 41.8\text{kg}$$

   $$\frac{x\,\text{mg}}{41.8\text{kg}} = \frac{3.5\text{mg}}{1\text{kg}}$$

   $$(x)(1) = (41.8)(3.5)$$

   $$\frac{146.3\text{mg}}{1} = 146.3\text{mg}$$

6. **B**

   If a manufacturer indicates a month and year only, you can assume it is the last day of this month, so 12/26 would be 12/31/2026.

7. **C**

1,750mg.

$$\frac{x\,\text{g}}{5\text{mL}} = \frac{35\text{g}}{100\text{mL}}$$

$$(x)(100) = (5)(35)$$

$$\frac{175}{100} = 1.75\text{g}$$

Convert to mg: $(1.75)(1000) = 1,750\text{mg}$

8. **B**

A nebulizer is a machine that uses a nebule (vial of solution) and turns it into a mist to be inhaled.

9. **D**

7.5mL.

$$\frac{x\,\text{mL}}{150\text{mL}} = \frac{5\text{mL}}{100\text{mL}}$$

$$(x)(100) = (150)(5)$$

$$\frac{750}{100} = 7.5\text{mL}$$

10. **C**

To draw blood, a patient may use a lancet, which is a device that quickly pricks the skin.

11. **A**

150mg.

$$\frac{x\,\text{g}}{15\text{g}} = \frac{1\text{g}}{100\text{g}}$$

$$(x)(100) = (15)(1)$$

$$\frac{15}{100} = 0.15\text{g}$$

Convert to mg: $(0.15)(1,000) = 150\text{mg}$

12. **D**

21g. The size of gauge used depends on what procedure is being administered. Smaller gauge or large needles are used for viscous or thick liquids to help draw fluid into the syringe.

13. **C**

105mL.

$$TID = 3 \times \text{ daily}$$

$$(5mL)(3) = 15mL \text{ daily}$$

$$\frac{x \text{ mL}}{7 \text{ day}} = \frac{15mL}{1 \text{ day}}$$

$$(x)(1) = (7)(15) = 105mL$$

14. **C**

120mL.

$$\frac{x \text{ mL}}{4 \text{ fl oz}} = \frac{30mL}{1 \text{ fl oz}}$$

$$(x)(1) = (4)(30) = 120mL$$

15. **A**

When you are measuring a liquid, it is important to read the measurement at the bottom of the curved fluid surface, which is known as the meniscus. This allows for a more accurate measurement, as reading the top of the meniscus would be an inaccurately high value and too much liquid would be used.

16. **B**

If tablets or powders must be crushed or mixed, a mortar and pestle may be used. A mortar is a bowl, and a pestle is a tool with a rounded end that is used for crushing and grinding.

17. **C**

53.3mg.

$$\frac{x \text{ mg}}{64kg} = \frac{2.5mg}{1kg}$$

$$(x)(1) = (64)(2.5) = 160mg / day$$

$$\frac{x \text{ mg}}{1 \text{ dose}} = \frac{160mg}{3 \text{ dose}}$$

$$(x)(3) = (1)(160)$$

$$\frac{160}{3} = 53.3mg$$

18. **C**

Trituration is the process of reducing a particle to a powder through grinding using a mortar and pestle.

19. **C**

Solutions are composed of a liquid with a completely dissolved active ingredient.

20. **D**

A unit dose medication is a drug packaged for a single administration.

21. **D**

18,000mg

$$\frac{x\,\text{g}}{150\text{mL}} = \frac{12\text{g}}{100\text{mL}}$$

$$(x)(100) = (150)(12)$$

$$\frac{(150)(12)}{100} = 18\text{g}$$

$$(18\text{g})(1,000) = 18,000\text{mg}$$

22. **B**

2 vials.

First, determine how many units the patient is using per day:
30+20 = 50 units.

$$\frac{x\,\text{day}}{1,000\,\text{units}} = \frac{1\,\text{day}}{50\,\text{units}}$$

$$(x)(50) = (1,000)(1)$$

$$\frac{1,000}{50} = 20\,\text{days}$$

$$\frac{x\,\text{vial}}{30\,\text{days}} = \frac{1\,\text{vial}}{20\,\text{days}}$$

$$(x)(20) = (30)(1) = 1.5\,\text{vials}$$

Because the pharmacy cannot dispense a half of a vial, the patient will need 2 vials.

23. **C**

    1 tablet by mouth every 4 to 6 hours as needed for headache.

    tab = tablet

    PO = by mouth

    Q4–6h = every 4 to 6 hours

    PRN = as needed for

    HA = headache

24. **C**

    750mg.

    $$\frac{x\,\text{mg}}{15\text{mL}} = \frac{250\text{mg}}{5\text{mL}}$$

    $$(x)(5) = (15)(250)$$

    $$\frac{(15)(250)}{5} = 750\text{mg}$$

25. **D**

    2,835mg.

    $$\frac{x\,\text{kg}}{189\,\text{lb}} = \frac{1\text{kg}}{2.2}$$

    $$(x)(2.2) = (189)(1)$$

    $$\frac{189}{2.2} = 85.9\text{kg}$$

    $$\frac{x\,\text{mg}}{189\text{kg}} = \frac{5\text{mg}}{1\text{kg}}$$

    $$(x)(1) = (189)(5) = 945\text{mg for one dose}$$

    Q8H = 3× daily

    $$(945)(3) = 2,835\text{mg}$$

26. **C**

    100mL.

    QID = 4× daily

    $$(0.025)(4) = 0.1\text{L}$$

    $$(0.1)(1,000) = 100\text{mL}$$

27. **C**
4.14mg.

$$\frac{x \text{ mg}}{1.8\text{m}^2} = \frac{2.3\text{mg}}{1\text{m}^2}$$

$$(x)(1) = (1.8)(2.3) = 4.14\text{mg}$$

28. **D**
An inert or inactive substance is known as an excipient.

29. **A**
Spatulation is the process of using a spatula to mix substances together.

30. **B**
8 mL.

$$\frac{x \text{ mL}}{16\text{mEq}} = \frac{1\text{mL}}{2\text{mEq}}$$

$$(x)(2) = (16)(1)$$

$$\frac{16}{2} = 8\text{mL}$$

31. **B**
Levigation is a technique used to mix substances together, specifically grinding powder, but with a small amount of liquid.

32. **C**
Suppositories are solid dosage forms that inserted into the body and melt at body temperature or dissolve into the mucous membranes. They are compounded using a mold depending on the type of suppository.

33. **C**
42.9mL of stock and 7.1mL of diluent.

$$C1V1 = C2V2$$

$$C1 = 35$$

$$V1 = x$$

$$C2 = 10$$

$$V2 = 50$$

$$(35)(x) = (10)(50)$$

$$\frac{500}{35} = 42.9\text{mL}$$

$$50 - 42.9 = 7.1\text{mL}$$

34. **B**

3.3g of 10% and 26.7g of 1%.

10			1
		2	
1			8

$1 + 8 = 9$ total parts

$$\frac{x\,g}{30\ parts} = \frac{1g}{9\ parts}$$

$$(x)(9) = (30)(1)$$

$$\frac{30}{9} = 3.3g\ of\ 10\%$$

$$\frac{x\,g}{30\ parts} = \frac{8g}{9\ parts}$$

$$(x)(9) = (30)(8)$$

$$\frac{240}{9} = 26.7g\ of\ 1\%$$

35. **D**

6 fl oz.

$$\frac{x\ fl\ oz}{160mL} = \frac{1\ fl\ oz}{30mL}$$

$$(x)(30) = (160)(1)$$

$$\frac{160}{30} = 5.3\,fl\ oz$$

The best size would be 6 fl oz to accommodate all of the liquid.

36. **A**

The barrel is a tube with the calibration lines used for measuring volume.

37. **D**

    150 doses.

$$\frac{x \text{ mL}}{100 \text{mg}} = \frac{5 \text{mL}}{250 \text{mg}}$$

$$(x)(250) = (100)(5)$$

$$\frac{500}{250} = 2 \text{mL per dose}$$

$$\frac{x \text{ dose}}{300 \text{mL}} = \frac{1 \text{ dose}}{2 \text{mL}}$$

$$(x)(2) = (300)(1)$$

$$\frac{300}{2} = 150 \text{ doses}$$

38. **A**

    4.2g.

$$\frac{x \text{ g}}{50 \text{mL}} = \frac{8.4 \text{g}}{100 \text{mL}}$$

$$(x)(100) = (50)(8.4)$$

$$\frac{420}{100} = 4.2 \text{g}$$

39. **D**

    Patients with diabetes will need to continuously monitor blood glucose levels. To do this at home, a glucometer is recommended.

40. **A**

    0.29mL.

$$\frac{23 \text{lb}}{2.2} = 10.5 \text{kg}$$

$$\frac{x \text{ mcg}}{10.5 \text{kg}} = \frac{3.5 \text{mcg}}{1 \text{kg}}$$

$$(x)(1) = (10.5)(3.5)$$

$$(10.5)(3.5) = 36.75 \text{mcg}$$

36.75mcg in one dose.

$$\frac{x \text{ mL}}{36.75 \text{mcg}} = \frac{1 \text{mL}}{125 \text{mcg}}$$

$$(x)(125) = (36.75)(1)$$

$$\frac{36.7}{125} = 0.29 \text{mL}$$

41. **B**

A lot number is a number assigned to a batch of medication. It allows the manufacturer to trace potential adverse incidents in a particular group of drugs. If a recall is necessary, lot numbers are used to identify the specific drugs impacted.

42. **D**

58 tabs

$$(3 \text{ tab})(3 \times \text{ daily}) = 9 \text{ tab daily}$$

$$\times 3 \text{ days} = 27 \text{ tabs}$$

$$(2 \text{ tab})(3 \times \text{ daily}) = 6 \text{ tab daily}$$

$$\times 3 \text{ days} = 18 \text{ tabs}$$

$$(1 \text{ tab})(2 \times \text{ daily}) = 2 \text{ tab daily}$$

$$\times 5 \text{ days} = 10 \text{ tabs}$$

$$1 \text{ tab} \times 3 \text{ days} = 3 \text{ tabs}$$

$$27 + 18 + 10 + 3 = 58 \text{ tabs}$$

43. **B**

The second set of numbers is the product code. This identifies the product, including the drug strength and dosage form.

44. **B**

4 patches will last the patient over 30 days.

$$\frac{x \text{ patch}}{30 \text{ days}} = \frac{1 \text{ patch}}{7 \text{ days}}$$

$$(x)(7) = (30)(1)$$

$$\frac{30}{7} = 4.3 \text{ patchs}$$

45. **D**

95.4°F.

$$°F = (1.8 \times 35.3) + 32$$

$$63.36 + 32 = 95.4°F$$

46. **B**

0.34mL.

$$\frac{x\,\text{mL}}{34\,\text{units}} = \frac{10\text{mL}}{1,000\,\text{units}}$$

$$(x)(1,000) = (34)(10)$$

$$\frac{340}{1,000} = 0.34\text{mL}$$

47. **B**

3 tabs.

$$\frac{x\,\text{mg}}{150\text{mL}} = \frac{0.5\text{mg}}{1\text{mL}}$$

$$(x)(1) = (150)(0.5) = 75\text{mg}$$

$$\frac{75\text{mg}}{25\text{mg}} = 3\text{ tabs}$$

48. **D**

160mL.

$$C1 = 50$$

$$V1 = x$$

$$C2 = 10$$

$$V2 = 200$$

$$(50)(x) = (10)(200)$$

$$\frac{2,000}{50} = 40\text{mL of dextrose}$$

To determine how much diluent needed, subtract from total: 200mL – 40mL = 160mL diluent.

49. **C**

64mL.

$$\frac{x\,\text{mL}}{32\text{g}} = \frac{100\text{mL}}{50\text{g}}$$

$$(x)(50) = (32)(100)$$

$$\frac{3,200}{50} = 64\text{mL}$$

50. **D**

750mg.

$$\frac{x \text{ mg}}{7.5\text{mL}} = \frac{250\text{mg}}{5\text{mL}}$$

$$(x)(5) = (7.5)(250)$$

$$\frac{1,875}{5} = 375\text{mg}$$

$$\text{BID} = 2 \times \text{ daily} = (375)(2) = 750\text{mg daily}$$

Practice Test 1

The following practice exam tests your readiness for the PTCE. To best prepare, give yourself only 1 hour 50 minutes to complete the exam.

1. Which of the following is an ACE inhibitor?
   A. atorvastatin
   B. lisinopril
   C. losartan
   D. metoprolol

2. Which organization publishes a high-alert/high-risk medication list that pharmacies can use to develop their own list?
   A. DEA
   B. FDA
   C. OSHA
   D. ISMP

3. Heroin is which schedule of controlled substance?
   A. Schedule I
   B. Schedule II
   C. Schedule III
   D. Schedule IV

4. The first set of numbers in an NDC represent the
   A. drug
   B. manufacturer
   C. package size
   D. dosage

5. The generic for Coreg is
   A. clonazepam
   B. citalopram
   C. carvedilol
   D. fluoxetine

6. Which of the following is an NSAID?
   A. clonazepam
   B. meloxicam
   C. tramadol
   D. cyclobenzaprine

7. Bolded, uppercase letters designed to draw attention to the difference in drug names are known as
   A. BCMA
   B. tall man lettering
   C. five rights
   D. LASA

8. Which type of syringe is measured in both mL and units?
   A. hypodermic
   B. oral
   C. tuberculin
   D. insulin

9. Which schedule of controlled substance is Percocet?
   A. I
   B. II
   C. III
   D. IV

10. Topiramate and pregabalin are which type of medications?
    A. antipsychotic
    B. antihistamine
    C. anticonvulsant
    D. antiemetic

11. Keppra is the name brand for
    A. tizanidine
    B. cephalexin
    C. rivaroxaban
    D. levetiracetam

12. A patient has a prescription for 180mL. How many fl oz is this?

   A. 3 fl oz
   B. 4 fl oz
   C. 5 fl oz
   D. 6 fl oz

13. Which of the following would be used in nonsterile compounding to measure the volume of a liquid?

   A. stirring rod
   B. mortar and pestle
   C. levigating agent
   D. graduated cylinder

14. Which of the following can be a cause of a medication error?

   A. human error
   B. bar code scanning
   C. tall man lettering
   D. CPOE

15. Which of the following is one of the five rights of medication administration?

   A. right route
   B. right computer
   C. right meal plan
   D. right visitor

16. Temazepam is which schedule controlled substance?

   A. I
   B. II
   C. III
   D. IV

17. Which of the following is an antiparkinson agent?

   A. aripiprazole
   B. ropinirole
   C. isosorbide
   D. methotrexate

18. A prescriber writes an order for Lipitor 40mg PO HS. What might this be mistaken for?

    A. discontinue Lipitor
    B. Lipitor in the morning
    C. Lipitor half strength
    D. Lipitor every other day

19. Which gauge needle would be the smallest?

    A. 18G
    B. 21G
    C. 25G
    D. 30G

20. A patient has the following prescription:

    2tsp PO QID × 5d

    How much (in mL) is required to fill this prescription?

    A. 50mL
    B. 150mL
    C. 200mL
    D. 600mL

21. How many times can a prescription for hydrocodone with acetaminophen (Norco) be refilled?

    A. as many times as issued by provider
    B. two refills
    C. no refills
    D. up to 5 times within 6 months

22. Which of the following is a calcium channel blocker?

    A. verapamil
    B. benazepril
    C. nebivolol
    D. temazepam

23. Which of the following drugs must be identified with a sticker or segregated in the pharmacy?

    A. MDIs
    B. suspensions
    C. high-alert medications
    D. direct oral anticoagulants

24. Carbamazepine is the generic for

    A. Bentyl

    B. Lotrel

    C. Topamax

    D. Tegretol

25. Define the directions for the following prescription:

    1 gtt AU TID × VII d

    A. Instill one drop into each eye three times daily for 12 days.

    B. Instill one drop into both ears four times daily for 4 days.

    C. Instill one drop into the right eye three times daily for 6 days.

    D. Instill one drop into both ears three times daily for 7 days.

26. A patient with bradycardia has a

    A. slow heart rate

    B. rapid heart rate

    C. normal heart rate

    D. large heart rate

27. DEA Form 222 is used for

    A. theft or loss of a controlled substance

    B. ordering Schedule I or II controlled substances

    C. registration of a new DEA number

    D. destruction of a controlled substance

28. A medication error that was caught before reaching the patient is a(n)

    A. prescribing error

    B. allergic reaction

    C. near miss

    D. adverse drug reaction

29. A patient fills a 60-day supply of a medication 2 times in 6 months. What is the adherence rate for this patient?

    A. 67%

    B. 35%

    C. 70%

    D. 90%

30. The FDA manages known patient safety issues of medications through which program?

    A. CSOS

    B. SDS

    C. REMS

    D. take back

31. Levofloxacin is which type of antibiotic?

    A. penicillin

    B. cephalosporin

    C. tetracycline

    D. fluoroquinolone

32. To be considered therapeutically equivalent, which of the following must be met?

    A. The drugs must be produced by the same manufacturer.

    B. The drugs must contain the same inactive ingredients.

    C. The drugs must be the same dosage form, route of administration, and strength.

    D. The drugs must go through complete clinical trials to demonstrate equivalency.

33. A VIS is given to patients in a pharmacy receiving a

    A. new insurance card

    B. vaccine

    C. counseling session

    D. new prescription

34. The process of mixing together powders of unequal sizes by adding the smallest quantity first and an equal amount of the larger quantity until the mixture is completed is known as

    A. levigation

    B. spatulation

    C. geometric dilution

    D. trituration

35. Which organization manages the REMS program?

    A. DEA

    B. FDA

    C. USP

    D. OSHA

36. A patient has the following prescription:

    Novolin R Insulin 1,000 units/10mL

    Inject 15 units subcutaneously in the morning and 25 units in the evening

    How many vials will the patient need for a 30-day supply?

    A. 1 vial
    B. 2 vials
    C. 3 vials
    D. 4 vials

37. A patient has a prescription for amoxicillin suspension 125mg TID. The pharmacy has 150mL stock bottles of 125mg/5mL. How many doses can the patient get from one bottle?

    A. 12 doses
    B. 18 doses
    C. 30 doses
    D. 32 doses

38. Which medication has a narrow therapeutic index?

    A. digoxin
    B. loratadine
    C. acetaminophen
    D. rosuvastatin

39. A sweetened lozenge that helps medication dissolve slowly for local treatment to the mouth or throat is a

    A. buccal tablet
    B. ODT
    C. SR capsule
    D. troche

40. Which of the following would be an acceptable purchase under the CMEA?

    A. 4 boxes of 90 tablets, 30mg pseudoephedrine in one day
    B. 3 boxes of 20 tablets, 90mg pseudoephedrine in one day
    C. 2 boxes of 30 tablets, 90mg pseudoephedrine in one month
    D. 3 boxes of 90 tablets, 90mg pseudoephedrine in one month

41. A patient is admitted to the hospital and is currently prescribed Lotensin. The hospital uses a therapeutic substitution program. Which of the following could be substituted for Lotensin?

    A. losartan

    B. atorvastatin

    C. metoprolol

    D. lisinopril

42. Which drug requires REMS due to the potential for severe neutropenia?

    A. tramadol

    B. pseudoephedrine

    C. clozapine

    D. isotretinoin

43. If a medication is administered intrathecal, it is injected into the

    A. cartilage

    B. joint

    C. artery

    D. spinal column

44. Special instructions for diuretics include

    A. may cause urinary retention

    B. take in morning to avoid nighttime urination

    C. avoid cough and cold agents

    D. should be taken at least 30 minutes prior to eating

45. A Class II recall occurs when

    A. the product can be used after the labeled expiration date

    B. the product may cause a temporary health problem or slight threat

    C. the product is unlikely to cause an issue

    D. the product could cause serious health problems or death

46. A chronic condition is one in which an illness

    A. has a rapid onset and short duration

    B. has a known treatment and resolves quickly

    C. causes death

    D. persists for a long time

47. Which type of error occurs when there is a difference in what is prescribed and what is given to the patient?

    A. administering
    B. monitoring
    C. prescribing
    D. dispensing

48. A physician prescribes a medication for a 66 lb patient as 10mg/kg/day in three divided doses. The medication is available as 150mg/10mL. How many mL will be needed for one dose?

    A. 1.5mL
    B. 2.9mL
    C. 4.2mL
    D. 6.7mL

49. A patient has the following prescription:

    Prednisone 10mg Take 6 tabs PO QD × 5 days, then 5 tabs PO QD × 4 days, then 4 tabs PO QD × 3 days, then 3 tabs PO QD × 2 days, then 2 tabs PO QD × 2 days, then 1 tab PO QD × 2 days.

    How many 10mg tablets are required to fill this prescription?

    A. 52 tabs
    B. 56 tabs
    C. 68 tabs
    D. 74 tabs

50. A patient taking atorvastatin may have a drug–nutrient interaction if which nutrients from which drink are consumed?

    A. milk
    B. grapefruit juice
    C. coffee
    D. tea

51. Which of the following can treat both hypertension and BPH?

    A. clonidine
    B. terazosin
    C. propranolol
    D. verapamil

52. A pharmacy technician is compounding a medication that is light sensitive. The finished compound is not dispensed in a light-resistant container and the medication degrades. Which type of incompatibility is this?

    A. physical
    B. chemical
    C. therapeutic
    D. viscosity

53. A desiccant is packaged with medications to protect from degradation due to

    A. light
    B. moisture
    C. air
    D. chemical incompatibility

54. A dry cough is a side effect of which class of medications?

    A. oral contraceptives
    B. iron supplements
    C. ACE inhibitors
    D. statins

55. The Drug Supply Chain Security Act requires pharmacies to

    A. inspect all manufacturers for product integrity issues
    B. audit tax returns of manufacturers
    C. verify licensing of wholesalers and registration of manufacturers
    D. keep transaction data stored for 20 years

56. When conducting a root cause analysis, contributing factors include

    A. punitive responses.
    B. mistakes made by the patient.
    C. conditions that may increase the probability of an adverse event.
    D. the human error component.

57. A pharmacy technician drawing up 34 units into an insulin U-100 syringe has drawn up how many mL?

    A. 0.034mL
    B. 0.34mL
    C. 3.4mL
    D. 34mL

58. What volume of amoxicillin 400mg/5mL suspension is needed for a 375mg dose?

    A. 24mL

    B. 4.7mL

    C. 12.8mL

    D. 9.4mL

59. A nurse gives a medication as an IV push instead of a subcutaneous injection. This type of error would be considered a(n)

    A. administering error

    B. monitoring error

    C. dispensing error

    D. prescribing error

60. How many 2mg clonazepam tablets are required to prepare clonazepam 0.1mg/mL oral suspension with a total volume of 100mL?

    A. 5 tabs

    B. 7 tabs

    C. 2 tabs

    D. 12 tabs

61. An order is written for 250mL of a 3% solution. You have a 6% solution in stock. How much stock solution and how much diluent is needed to compound this order?

    A. 135mL diluent is added to 115mL stock.

    B. 200mL diluent is added to 50mL stock.

    C. 125mL diluent is added to 125mL stock.

    D. 152mL diluent is added to 98mL stock.

62. Clavulanate increases the action of amoxicillin to increase inhibition of bacterial growth. This is known as which type of drug–drug interaction?

    A. additive

    B. antagonistic

    C. potentiated

    D. synergistic

63. A patient with hypertension should avoid which of the following?

    A. acetaminophen

    B. spironolactone

    C. pseudoephedrine

    D. hydroxyzine

64. Reverse distribution occurs when

    A. a prescription is reversed from the insurance and returned to stock
    B. a medication is returned to the wholesaler for credit
    C. expired or damaged medications are removed from a pharmacy and processed for credit
    D. a pharmacy disposes of expired medications through drop boxes

65. An oral syringe has which type of tip?

    A. Luer lock
    B. filter
    C. insulin
    D. slip

66. An order is written for 1000mL of a 40% solution. You have a 50% solution in stock. How much stock solution and how much diluent is needed to compound this order?

    A. 333mL diluent is added to 667mL stock.
    B. 200mL diluent is added to 800mL stock.
    C. 400mL diluent is added to 600mL stock.
    D. 667mL diluent is added to 333mL stock.

67. Which of the following is indicated to treat hypertension and CHF?

    A. nortriptyline
    B. acyclovir
    C. liraglutide
    D. benazepril

68. Benzonatate and dextromethorphan could both be used for

    A. relief of congestion
    B. relief of cough
    C. runny nose
    D. allergic rhinitis

69. A pharmacist review of a prescription for drug interactions, allergies, contraindications, or compliance issue before and after dispensing is known as

    A. Omnibus Budget Reconciliation Act
    B. drug utilization review
    C. DSCSA
    D. product integrity

70. Taking a prescription that is not prescribed to you or using a medication for a high is considered
    A. overdosing
    B. adherence
    C. a therapeutic substitution
    D. misuse

71. Which of the following is indicated for the treatment of type I diabetes?
    A. metformin
    B. pioglitazone
    C. insulin lispro
    D. glyburide

72. A patient is admitted to the hospital taking Januvia. Which of the following could be used as a therapeutic substitution?
    A. metformin
    B. glipizide
    C. linagliptin
    D. glimeperide

73. A contributing factor to ADEs can be if a patient is taking multiple drugs, often for the same disease. This is known as
    A. ADR
    B. Beers list
    C. polypharmacy
    D. VAERS

74. Temazepam is indicated for
    A. insomnia
    B. panic attacks and seizures
    C. OCD and schizophrenia
    D. depression

75. A pharmacy technician forgets to clean the counting tray after counting amoxicillin tablets. This left a powdery residue, which isn't cleaned prior to counting the next patient's medications. What might occur?
    A. inappropriate polypharmacy
    B. cross-contamination with the potential for patient harm
    C. the patient could develop a tetracycline allergy
    D. near miss

76. A HEPA filter in a horizontal or vertical flow hood must be certified every
    A. 7 days
    B. 6 months
    C. 1 year
    D. 30 days

77. Which of the following is indicated for moderate dementia caused by Alzheimer's disease?
    A. pregabalin
    B. carbidopa-levodopa
    C. dexmethylphenidate
    D. memantine

78. A patient is suffering from regular insomnia and wants a natural remedy. What can be recommended for treatment?
    A. aloe vera
    B. chondroitin
    C. melatonin
    D. saw palmetto

79. In the buffer room, the ISO level must not be greater than
    A. ISO class 9
    B. ISO class 5
    C. ISO class 8
    D. ISO class 7

80. Which of the following PPE would be donned first when preparing for sterile compounding?
    A. sterile gloves
    B. gown
    C. goggles
    D. shoe covers

81. Which of the following is indicated for the treatment of gout?
    A. methotrexate
    B. allopurinol
    C. celecoxib
    D. naproxen

82. A patient with rheumatoid arthritis may be prescribed which of the following for treatment?

    A. baclofen
    B. diclofenac
    C. allopurinol
    D. brimonidine

83. A patient taking which of the following medications may experience flushing of the face and neck as a side effect?

    A. canagliflozin
    B. mirabegron
    C. nitroglycerin
    D. amoxicillin

84. A patient fills a 90-day supply of a medication 3 times in 9 months. What is the adherence rate for this patient?

    A. 72%
    B. 30%
    C. 100%
    D. 80%

85. A pharmacy technician is assisting a new patient to fill a prescription. The patient says they have no allergies at all. The pharmacy technician should document this as

    A. NKA
    B. NKDA
    C. NTG
    D. NPO

86. Which of the following is indicated for the treatment of breast cancer, rheumatoid arthritis, and control of psoriasis?

    A. timolol
    B. adilumumab
    C. menthol
    D. methotrexate

87. Which of the following is a side effect of warfarin?

    A. neuropathy
    B. hypertension
    C. photosensitivity
    D. unexpected bleeding

88. A pharmacy technician is preparing to reconstitute azithromycin suspension. The patient asks how many days the suspension will be good for at room temperature. The pharmacy technician tells the patient

    A. 10 days

    B. 7 days

    C. 28 days

    D. expiration date on the bottle

89. Which of the following is exposed to air after opening and has a short stability?

    A. MDV

    B. ampule

    C. SDV

    D. epidural

90. A patient is prescribed a medication with the stem *-gliptin*. This patient has

    A. hypertension

    B. diabetes

    C. CHF

    D. depression

Practice Test 1 Answer Key

1. **B**

   Lisinopril is an ACE inhibitor.

2. **D**

   To help prevent errors, ISMP has developed a list of high-alert medications, which are drugs that may cause greater harm if used in error.

3. **A**

   Heroin is a Schedule I controlled substance.

4. **B**

   The first series of numbers is known as the labeler code, and represents the manufacturer, repackager, or distributor.

5. **C**

   Carvedilol is the generic for Coreg.

6. **B**

   Meloxicam is an NSAID.

7. **B**

   Uppercase and bolded letters that are used to draw attention to the differences in each drug name are known as tall man lettering. This helps distinguish between two drugs that look or sound similar.

8. **D**

   Insulin syringes are also used for patients with diabetes when administering insulin. These syringes hold 1mL or less, and are measured in both mL and insulin units.

9. **B**

   Percocet is a Schedule II controlled substance.

10. **C**

    Topiramate and pregabalin are both anticonvulsant medications.

11. **D**

    Levetiracetam is the generic for Keppra.

12. **D**

    6 fl oz.

$$\frac{x \text{ fl oz}}{180 \text{mL}} = \frac{1 \text{ fl oz}}{30 \text{mL}}$$

$$(x)(30) = (180)(1)$$

$$\frac{180}{30} = 6 \text{ fl oz}$$

13. **D**

    A graduated cylinder is a tall, narrow container that has straight sides and is used for measuring liquids.

14. **A**

    Medication errors can be caused by many factors, though some common causes can be: communication failures, failure in procedure, and human error.

15. **A**

    The five rights are:

    - Right patient
    - Right drug
    - Right dose
    - Right route
    - Right time

16. **D**

    Temazepam is a Schedule IV controlled substance.

17. **B**

    Ropinirole is an antiparkinson agent.

18. **C**

    HS is the abbreviation for at bedtime but can be confused for half-strength.

19. **D**

    30G. The size of the needle decreases as the gauge increases. This means the larger gauge value will also be the smallest needle.

20. **C**

    200mL

    $$2 \text{ tsp} = 5\text{mL} \times 2 = 10\text{mL}$$

    $$QID = 4\times \text{ daily} = (10\text{mL} \times 4) = 40\text{mL daily}$$

    $$(40\text{mL}) \times 5d = 200\text{mL}$$

21. **C**

    Hydrocodone with acetaminophen is a Schedule II controlled substance, and refills are not permitted.

22. **A**

    Verapamil is a calcium channel blocker.

23. **C**

High-alert medications require a method of distinction to identify, such as a high-alert sticker, or be stored in a segregated area in the pharmacy.

24. **D**

Tegretol is the name brand of carbamazepine.

25. **D**

Instill one drop into both ears three times daily for 7 days.

> 1 gtt = 1 drop
>
> AU = both ears
>
> TID = 3× daily
>
> VII d = for 7 days

26. **A**

Bradycardia is a slow heart rate. The prefix *brady-* is for slow, and *cardio-* is the root word for heart.

27. **B**

DEA Form 222 is used for ordering Schedule I or II controlled substances.

28. **C**

A near miss is a potential medication error that was caught before it reached the patient.

29. **A**

67%

$$60 \text{ day supply filled twice} = (60)(2) = 120 \text{ days' supply of patient fills}$$

$$6 \text{ months} \times 30\frac{\text{days}}{\text{month}} = 180 \text{ total days}$$

$$\frac{120 \text{ total days' supply}}{180 \text{ total days}} \times 100 = 67\%$$

30. **C**

Though medications must pass rigorous testing and clinical trials prior to FDA approval, some are approved or are later identified to require restrictions due to known patient safety issues. The FDA manages these through risk evaluation and mitigation strategies (REMS). The manufacturer is required to develop a REMS program to accompany the new drug approval or after approval if the FDA identifies a need.

31. **D**

Levofloxacin is a fluoroquinolone antibiotic.

32. **C**

For a drug to be considered therapeutically equivalent, the following must be demonstrated:

- Must contain the same active ingredient
- Must be the same dosage form, route of administration, and strength
- Clinical effect and safety profile are the same when administered to patients under same conditions as specified in labeling
- Bioequivalence is demonstrated

33. **B**

Pharmacy technicians can assist the pharmacist for patients requesting vaccines by completing documentation for the patient, including informed consent for the vaccine risks and supplying a vaccine information statement (VIS).

34. **C**

When mixing together powders that are of unequal size, geometric dilution is the process that can be used to ensure a well-mixed compound. In this process, the smallest amount of powder is added first and mixed with an equal amount of the powder in the larger quantity.

35. **B**

Though medications must pass rigorous testing and clinical trials prior to FDA approval, some are approved or are later identified to require restrictions due to known patient safety issues. The FDA manages these through risk evaluation and mitigation strategies (REMS). The manufacturer is required to develop a REMS program to accompany the new drug approval or after approval if the FDA identifies a need.

36. **B**

2 vials.

$$15 + 25 = 40 \text{ total units daily}$$

$$\frac{x \text{ vial}}{40 \text{ units}} = \frac{1 \text{ vial}}{1{,}000 \text{ units}}$$

$$(x)(1{,}000) = (1)(40)$$

$$\frac{40}{1{,}000} = 0.04 \text{ vial for 1 day}$$

$$(0.04)(30) = 1.2 \text{ vials} = 2 \text{ total vials needed.}$$

37. **C**

30 doses.

$$\frac{x\,\text{mL}}{125\text{mg}} = \frac{5\text{mL}}{125\text{mg}}$$

$$(x)(125) = (125)(5)$$

$$x = 5\text{mL / dose}$$

$$\frac{x\,\text{dose}}{150\text{mL}} = \frac{1\,\text{dose}}{5\text{mL}}$$

$$(x)(5) = (150)(1)$$

$$\frac{150}{5} = 30\,\text{doses}$$

38. **A**

Digoxin has a narrow therapeutic index.

39. **D**

Lozenges or troches are another type of solid dosage form that are sweetened or flavored to help medication slowly dissolve locally to the throat or mouth.

40. **C**

2 boxes of 30 tablets, 90mg pseudoephedrine in one month.

$$(2)(30)(90) = 5,400\text{mg} = 5.4\text{g, which is under the 30-day limit of 9g}$$

41. **D**

Lotensin (benazepril) can be therapeutically substituted by lisinopril as they are both ACE inhibitors.

42. **C**

Clozapine (Clozaril) is a medication used for the treatment of schizophrenia and has been associated with causing severe neutropenia.

43. **D**

Intrathecal injections are injected into the spinal column.

44. **B**

Diuretics should be taken in the morning to avoid urination at nighttime.

45. **B**

Class II recalls are those in which the product causes a temporary health problem or slight threat.

46. **D**

Chronic conditions are those in which an illness persists for a long time, such as months, years, or even the rest of your life, such as diabetes or hypertension.

47. **D**

A dispensing error is a difference in what was prescribed and what is dispensed to a patient.

48. **D**

6.7mL.

$$\frac{66}{2.2} = 30\text{kg}$$

$$\frac{x \text{ mg}}{30\text{kg}} = \frac{10\text{mg}}{1\text{kg}}$$

$$(x)(1) = (30)(10)$$

$$x = 300\text{mg per day}$$

$$\frac{300\text{mg}}{3} = 100\text{mg per dose}$$

$$\frac{x \text{ mL}}{100\text{mg}} = \frac{10\text{mL}}{150\text{mg}}$$

$$(x)(150) = (100)(10)$$

$$\frac{1,000}{150} = 6.7\text{mL}$$

49. **D**

74 tabs

(6 tabs)(5 days) = 30 tabs

(5 tabs)(4 days) = 20 tabs

(4 tabs)(3 days) = 12 tabs

(3 tabs)(2 days) = 6 tabs

(2 tab)(2 days) = 4 tabs

(1 tab)(2 days) = 2 tab

$$30 + 20 + 12 + 6 + 4 + 2 = 74 \text{ tabs}$$

50. **B**

A nutrient in grapefruit juice prevents the breakdown of statins and can lead to an increase in toxic accumulation.

51. **B**

Terazosin can treat both hypertension and BHP.

52. **B**

A chemical incompatibility could occur in a compound with a light-sensitive ingredient not stored in a light-resistant container. The light could cause a breakdown in the medication, causing a lack of effectiveness.

53. **B**

A desiccant is used as a drying agent. This absorbs any moisture that could potentially degrade the medication.

54. **C**

A side effect of ACE inhibitors is a dry cough.

55. **C**

The Drug Supply Chain Security Act (DSCSA) was enacted in 2013 to help detect and remove counterfeit, stolen, or contaminated drugs from the US supply chain. Under the DSCSA, pharmacies must verify licensing of wholesalers and registration of manufacturers.

56. **C**

RCA identifies factors that may enhance the possibility of an error occurring. These are called contributing factors and can include circumstances or conditions that may increase the probability of an adverse event.

57. **B**

0.34mL.

$$\frac{x \text{ mL}}{34 \text{ units}} = \frac{1\text{mL}}{100 \text{ units}}$$

$$(x)(100) = (34)(1)$$

$$\frac{34}{100} = 0.34\text{mL}$$

58. **B**

4.7mL.

$$\frac{x \text{ mL}}{375\text{mg}} = \frac{5\text{mL}}{400\text{mg}}$$

$$(x)(400) = (375)(5)$$

$$\frac{1,875}{400} = 4.7\text{mL}$$

59. **A**

An administration error occurs when there is a difference in what the patient is administered and what was prescribed. This includes administering the wrong drug, the wrong dose, or at the wrong time.

60. **A**

    5 tabs.

    $$\frac{x \text{ mg}}{100 \text{mL}} = \frac{0.1 \text{mg}}{1 \text{mL}}$$

    $$(x)(1) = (100)(0.1) = 10 \text{mg}$$

    $$\frac{x \text{ tab}}{10 \text{mg}} = \frac{1 \text{tab}}{2 \text{mg}}$$

    $$(x)(2) = (10)(1)$$

    $$\frac{10}{2} = 5 \text{ tabs}$$

61. **C**

    125mL diluent is added to 125mL stock.

    $$C1 = 6$$

    $$V1 = x$$

    $$C2 = 3$$

    $$V2 = 250$$

    $$(6)(x) = (3)(250)$$

    $$\frac{750}{6} = 125 \text{mL of stock solution}$$

    This question also asks for quantity of diluent needed with the stock solution. This can be found by taking the final volume and subtracting the stock volume calculated.

    $$250 \text{mL} - 125 \text{mL} = 125 \text{mL}$$

    125mL diluent is added to 125mL stock solution to get a final volume of 250mL.

62. **C**

    A potentiated reaction occurs when two drugs given together cause an increase in duration of one of the drugs. Clavulanate potentiates the action of amoxicillin and increases inhibition of bacterial growth.

63. **C**

    Pseudoephedrine is a decongestant and can increase blood pressure.

64. **C**

    A reverse distributor processes expired or damaged drugs from a pharmacy and removes them to be returned back to the manufacturers for credit.

65. **D**

An injectable syringe should use a Luer lock so a needle can be screwed on the top, whereas an oral syringe has a flat or slip tip that a cap can slip onto.

66. **B**

200mL diluent is added to 800mL stock.

$$C1 = 50$$

$$V1 = x$$

$$C2 = 40$$

$$V2 = 1,000$$

$$(50)(x) = (40)(1,000)$$

$$\frac{40,000}{50} = 800\text{mL stock solution}$$

This question also asks for quantity of diluent needed with the stock solution. This can be found by taking the final volume and subtracting the stock volume calculated.

$$1,000\text{mL} - 800\text{mL} = 200\text{mL}$$

200mL diluent is added to 800mL stock solution to get a final volume of 1,000mL.

67. **D**

Benazepril is indicated to treat hypertension and CHF.

68. **B**

Benzonatate and dextromethorphan are both indicated for the relief of cough.

69. **B**

A pharmacist completes a DUR by reviewing a prescription for potential drug interactions, allergies, contraindications, and compliance issues. A DUR provides a comprehensive review of prescriptions and medication data before and after dispensing to ensure a positive outcome.

70. **D**

Misuse of a prescription is when a patient intentionally or unintentionally takes a medication outside of the prescribed directions. This could include taking a prescription that is not prescribed to you or using a medication for a high or euphoric feeling.

71. **C**

Insulin lispro is indicated for treatment of type I diabetes.

72. **C**

Januvia (sitagliptin) is a gliptin that can be therapeutically substituted with linagliptin.

73. **C**

Contributing factor to ADEs can be polypharmacy, or when a patient is taking multiple drugs, often for the same disease.

74. **A**

Temazepam is indicated for treatment of insomnia.

75. **B**

Counting trays should be cleaned with 70% isopropyl alcohol (IPA). Cleaning counting trays regularly helps prevent cross-contamination, which is the contamination of another medication due to residual residue left on a counting tray. Drugs that leave a powder on the tray can contaminate the next prescription if the tray is not cleaned in between prescriptions. This is especially true for medications that have allergy implications. For example, if a counting tray is not cleaned following the counting of amoxicillin, and a patient has a penicillin allergy, this could result in an allergic reaction if residue is on the tray when the next prescription is counted.

76. **B**

The HEPA filter must be certified every 6 months.

77. **D**

Memantine is indicated for moderate dementia caused by Alzheimer's disease.

78. **C**

Melatonin is a supplement used for insomnia.

79. **D**

In the buffer area, the air should be no higher than ISO class 7.

80. **D**

Here is the proper order of PPE donning for sterile compounding:

- Start by removing any jewelry, makeup, artificial nails or polish before donning PPE.
- Put on shoe covers.
- Don hair cover—including beard cover if needed.
- Put on a face mask or shield. A face shield or goggles are typically only required when compounding hazardous drugs.
- Perform hand hygiene.
- Don nonshedding gown over clean scrubs.
- Use surgical (alcohol-based) hand scrub prior to putting on gloves. Allow to dry.
- Don sterile gloves. Two pairs of chemotherapy gloves should be used if compounding a hazardous drug.

81. **B**

Allopurinol is indicated for the treatment of gout.

82. **B**

Diclofenac is indicated for rheumatoid arthritis, osteoarthritis, ankylosing spondylitis, and pain.

83. **C**

Nitroglycerin and other nitrates have a side effect of flushing of the face and neck.

84. **C**

100%.

$$90 \text{ day supply filled three times} = (90)(3) = 270 \text{ days' supply of patient fills}$$

$$9 \text{ months} \times 30\frac{\text{days}}{\text{month}} = 270 \text{ total days}$$

$$\frac{270 \text{ total days' supply}}{270 \text{ total days}} \times 100 = 100\%$$

85. **A**

If a patient has no known allergies, including all substances and drugs, this is NKA.

86. **D**

Methotrexate is indicated for treatment of breast cancer, control of psoriasis, treatment of rheumatoid arthritis, head and neck cancer, lymphoma, and osteosarcoma.

87. **D**

Warfarin may cause unexpected bleeding.

88. **A**

Azithromycin is stable for 10 days after reconstitution.

89. **B**

Ampules are also single use and do not contain a preservative. They are a glass container that is designed to be broken at the neck. The medication inside is removed using a filter needle, to protect against any residual glass that may have fallen in the contents. As soon as the ampule is open, it is exposed to air, and the stability is limited.

90. **B**

Linagliptin is an example of a drug with the stem *-gliptin* indicated for type II diabetes.

Practice Test 2

The following practice exam tests your readiness for the PTCE. To best prepare, give yourself only 1 hour 50 minutes to complete the exam.

1. Schedule I substances have
   A. no accepted medical use
   B. accepted medical use and high potential for abuse
   C. the lowest potential for abuse
   D. slight potential for abuse but less than oxycodone

2. The name brand of omeprazole is
   A. Prilosec
   B. Nexium
   C. Prevacid
   D. Protonix

3. The middle set of numbers in an NDC is known as the
   A. product code
   B. labeler code
   C. package code
   D. dosage code

4. High-alert/risk medications are drugs that
   A. are all controlled substances
   B. can be devastating if used in error
   C. look like other drugs
   D. have an error-prone abbreviation

5. Lantus is the name brand of which insulin?

   A. insulin detemir

   B. insulin aspart

   C. insulin regular

   D. insulin glargine

6. Which of the following is a beta blocker?

   A. allopurinol

   B. zolpidem

   C. ranitidine

   D. atenolol

7. Which of the following should always be used and comes before the decimal point?

   A. trailing zero

   B. leading zero

   C. μg

   D. AD, AS, AU

8. Other than a vial, what is another way that insulin can be dispensed for patient use?

   A. lancet

   B. glucometer

   C. insulin pen

   D. nebulizer

9. Which of the following schedules has the lowest potential for abuse?

   A. I

   B. II

   C. III

   D. IV

10. Which medication is an H2 antagonist?

    A. famotidine

    B. paroxetine

    C. cetirizine

    D. clonidine

11. Which of the following is a COX-2 inhibitor?
    A. hydralazine
    B. diclofenac
    C. celecoxib
    D. famotidine

12. A patient is receiving TPN in a 3L bag. How many mL is in this bag?
    A. 0.003mL
    B. 0.03mL
    C. 3mL
    D. 3,000mL

13. The package code of an NDC consists of how many digits (assuming an 11-digit format)?
    A. 2
    B. 3
    C. 4
    D. 5

14. When filling prescriptions in a retail pharmacy what may be scanned to confirm the correct product has been selected?
    A. bar code of the expiration date
    B. bar code of the NDC
    C. bar code of the manufacturer
    D. bar code of the lot number

15. Which of the following is one of the five rights of medication administration?
    A. right signature
    B. right tubing
    C. right drug
    D. right insurance plan

16. Which of the following must be included on a prescription for a controlled substance?
    A. patient's Social Security number
    B. prescriber NPI number
    C. patient's full address
    D. prescriber's Medicaid number

17. The generic for Valium is

    A. lorazepam

    B. clonazepam

    C. alprazolam

    D. diazepam

18. According to the ISMP, which of the following should be used instead of µg?

    A. kg

    B. grains

    C. g

    D. mg

19. A pharmacy technician is compounding a prescription and the mixture of powder and liquid does not fully dissolve. This is which type of liquid?

    A. suspension

    B. solution

    C. syrup

    D. suppository

20. A patient weighs 132 pounds. How many kg does this patient weigh?

    A. 58.2kg

    B. 94.2kg

    C. 164.8kg

    D. 290.4kg

21. If a Schedule II controlled substance is partially filled for a patient who is not in hospice or a long-term-care facility, the full prescription must be picked up within what time frame before a new prescription is needed?

    A. 24 hours

    B. 72 hours

    C. 7 days

    D. 30 days

22. Oseltamivir is the generic for

    A. Lotrel

    B. Tamiflu

    C. Tamsulosin

    D. Digoxin

23. Medications that are recalled must be
    A. sent back to the wholesaler
    B. quarantined and removed from stock
    C. dispensed immediately to patients
    D. thrown away

24. Which of the following is an antifungal agent?
    A. fluconazole
    B. progesterone
    C. terazosin
    D. glyburide

25. Which of the following may be used during nonsterile compounding?
    A. filter needle
    B. conical cylinder
    C. ampule
    D. CSTD

26. A pulmonologist is one who
    A. specializes in lungs
    B. records the heart
    C. examines the stomach
    D. treats the brain

27. According to federal law, how many times can a prescription for clonazepam be refilled?
    A. up to 5 times within 6 months
    B. 12 times in 1 year
    C. no refills
    D. up to 5 times in 30 days

28. Medication errors, ADRs, and allergic reactions are all considered
    A. high-alert
    B. hazardous drugs
    C. ADEs
    D. overdoses

29. A patient fills a 30-day supply of a medication 1 time in 6 months. What is the adherence rate for this patient?

    A. 33%

    B. 50%

    C. 17%

    D. 60%

30. A program sponsored by the DEA that allows patients to dispose of unused medications safely is a

    A. reverse distributor

    B. credit rebill

    C. take-back day

    D. REMS

31. Which of the following is an antitussive agent?

    A. benzonatate

    B. timolol

    C. pioglitazone

    D. promethazine

32. Therapeutically equivalent drugs must

    A. have the same NDC

    B. demonstrate bioequivalence

    C. have a B code

    D. be produced by the same manufacturer

33. A handout for patients, which provides information on specific vaccines, including reactions to look for post-immunization is a

    A. DUR

    B. MedWatch

    C. VAERS

    D. VIS

34. Polyethylene glycol and petrolatum are bases that can be used to compound a(n)

    A. ointment

    B. elixir

    C. enema

    D. capsule

35. Which of the following drugs will require a medication guide to be dispensed?

    A. atorvastatin

    B. citalopram

    C. lisinopril

    D. albuterol

36. A patient has the following prescription:

    Novolog Insulin 1,000 units/10mL

    Inject 37 units subcutaneously immediate before meals 3 times daily

    How many vials will the patient need for a 30-day supply?

    A. 1 vial

    B. 2 vials

    C. 3 vials

    D. 4 vials

37. A patient has a prescription for amoxicillin suspension 500mg Q12H × 7d. The pharmacy has 100mL stock bottles of 400mg/5mL. How many doses can the patient get from one bottle?

    A. 4 doses

    B. 9 doses

    C. 14 doses

    D. 16 doses

38. Which medication has a narrow therapeutic index?

    A. lovastatin

    B. ramipril

    C. levothyroxine

    D. levocetirizine

39. Which type of tablet dissolves in water and gives off carbon dioxide, causing a fizz?

    A. sublingual

    B. effervescent

    C. film-coated

    D. ODT

40. Which of the following would be an acceptable purchase under the CMEA?

    A. 5 boxes of 20 tablets, 90mg pseudoephedrine in one day

    B. 3 boxes of 30 tablets, 90mg pseudoephedrine in one month

    C. 6 boxes of 30 tablets, 30mg pseudoephedrine in one day

    D. 3 boxes of 30 tablets, 240mg pseudoephedrine in one month

41. A patient attempts to fill a prescription for Nexium, but the insurance rejects the prescription saying a cheaper alternative must be tried first. Which of the following is a potential therapeutic substitution?

    A. ranitidine

    B. omeprazole

    C. ezetimibe

    D. rosuvastatin

42. The goal of the opioid REMS is to educate on

    A. potential for birth defects

    B. severe neutropenia

    C. risk of bleeding

    D. the risk of addiction, unintentional overdose, and death

43. Which of the following contain handling requirements of hazardous drugs and chemicals?

    A. USP<797>

    B. SDS

    C. CMEA

    D. iPLEDGE

44. Which medication has the following special instructions: Must be swallowed with 8 ounces plain water immediately after rising for the day and must be 30 minutes before first food, beverage, or medication of the day?

    A. alendronate

    B. prednisone

    C. glimeperide

    D. furosemide

45. A Class III recall occurs when the product

    A. is unlikely to cause an issue

    B. could cause serious health problems or death

    C. may cause a temporary health problem or slight threat

    D. is declared counterfeit

46. Which of the following is a long-acting insulin?

    A. aspart

    B. detemir

    C. glargine

    D. lispro

47. Which type of error occurs when an order is written for a drug known to be a contraindicated medication with the patient's drug therapy?

   A. monitoring
   B. administering
   C. prescribing
   D. dispensing

48. A physician prescribes a medication as 2.4mcg/kg BID for a 9 lb baby. The medication is available as 25mcg/mL in a 50mL bottle. How much in mL is required for each dose?

   A. 0.39mL
   B. 0.48mL
   C. 0.92mL
   D. 1.4mL

49. A patient has the following prescription:

   Prednisone 20mg. Take 3 tabs PO QD × 3 days, then 2 tabs PO QD × 3 days, then 1 tab PO QD × 3 days.

   How many prednisone 20mg tab are required to fill this order?

   A. 14 tabs
   B. 18 tabs
   C. 22 tabs
   D. 30 tabs

50. Which of the following would cause an antagonistic drug–drug interaction with naloxone?

   A. ibuprofen
   B. aspirin
   C. ketoconazole
   D. oxycodone

51. Lansoprazole is indicated for the treatment of

   A. Crohn's disease
   B. gastric ulcers and GERD
   C. ulcerative colitis
   D. vertigo and motion sickness

52. An interaction in which two or more substances cause a change in the properties of a drug and may often be unseen is which type of interaction?
    A. physical
    B. chemical
    C. therapeutic
    D. sublingual

53. A medication to be stored at room temperature should be stored in which range?
    A. 20°C to 25°C
    B. 2°C to 8°C
    C. 86°F to 104°F
    D. 46°F to 59°F

54. Muscle pain and dyspepsia is a side effect of which class of medications?
    A. calcium channel blockers
    B. statins
    C. nitrates
    D. H2 antagonists

55. The FDA uses information from MedWatch to
    A. initiate recalls
    B. send information to patients
    C. take legal action against those who don't report
    D. develop safe drug lists

56. The process to identify the cause of an error through a comprehensive review of all workflows and systems is known as a
    A. BCMA
    B. RCA
    C. DSCSA
    D. MERP

57. A pharmacy technician drawing up 42 units into an insulin U-100 syringe has drawn up how many mL?
    A. 42mL
    B. 0.042mL
    C. 4.2mL
    D. 0.42mL

58. How many mg of cephalexin 250mg/5mL suspension is needed for a 0.5 tsp dose?

    A. 125mg

    B. 75mg

    C. 25mg

    D. 100mg

59. A patient is admitted to the hospital and the nurse misses her 9 PM doses. What type of error has occurred?

    A. dispensing

    B. prescribing

    C. monitoring

    D. administering

60. How many 90mg diltiazem tablets are needed to compound diltiazem 12mg/mL suspension with a total volume of 120mL?

    A. 8 tabs

    B. 24 tabs

    C. 16 tabs

    D. 13 tabs

61. An order is written for 100mL of a 23% solution. You have a 42% solution in stock. How much stock solution and how much diluent are needed to compound this order?

    A. 84mL diluent is added to 16mL stock.

    B. 45.2mL diluent is added to 54.8mL stock.

    C. 36mL diluent is added to 64mL stock.

    D. 28.4mL diluent is added to 71.6mL stock.

62. When two drugs are given together and have the same effect if each were taken separately, this is which type of drug interaction?

    A. additive

    B. antagonistic

    C. potentiated

    D. synergistic

63. Ethinyl estradiol and desogestrel may interact with which class of drugs?

    A. antifungal agents

    B. antibiotics

    C. antiviral agents

    D. statins

64. A credit return occurs when
    A. an eligible drug is returned to the wholesaler for credit
    B. a reverse distributor returns drugs to manufacturers for credit
    C. a patient is credited the prescription and it is returned to stock
    D. a pharmacy sends a medication back to the manufacturer directly

65. The Poison Prevention Packaging Act of 1970 requires most prescription and OTC drugs to be packaged in containers that are
    A. light resistant
    B. child resistant
    C. moisture resistant
    D. temperature resistant

66. A patient has an order for a medication for 6mg/m^2. The patient has a BSA of 1.4m^2. The medication is available as a 100mg/15mL vial. How many mL are needed per dose?
    A. 0.8mL
    B. 4.2mL
    C. 9.6mL
    D. 1.3mL

67. Adalimumab is indicated for the treatment of
    A. nausea and vomiting
    B. Crohn's disease and ulcerative colitis
    C. vertigo and motion sickness
    D. GERD

68. Which of the following is the indication for glipizide?
    A. urinary retention
    B. nausea and dizziness
    C. headache
    D. adjunct to diet and exercise for type II diabetes

69. A prospective DUR occurs
    A. after the drug is dispensed as a review
    B. only on refilled prescriptions
    C. on prescriptions before they are dispensed
    D. in physician offices

70. Which of the following drugs is most likely to be abused?

    A. Norco

    B. Naprosyn

    C. Coreg

    D. Aldactone

71. Which is the following is indicated for treatment and prevention of osteoporosis in postmenopausal women?

    A. levothyroxine

    B. norethindrone

    C. testosterone

    D. alendronate

72. A patient has a prescription for diclofenac oral tablets. The insurance company requires a therapeutic substitution. Which of the following can be used as an alternative?

    A. acetaminophen

    B. meloxicam

    C. tolterodine

    D. zolpidem

73. The Beers list is a list of medications and drugs that may be inappropriate for which type of patient?

    A. patients on anticoagulants

    B. immunocompromised

    C. pediatric

    D. geriatric

74. Ropinirole is indicated for

    A. insomnia

    B. Alzheimer's disease

    C. Parkinson's disease and restless leg syndrome

    D. seizure disorder and migraines

75. Which of the following may occur if counting trays are not cleaned properly after counting high-residue medications?

    A. cross-contamination

    B. loss of product integrity

    C. polypharmacy

    D. adherence

76. In an ante room, the ISO level must not be greater than
    A. ISO class 5
    B. ISO class 8
    C. ISO class 7
    D. ISO class 6

77. Which of the following is used to treat iron deficiency anemia?
    A. potassium
    B. magnesium
    C. ferrous sulfate
    D. vitamin D

78. Saint John's wort is a supplement that can be used for
    A. depression and anxiety
    B. arthritis
    C. lowering cholesterol
    D. BPH

79. USP<797> outlines standards for which of the following related to sterile compounding?
    A. handling of hazardous drugs
    B. reconstituting oral antibiotics
    C. engineering controls for compounding equipment
    D. expiration dating from manufacturer

80. Per USP<797>, cleaning walls, ceilings, and shelving should occur how frequently in a hospital clean room?
    A. daily
    B. yearly
    C. monthly
    D. weekly

81. A patient has been diagnosed with a UTI. Which of the following may be prescribed to treat the infection?
    A. fluconazole
    B. sulfamethoxazole and trimethoprim
    C. acyclovir
    D. hydrocortisone

82. A patient has been prescribed nitrofurantoin. What is this indicated to treat?

    A. herpes zoster

    B. influenza

    C. cystitis and bacteriuria

    D. osteomyelitis

83. A fungal infection, such as thrush, is a side effect of which medication?

    A. montelukast

    B. cetirizine

    C. fluticasone and salmeterol

    D. omeprazole

84. A patient fills a 90-day supply of a medication 1 time in 9 months. What is the adherence rate for this patient?

    A. 33%

    B. 45%

    C. 60%

    D. 90%

85. A nurse disconnects tubing from a patient and it is visibly bloody. Where should the tubing be discarded?

    A. in the trash

    B. in the biohazard waste

    C. chemotherapy waste

    D. sharps container

86. Photosensitivity is a side effect of which medication?

    A. doxycycline

    B. finasteride

    C. sumatriptan

    D. atomoxetine

87. Tardive dyskinesia is a side effect of which of the following?

    A. venlafaxine

    B. citalopram

    C. risperidone

    D. clonazepam

88. A bottle of cephalexin is reconstituted for a patient prescription. How long will this bottle be stable if stored in the refrigerator?

    A. 6 months

    B. expiration date on the bottle

    C. 14 days

    D. 7 days

89. A medication ending in -*sartan* is which class of drugs?

    A. beta blockers

    B. ACE inhibitors

    C. ARBs

    D. diuretic

90. Which of the following drug classes often end in -*vir*?

    A. corticosteroid

    B. antibiotic

    C. antiviral

    D. antifungal

Practice Test 2 Answer Key

1. **A**

   Schedule I controlled substances have no accepted medical use.

2. **A**

   The name brand of omeprazole is Prilosec.

3. **A**

   The second set of numbers is the product code. This identifies the product, including the drug strength and dosage form.

4. **B**

   High-alert/risk drugs do not have a higher rate of error, but can be more devastating if used in error. ISMP publishes this high-alert list to help organizations identify which medications should have special strategies for error prevention, such as limiting access, using auxiliary labels, and standardizing ordering and preparation of these medications.

5. **D**

   Lantus is the name brand of insulin glargine.

6. **D**

   Atenolol is a beta blocker.

7. **B**

   Leading zeros help minimize errors and should always be used. The leading zero comes before the decimal point, such as <u>0</u>.7. If a leading zero is not used, .7 can be misread as 7 and a tenfold error could occur.

8. **C**

   Newer forms of insulin are administered through an insulin pen, which is a prefilled cartridge that has a dial for measuring doses, instead of using a syringe and needle. Insulin pens use pen needles, which are smaller, often less painful, needles.

9. **D**

   Schedule IV controlled substances have the lowest potential for abuse of Schedules I–IV.

10. **A**

    Famotidine is an H2 antagonist.

11. **C**

    Celecoxib is a COX-2 inhibitor.

12. **D**

    3,000mL.

    $$(3)(1,000) = 3,000mL$$

13. **A**

The package code is the third set of numbers and is 2 digits.

14. **B**

When filling prescriptions in a pharmacy, the bar code of the correct NDC is scanned to confirm product selection.

15. **C**

The five rights are:

- Right patient
- Right drug
- Right dose
- Right route
- Right time

16. **C**

Prescriptions written for a controlled substance must follow DEA requirements before it can be filled by a pharmacy. The prescription must contain the following:

- Drug name
- Strength
- Dosage form
- Quantity prescribed (written out in word format, e.g., 10 tablets [ten])
- Directions for use
- Refills, if any authorized
- Date issued
- Patient's full name
- Patient's full address
- Prescriber's full name
- Prescriber's full address
- Prescriber's DEA number

17. **D**

Diazepam is the generic for Valium.

18. **D**

Milligrams is abbreviated mg and the use of µg is considered dangerous.

19. **A**

A suspension is a powder with a specified amount of diluent added. The powder never fully dissolves, so it must be shaken before administration.

20. **A**

58.2kg.

$$\frac{128}{2.2} = 58.2\text{kg}$$

21. **B**

If a pharmacy does not have enough medication to fill the entire prescription, a partial fill may be dispensed if the remaining quantity can be given within 72 hours. After these 72 hours, if the prescription has not been picked up or is not available from the pharmacy, the patient must get a new prescription.

22. **B**

Tamiflu is the name brand of oseltamivir.

23. **B**

Recalled medications must be quarantined and removed from stock and sent back to manufacturer.

24. **A**

Fluconazole is an antifungal agent.

25. **B**

A conical cylinder is cone-shaped (wider at the top than the bottom) and used for measuring liquid during nonsterile compounding.

26. **A**

Pulmonologist = *pulmon/o* is the root word for lungs and *-ologist* is the suffix for specialist.

27. **A**

Clonazepam is a Schedule IV controlled substance and can be refilled up to 5 times within 6 months.

28. **C**

Adverse drug events (ADE) occur when a medication causes harm to a patient. ADEs consist of medication errors, adverse drug reactions, allergic reactions, or overdose.

29. **C**

17%.

$$6 \text{ months} \times 30 \frac{\text{days}}{\text{month}} = 180 \text{ total days}$$

$$\frac{30 \text{ total days' supply}}{180 \text{ total days}} \times 100 = 17\%$$

30. **C**

If a patient has an outdated or unused controlled substance, it may become dangerous if these unused drugs end up in the wrong hands. Patients can dispose of these medications through take-back programs. These are designated days throughout the country, which are sponsored by the DEA. A take-back day allows patients to dispose of unwanted medications safely and anonymously in a nearby location.

31. **A**

Benzonatate is an antitussive agent.

32. **B**

For a drug to be considered therapeutically equivalent, bioequivalence must be demonstrated. Bioequivalence means there is no significant difference in the rate at which the active ingredient is distributed in the body and available at the site of action.

33. **D**

The VIS provides information on the vaccine, including risks of a reaction, reporting procedures for post-immunization follow-up, who should get vaccinated, and information that patients should tell their healthcare provider.

34. **A**

Some examples of bases used in compounding ointments include:

- Petrolatum (Vaseline)
- Lanolin
- Paraffin
- Eucerin
- Polyethylene glycol (PEG)

35. **B**

Citalopram is an SSRI and requires a medication guide to be dispensed when filling a prescription.

36. **C**

3 vials.

$$30 \times 3 = 90 \text{ total units daily}$$

$$\frac{x \text{ vial}}{90 \text{ units}} = \frac{1 \text{ vial}}{1,000 \text{ units}}$$

$$(x)(1000) = (1)(90)$$

$$\frac{90}{1,000} = 0.09 \text{ vial for 1 day}$$

$$(0.09)(30) = 2.7 \text{ vials} = 3 \text{ total vials needed}$$

37. **D**
    16 doses.

$$\frac{x \text{ mL}}{500\text{mg}} = \frac{5\text{mL}}{400\text{mg}}$$

$$(x)(400) = (500)(5)$$

$$\frac{2,500}{400} = 6.25\text{mL per dose}$$

$$\frac{x \text{ dose}}{100\text{mL}} = \frac{1\text{dose}}{6.25\text{mL}}$$

$$(x)(6.25) = (100)(1)$$

$$\frac{100}{6.25} = 16 \text{ doses}$$

38. **C**
    Levothyroxine has a narrow therapeutic index.

39. **B**
    Effervescent tablets dissolve in water and give off a fizz.

40. **B**
    3 boxes of 30 tablets, 90mg pseudoephedrine in one month.

$$(3)(30)(90) = 8,100mg = 8.1\text{g which is under the 30 day limit of 9g}$$

41. **B**
    Nexium (esomeprazole) can be therapeutically substituted by omeprazole as they are both proton pump inhibitors.

42. **D**
    This REMS helps identify the risks of opioids, including the risk of addiction, unintentional overdose, and death.

43. **B**
    SDS contain handling requirements of hazardous drugs and chemicals. These documents are produced by the manufacturer of a chemical or drug if it is considered hazardous. OSHA requires specific information be included in a 16-section format for standardization. The first 8 sections contain information regarding the chemical, including safe handling practices, emergency control measures, and composition. The remaining sections contain other information such as physical or chemical properties and date of last revision.

44. **A**
    Alendronate must be swallowed with 8 ounces plain water immediately after rising for the day and must be 30 minutes before first food, beverage, or medication of the day.

45. **A**

Class III recalls are those in which the products are unlikely to cause any reaction, but violate FDA labeling or manufacturing requirements.

46. **A**

Insulin aspart is a long-acting insulin.

47. **C**

Prescribing errors occur from the written order of a provider, either a prescription or a medication order. This includes errors in prescribed dosage or drug strength, quantity (excessive or insufficient) needed for drug therapy, route or dosage form, rate of infusion, or drug ordered. A prescribing error can also include omitting necessary refills or approving early refills that may alter appropriate therapy. Incorrect patient errors can also occur during prescribing, including writing an order for a medication to a patient with a known allergy or contraindication.

48. **A**

0.39mL.

$$\frac{9 \text{ lb}}{2.2} = 4.1\text{kg}$$

$$\frac{x \text{ mcg}}{4.1\text{kg}} = \frac{2.4\text{mcg}}{1\text{kg}}$$

$$(x)(1) = (4.1)(2.4) = 9.8\text{mcg}$$

$$\frac{x \text{ mL}}{9.8\text{mcg}} = \frac{1\text{mL}}{25\text{mcg}}$$

$$(x)(25) = (9.8)(1)$$

$$\frac{9.8}{25} = 0.39\text{mL}$$

49. **B**

18 tabs.

$$(3 \text{ tabs})(3 \text{ days}) = 9 \text{ tabs}$$

$$(2 \text{ tabs})(3 \text{ days}) = 6 \text{ tabs}$$

$$(1 \text{ tab})(3 \text{ days}) = 3 \text{ tabs}$$

$$9 + 6 + 3 = 18 \text{ tabs}$$

50. **D**

Naloxone blocks the opioid receptors and inhibits the effect of oxycodone.

51. **B**

Lansoprazole is indicated for the treatment of gastric ulcers, healing of erosive esophagitis, and GERD.

52. **B**

    A chemical incompatibility is a reaction between two or more substances, which causes a change in the chemical properties of a drug. Chemical incompatibilities are often unseen but can be observed through a temperature or color change due to oxidation.

53. **A**

    20°C to 25°C is the range for controlled room temperature.

54. **B**

    Statins may cause muscle pain and dyspepsia as a side effect.

55. **A**

    The FDA uses information from MedWatch to initiate recalls, investigate manufacturers, or make recommendations on medications. Reporting is therefore crucial for patient safety, though there is no legal requirement to report adverse events.

56. **B**

    An RCA is a process to find the "root cause" of a problem through a comprehensive review of all workflows and systems in place.

57. **D**

    0.42mL.

    $$\frac{x \text{ mL}}{42 \text{ units}} = \frac{1 \text{mL}}{100 \text{ units}}$$

    $$(x)(100) = (42)(1)$$

    $$\frac{42}{100} = 0.42 \text{mL}$$

58. **A**

    125mg.

    $$\frac{x \text{ mL}}{0.5 \text{tsp}} = \frac{5 \text{mL}}{1 \text{tsp}}$$

    $$(x)(1) = (5)(0.5) = 2.5 \text{mL}$$

    $$\frac{x \text{ mg}}{2.5 \text{mL}} = \frac{250 \text{mg}}{5 \text{mL}}$$

    $$(x)(5) = (2.5)(250)$$

    $$\frac{625}{5} = 125 \text{mg}$$

59. **D**

    An omission error is also considered an administration error and occurs if a patient does not receive a medication at all.

60. **C**

16 tabs.

$$\frac{x \text{ mg}}{120\text{mL}} = \frac{12\text{mg}}{1\text{mL}}$$

$$(x)(1) = (120)(12) = 1,440\text{mg}$$

$$\frac{x \text{ tab}}{1,440\text{mg}} = \frac{1 \text{ tab}}{90\text{mg}} \quad (x)(90) = (1,440)(1)$$

$$\frac{1,440}{90} = 16 \text{ tabs}$$

61. **B**

45.2mL diluent is added to 54.8mL stock.

$$C1 = 42$$

$$V1 = x$$

$$C2 = 23$$

$$V2 = 100$$

$$(42)(x) = (23)(100)$$

$$\frac{2,300}{42} = 54.8\text{mL of stock solution}$$

This question also asks for quantity of diluent needed with the stock solution. This can be found by taking the final volume and subtracting the stock volume calculated.

$$100\text{mL} - 54.8\text{mL} = 45.2\text{mL}$$

54.8mL stock solution and 45.2mL of diluent to get a final volume of 100mL.

62. **A**

An additive drug interaction occurs when two drugs given together have the same effect if each were taken separately.

63. **B**

Antibiotics may lower the effectiveness of oral contraceptives.

64. **A**

A credit return is a credit from the wholesaler to an invoice after sending back eligible drugs.

65. **B**

The Poison Prevention Packaging Act of 1970 (PPPA) requires most OTC and prescription drugs be packaged in containers that cannot be opened by 80% of children under five years old, but can be opened by 90% of adults.

66. **D**

1.3mL.

$$\frac{x \text{ mg}}{1.4\text{m}^2} = \frac{6\text{mg}}{1\text{m}^2}$$

$$(x)(1) = (1.4)(6) = 8.4\text{mg}$$

$$\frac{x \text{ mL}}{8.4\text{mg}} = \frac{15\text{mL}}{100\text{mg}}$$

$$(x)(100) = (8.4)(15)$$

$$\frac{126}{100} = 1.26 = 1.3\text{mL}$$

67. **B**

Adalimumab is indicated for the treatment of Crohn's disease and ulcerative colitis.

68. **D**

Glipizide is indicated as an adjunct to diet and exercise for type II diabetes.

69. **C**

A DUR can be considered prospective (screening of medication before it is dispensed) or retrospective (ongoing review of claims data).

70. **A**

Norco is an opioid analgesic that is more likely to be abused than Naprosyn (NSAID), Coreg (beta blocker), or Aldactone (diuretic).

71. **D**

Alendronate is indicated for the treatment and prevention of osteoporosis in postmenopausal women.

72. **B**

Diclofenac is an NSAID and can be therapeutically substituted with meloxicam.

73. **D**

The Beers list is published by the American Geriatrics Society and is a list of medications and drug classes that may be inappropriate for geriatric use.

74. **C**

Ropinirole is indicated for Parkinson's disease and restless leg syndrome.

75. **A**

Cleaning counting trays regularly helps prevent cross-contamination, which is the contamination of another medication due to residual residue left on a counting tray.

76. **B**

In the ante area outside the buffer area, the air should be no higher than ISO class 8.

77. **C**

Ferrous sulfate is indicated for treatment of iron deficiency anemia.

78. **A**

Saint John's wort is a supplement that can be used to treat depression and anxiety.

79. **C**

USP<797> provides standards and requirements on the following:

- Engineering controls for compounding equipment
- Training and competencies
- Certification requirements for hoods
- Beyond-use-dating
- Layout of facility
- Clean room design
- Environmental monitoring for potential contaminants

80. **C**

Hospital pharmacies, or those with a clean room, follow standards in USP<797>, which require monthly cleaning of walls, ceilings, and shelves that are in the buffer or ante room. This cleaning must be documented in a log each month.

81. **B**

Sulfamethoxazole and trimethoprim is indicated to treat UTI, otitis media, and traveler's diarrhea.

82. **C**

Nitrofurantoin is indicated to treat cystitis and bacteriuria.

83. **C**

Fluticasone and salmeterol may cause thrush as a side effect.

84. **A**

33%.

$$9 \text{ months} \times 30 \frac{\text{days}}{\text{month}} = 270 \text{ total days}$$

$$\frac{90 \text{ total days' supply}}{270 \text{ total days}} \times 100 = 33\%$$

85. **B**

Visibly bloody IV tubing should be discarded in the biohazard waste.

86. **A**

    Doxycycline is a tetracycline antibiotic and may cause photosensitivity as a side effect.

87. **C**

    Risperidone is an antipsychotic that may cause tardive dyskinesia as a side effect.

88. **C**

    Cephalexin is stable for 14 days if refrigerated after reconstitution.

89. **C**

    ARBs end in *-sartan*.

90. **C**

    Antiviral medications, such as acyclovir or valacyclovir, end in *-vir*.

Practice Test 3

The following practice exam tests your readiness for the PTCE. To best prepare, give yourself only 1 hour 50 minutes to complete the exam.

1. Gabapentin is the generic for
   A. Lyrica
   B. Valium
   C. Cozaar
   D. Neurontin

2. Using both brand and generic names on prescriptions and labels, and tall man lettering, are a way to prevent mix-up between
   A. LASA drugs
   B. high risk/alert drugs
   C. controlled substances
   D. fast movers

3. Schedule II controlled substances have
   A. no accepted medical use
   B. high potential for abuse and may lead to physical dependence
   C. low potential for abuse
   D. accepted medical use and low potential for abuse

4. The process of taking a bulk bottle of medication and packaging it into smaller individual doses is known as
   A. unit dose
   B. unit-of-use
   C. repackaging
   D. BCMA

5. Which of the following is a proton pump inhibitor?

   A. pantoprazole

   B. sertraline

   C. levothyroxine

   D. amlodipine

6. Clopidogrel is the generic for

   A. Tenormin

   B. Desyrel

   C. Plavix

   D. Flexeril

7. An event that leads to patient harm or inappropriate medication use is a

   A. near miss

   B. medication error

   C. high risk/alert drug

   D. LASA

8. A 28-day package of oral contraceptive would be considered

   A. unit dose

   B. unit-of-use

   C. repackaging

   D. days' supply

9. Which of the following is a Schedule III controlled substance?

   A. pregabalin

   B. marijuana

   C. methadone

   D. ketamine

10. Which medication is an antigout agent?

    A. ergocalciferol

    B. allopurinol

    C. propranolol

    D. fluoxetine

11. Which of the following is an overactive bladder agent?

    A. sitagliptin

    B. finasteride

    C. valsartan

    D. oxybutynin

12. A patient has a prescription for digoxin 125mcg PO BID. How many mg does the patient take in one day?

    A. 0.125mg

    B. 0.25mg

    C. 125mg

    D. 250mg

13. The product code of an NDC consists of how many digits (assuming an 11-digit format)?

    A. 1

    B. 2

    C. 4

    D. 5

14. At which point are medications scanned?

    A. after dispensing a prescription to a patient

    B. when the patient is asleep to not disturb

    C. before loading into dispensing cabinets to confirm inventory

    D. after patient administration

15. Which of the following is one of the five rights of medication administration?

    A. right insurance

    B. right dose

    C. right pharmacy

    D. right scanner

16. Schedule V controlled substances have

    A. a high potential for abuse

    B. a low to moderate potential for abuse

    C. no accepted medical use

    D. a low potential for abuse and are often antitussive or anticonvulsant medications

17. Which of the following is an antirheumatic and antimalarial agent?

    A. divalproex

    B. enalapril

    C. nifedipine

    D. hydroxychloroquine

18. The abbreviation U is on the confused abbreviation list. What should be used instead?

    A. universal

    B. unit

    C. ulcer

    D. unconscious

19. A syringe that holds up to 1mL and is used for intradermal administration of PPD to identify TB is a(n)

    A. insulin syringe

    B. hypodermic

    C. oral

    D. tuberculin

20. A patient has a prescription for 240mL of a solution. Which size bottle should be selected to fill this order?

    A. 4 fl oz

    B. 6 fl oz

    C. 8 fl oz

    D. 12 fl oz

21. In order to prescribe a verbal order for a Schedule II controlled substance, a valid written prescription must be provided for this order within what time period?

    A. 72 hours

    B. 7 days

    C. 10 days

    D. 24 hours

22. Which of the following is an antiviral medication?

    A. memantine

    B. valacyclovir

    C. doxazosin

    D. risperidone

23. Which of the following must be segregated from pharmacy inventory?

    A. expired medications

    B. Schedule IV controlled substances

    C. anticoagulants

    D. antibiotic suspensions

24. Which of the following is a diuretic?

    A. amiodarone

    B. atomoxetine

    C. chlorthalidone

    D. mupirocin

25. A pharmacy technician is compounding a medication, and the directions indicate the compound should be triturated. What should the pharmacy technician complete for this step?

    A. combine the powder with a liquid

    B. mix two substances together by adding even amounts of the smallest quantity first

    C. crush and grind powder using a mortar and pestle

    D. use a spatula to mix

26. A patient is suffering from cystitis, which is a(n)

    A. tumor of the heart

    B. inflammation of the bladder

    C. pain in the kidney

    D. low sugar level

27. How many times can a prescription for lorazepam be refilled?

    A. up to 3 times in 30 days

    B. as many times as issued by the provider

    C. no refills

    D. up to 5 times within 6 months

28. An adverse drug event occurs when

    A. a medication causes harm to a patient

    B. a potential medication error is caught before it reaches the patient

    C. a medication is scanned prior to administration

    D. an employee is exposed to a hazardous drug

29. A patient fills a 90-day supply of a medication 1 time in 6 months. What is the adherence rate for this patient?

    A. 30%

    B. 50%

    C. 75%

    D. 40%

30. DEA Form 106 is used for

    A. destruction of a controlled substance
    B. registration of a new DEA number
    C. theft or loss of a controlled substance
    D. ordering Schedule I or II controlled substance

31. Which of the following TE codes in the FDA Orange Book identifies a medication as therapeutically equivalent?

    A. A
    B. B
    C. C
    D. D

32. Insulin detemir is the generic for

    A. Lantus
    B. Novolog
    C. Levemir
    D. Imdur

33. Concerns regarding vaccine post-immunization follow-up should be reported to

    A. VAERS
    B. FDA
    C. MERP
    D. USP

34. A pharmacy is compounding a liquid that is sticky with a high sugar content. What kind of liquid is this?

    A. suspension
    B. elixir
    C. syrup
    D. enema

35. A handout that contains information for patients to read about potential for serious adverse events is a(n)

    A. medication guide
    B. reverse distributor
    C. iPledge
    D. REMS

36. A patient has a prescription for amoxicillin suspension 250mg Q8H × 10d. The pharmacy has 125mL stock bottles of 250mg/5mL. How many doses can the patient get from one bottle?

    A. 10 doses
    B. 15 doses
    C. 25 doses
    D. 30 doses

37. How much active ingredient is required to make 25mL of a 0.25% solution?

    A. 6.25g
    B. 0.625mg
    C. 16.25mg
    D. 60.5g

38. A drug that has a narrow therapeutic index

    A. requires special prescribing privileges to order
    B. has discounted pricing for patient safety
    C. requires careful dosing modifications if needed
    D. is unstable at room temperature

39. Which of the following would be considered an emulsion?

    A. enema
    B. solution
    C. cream
    D. suspension

40. Which of the following drugs will require a medication guide to be dispensed?

    A. fluoxetine
    B. enalapril
    C. lovastatin
    D. prednisone

41. Which of the following would be an acceptable purchase under the CMEA?

    A. 3 boxes of 30 tablets, 60mg pseudoephedrine in one day
    B. 1 box of 90 tablets, 30mg pseudoephedrine in one day
    C. 5 boxes of 90 tablets, 30mg pseudoephedrine in one month
    D. 7 boxes of 30 tablets, 60mg pseudoephedrine in one month

42. The goal of which REMS program is to prevent fetal exposure and inform providers, patients, and pharmacies of the potential of teratogenic effects?
    A. pseudoephedrine
    B. opioid analgesic
    C. clozapine
    D. iPLEDGE

43. What device allows chemotherapy to be compounded and administered with minimal risk of exposure to the compounder and patient?
    A. laminar flow hood
    B. OSHA
    C. SDS
    D. CSTD

44. A patient is admitted into the hospital taking Pepcid. The pharmacy completes a therapeutic substitution to which of the following?
    A. gemfibrozil
    B. pantoprazole
    C. ranitidine
    D. metronidazole

45. A special instruction for benzodiazepines is that they
    A. can cause insomnia
    B. should be taken with other depressants
    C. can be habit forming
    D. can increase urinary output

46. Which of the following medications can be given sublingually every 5 minutes up to 3 times in 15 minutes?
    A. nitroglycerin
    B. hydralazine
    C. metoprolol
    D. isosorbide mononitrate

47. Which type of error occurs when there is an error in the ordered medication dosage, strength, quantity, or route?
    A. dispensing
    B. prescribing
    C. administering
    D. monitoring

48. How much active ingredient is required to make 60mL of a 0.5% solution?

    A. 0.003g

    B. 30mg

    C. 13.3mg

    D. 0.3mg

49. A patient has been prescribed methylprednisone taper in a dose pack. Calculate how many methylprednisone 4mg tablets are needed for the following prescription:

    Methylprednisone 4mg tablets

    Day 1: Take 2 tabs before breakfast, 1 tab after lunch, 1 tab after supper, and 2 tabs at bedtime

    Day 2: Take 1 tab before breakfast, 1 tab after lunch, 1 tab after supper, and 2 tabs at bedtime

    Day 3: Take 1 tab before breakfast, 1 tab after lunch, 1 tab after supper, and 1 tab at bedtime

    Day 4: Take 1 tab before breakfast, 1 tab after lunch, and 1 tab at bedtime

    Day 5: Take 1 tab before breakfast and 1 tab at bedtime

    Day 6: Take 1 tab before breakfast

    A. 14 tabs

    B. 21 tabs

    C. 28 tabs

    D. 42 tabs

50. Saint John's wort has a dangerous interaction with which of the following drugs?

    A. metronidazole

    B. sertraline

    C. amoxicillin

    D. acetaminophen

51. Which of the following is indicated for prophylaxis, management, and treatment of angina?

    A. nitroglycerin

    B. lovastatin

    C. atenolol

    D. amiodarone

52. An interaction of two or more substances that results in a change in color, odor, taste, or viscosity is which type of interaction?

    A. physical
    B. intravenous
    C. therapeutic
    D. chemical

53. A medication to be stored in refrigerated temperature should be in which range?

    A. 20°C to 25°C
    B. −13°F to 14°F
    C. 2°C to 8°C
    D. −25°C to −10°C

54. Furosemide may have which of the following side effects?

    A. hypertension
    B. increased urination
    C. tendinitis
    D. bloating

55. Which of the following is a FDA voluntary reporting system used to report adverse or safety events?

    A. DSCSA
    B. CQA
    C. MedWatch
    D. MERP

56. When a medication error occurs, it may require a more thorough investigation to identify any underlying issues that could result in additional errors. This process is known as

    A. transaction history
    B. human error
    C. MedWatch
    D. root cause analysis

57. A pharmacy technician drawing up 26 units into an insulin U-100 syringe has drawn up how many mL?

    A. 2.6mL
    B. 26mL
    C. 0.26mL
    D. 0.026mL

58. What volume of amoxicillin 250mg/5mL suspension is needed for a 875mg dose?

    A. 12.75mL

    B. 7.5mL

    C. 17.5mL

    D. 25.25mL

59. A patient has an INR drawn that is elevated. The patient's warfarin is not adjusted based on this lab value and the patient develops a bleed. Which type of error has occurred?

    A. prescribing

    B. dispensing

    C. monitoring

    D. administering

60. How many 10mg amlodipine tablets are needed to prepare amlodipine oral suspension with a concentration of 1mg/1mL and a final volume of 60mL?

    A. 4 tabs

    B. 6 tabs

    C. 10 tabs

    D. 12 tabs

61. An order is written for 20mL of a 15% solution. You have a 21% solution in stock. How much stock solution and how much diluent are needed to compound this order?

    A. 4mL diluent is added to 16mL stock

    B. 6.2mL diluent is added to 13.8mL stock

    C. 6mL diluent is added to 14mL stock

    D. 5.7mL diluent is added to 14.3mL stock

62. Which drug causes an interaction with nitroglycerin and can lead to a hypotensive effect?

    A. bacitracin

    B. sildenafil

    C. metformin

    D. fenofibrate

63. Which drug may interact with potassium supplements and cause a hyperkalemic effect if taken?

    A. lisinopril

    B. metoprolol

    C. verapamil

    D. losartan

64. Return to stock prescriptions are those that

    A. are returned to a wholesaler for credit

    B. are returned via reverse distributor

    C. are restocked into inventory in the pharmacy

    D. can be dumped back into the stock bottle to be reused

65. Which of the following is a benefit of unit dose?

    A. provides the patient with a full course of therapy in one package

    B. higher cost for institutional pharmacies to stock

    C. allows return to stock if unused by patient

    D. nurses can waste drug if it's not taken by the patient

66. Prepare 200 grams of 1% hydrocortisone ointment using 5% and 0.5% hydrocortisone base. How many grams of each are required to compound this order?

    A. 160g of the 0.5% and 40g of the 5%

    B. 70.4g of the 0.5% and 129.6g of the 5%

    C. 177.8g of the 0.5% and 22.2g of the 5%

    D. 120g of the 0.5% and 80g of the 5%

67. Which of the following is used to control vertigo and motion sickness?

    A. tiotropium

    B. bisacodyl

    C. dicyclomine

    D. meclizine

68. A patient is suffering from pruritis. Which medication could be prescribed for treatment?

    A. hydroxyzine

    B. dextromethorphan

    C. fluticasone

    D. albuterol

69. Ongoing review of claims data is completed through a

    A. prospective DUR

    B. therapeutic substitution

    C. retrospective DUR

    D. duration review

70. If a patient intentionally or unintentionally takes a medication outside of the prescribed directions, this is known as
    A. DUR
    B. misuse
    C. ADR
    D. product integrity issues

71. Prednisone is indicated for
    A. migraines with aura
    B. allergic and inflammatory disease
    C. prevention of pregnancy
    D. absent thyroid function

72. A patient has a prescription for Crestor. The insurance requires a therapeutic substitution to a cheaper alternative. Which of the following could be an alternative?
    A. dexlansoprazole
    B. atorvastatin
    C. irbesartan
    D. quinapril

73. Which of the following provides recommendations on prescribing specific drug classes to geriatric patients to prevent ADEs?
    A. Orange Book
    B. Beer's list
    C. MedWatch
    D. VIS

74. Which medication is indicated for schizophrenia and bipolar disorder?
    A. zolpidem
    B. aripiprazole
    C. carbamazepine
    D. lamotrigine

75. Which of the following should be used to clean counting trays in a pharmacy?
    A. sterile water
    B. 2% chlorhexidine gluconate
    C. 70% IPA
    D. sodium chloride

76. Clean airflow within a laminar or vertical flow hood must be no greater than which ISO level?

    A. 9
    B. 7
    C. 5
    D. 8

77. Sumatriptan is indicated for

    A. CHF and renal dysfunction
    B. treatment of migraines
    C. cystitis
    D. hypokalemia

78. A patient is looking for a natural remedy for menopausal symptoms, such as hot flashes and night sweats. Which supplement can be recommended for use?

    A. black cohosh
    B. echinacea
    C. melatonin
    D. cranberry

79. Hazardous drugs are compounded in a(n)

    A. vertical flow hood
    B. CAI
    C. ante room
    D. laminar flow hood

80. Which of the following PPE would be doffed or removed first after completion of sterile compounding?

    A. face mask
    B. shoe covers
    C. sterile gloves
    D. gown

81. Which of the following is indicated for the treatment of vaginal candidiasis?

    A. valacyclovir
    B. fluticasone
    C. fluconazole
    D. nitrofurantoin

82. Levofloxacin is indicated to treat
    A. pneumonia, UTI, and chronic bronchitis
    B. chlamydia and gonorrhea
    C. genital herpes
    D. esophageal candidiasis

83. Drowsiness and dry mouth are side effects of which medication?
    A. prednisolone
    B. diphenhydramine
    C. guaifenesin
    D. testosterone

84. A patient fills a 90-day supply of a medication 2 times in 6 months. What is the adherence rate for this patient?
    A. 58%
    B. 25%
    C. 76%
    D. 100%

85. A pharmacy technician used an ampule to compound a medication for a patient. Where should the empty ampule be discarded?
    A. chemotherapy waste
    B. biohazard waste
    C. sharps container
    D. hazardous drug waste

86. Urine discoloration is a side effect of which medication?
    A. clindamycin
    B. amoxicillin
    C. cephalexin
    D. nitrofurantoin

87. Acetaminophen, when more than 4,000mg is taken per day, can lead to which side effect?
    A. hypertension
    B. liver toxicity
    C. peripheral neuropathy
    D. lymphedema

88. A pharmacy technician reconstitutes a prescription for amoxicillin suspension. How many days' stability will this prescription have?

    A. 28

    B. 10

    C. 7

    D. 14

89. Antibiotics ending in -*oxacin* belong to which class?

    A. tetracycline

    B. fluoroquinolone

    C. macrolide

    D. penicillin

90. After opening, how long is insulin aspart stable?

    A. 28 days

    B. 1 hour

    C. 7 days

    D. expiration date on bottle

Practice Test 3 Answer Key

1. **D**
   The generic for Neurontin is gabapentin.

2. **A**
   The ISMP also compiles a list of confused drug names, which includes look-alike/sound-alike (LASA) name pairs of medications. Pharmacies and healthcare facilities can use this list to develop their own list of LASA drugs and strategies to prevent mix-ups. This could include using both the brand and generic names on prescriptions or labels, including the medication purpose on prescriptions, and configuring ordering solutions to prevent LASA names from appearing next to each other.

3. **B**
   Schedule II controlled substances have a high potential for abuse that may lead to physical or psychological dependence.

4. **C**
   The FDA defines repackaging as "taking a finished drug product from the container in which it was distributed by the manufacturer and placing into a different container without further manipulation." In other words, a pharmacy technician removes the drug from a bulk bottle and packages into individual doses for distribution.

5. **A**
   Pantoprazole is a proton pump inhibitor.

6. **C**
   Plavix is the name brand of clopidogrel.

7. **B**
   A medication error is an event that leads to patient harm or inappropriate medication use that was preventable.

8. **B**
   Unit-of-use packaging is packaging that allows for a medication to be dispensed directly to a patient without any manipulation except applying a label. Whereas unit dose delivers enough medication for one dose, or for 24 hours, unit-of-use is designed to deliver medication for the duration of therapy.

9. **D**
   Ketamine is a Schedule III controlled substance.

10. **B**
    Allopurinol is an antigout agent.

11. **D**
    Oxybutynin is an overactive bladder agent.

12. **B**

0.25mg.

$$125\text{mcg} = 0.125\text{mg}$$
$$\text{BID} = 2\times$$
$$(2)(0.125) = 0.25\text{mg}$$

13. **C**

The product code consists of 4 numbers.

14. **C**

In a hospital pharmacy, medications are scanned prior to loading in automated dispensing cabinets to confirm the correct product was selected. The medication is scanned when loading stock, and after the nurse dispenses, the medication is scanned again prior to patient administration.

15. **B**

The five rights are:

- Right patient
- Right drug
- Right dose
- Right route
- Right time

16. **D**

Schedule V controlled substances have a low potential for abuse and many drugs are used as antitussive, anticonvulsant, or antidiarrheal purposes.

17. **D**

Hydroxychloroquine is both an antirheumatic agent and antimalarial medication.

18. **B**

Unit should be used instead of U, as U can be mistaken for 0 or 4.

19. **D**

Tuberculin syringes are small syringes that are designed for 1mL intradermal administration of tuberculin purified protein derivative (PPD). This injection helps diagnosis tuberculosis in a patient.

20. **C**

8 fl oz.

$$\frac{240\text{mL}}{30} = 8 \text{ fl oz}$$

21. **B**

Verbal orders for Schedule II prescriptions are discouraged, but may be accepted in emergency situations. If an emergency fill is required, the pharmacy must write out the verbal order as a valid prescription and dispense a quantity sufficient required only for the emergency period (e.g., a fill for Saturday and Sunday until the prescriber's office is open). The prescriber must then provide the pharmacy with a valid written prescription for this order within 7 days.

22. **B**

Valacyclovir is an antiviral medication.

23. **A**

Expired medications must be segregated from in-dated inventory to prevent dispensing expired drug to patient.

24. **C**

Chlorthalidone is a thiazide diuretic.

25. **C**

Trituration is the process of reducing a particle to a powder through grinding using a mortar and pestle.

26. **B**

Cystitis = *cyst/o* is the root word for bladder and *-itis* is the suffix for inflammation.

27. **D**

Lorazepam is a Schedule IV controlled substance and can be refilled up to 5 times within 6 months.

28. **A**

Adverse drug events (ADE) occur when a medication causes harm to a patient. ADEs consist of medication errors, adverse drug reactions, allergic reactions, or overdose.

29. **B**

50%.

$$90 \text{ day supply} = 90 \text{ days' supply of patient fills}$$

$$6 \text{ months} \times 30 \frac{\text{days}}{\text{month}} = 180 \text{ total days}$$

$$\frac{90 \text{ total days' supply}}{180 \text{ total days}} \times 100 = 50\%$$

30. **C**

DEA Form 106 is used for theft or loss of a controlled substance.

31. **A**

TE code A is considered therapeutically equivalent.

32. **C**

Levemir is the name brand of insulin detemir.

33. **A**

Any concerns reported by patients for vaccines should be reported to the Vaccine Adverse Event Reporting System (VAERS). This system is designed to detect possible problems with US vaccines.

34. **C**

Syrups are made of mostly sugar and water. Syrups are sticky, and become stickier with higher sugar content.

35. **A**

A medication guide contains FDA-approved information for patients in an easy-to-read format to help inform patients about the potential for serious adverse events. Medication guides are dispensed when the patient picks up a prescription.

36. **C**

25 doses.

$$\frac{x\ mL}{250mg} = \frac{5mL}{250mg}$$

$$(x)(250) = (250)(5) = 5mL\ per\ dose$$

$$\frac{x\ dose}{125mL} = \frac{1\ dose}{5mL}$$

$$(x)(5) = (125)(1)$$

$$\frac{125}{5} = 25\ doses$$

37. **B**

0.625mg.

$$\frac{x\ g}{25mL} = \frac{0.0025g}{100mL}$$

$$(x)(100) = (25)(0.0025)$$

$$\frac{0.0625}{100} = 0.000625g = 0.625mg$$

38. **C**

   If a drug has a narrow therapeutic index, a small difference in dosing could lead to a major therapeutic failure or adverse reaction that could be life-threatening. NTI drugs often have requirements for generic substitution, because if there are any even minor differences in bioequivalence, it could result in toxic effects or a lack of effectiveness, leading to treatment failure.

39. **C**

   A cream is an emulsion, which is a mixture consisting of two liquids that do not normally mix together.

40. **A**

   Fluoxetine is an SSRI and requires a medication guide to be dispensed when filling a prescription.

41. **B**

   1 box of 90 tablets, 30mg pseudoephedrine in one day.

   $$(1)(90)(30) = 2,700\text{mg} = 2.7\text{g which is under the daily maximum of 3.6g}$$

42. **D**

   The REMS program for isotretinoin is known as iPLEDGE. The goal of this REMS to prevent fetal exposure and inform pharmacist, providers, and patients of the potential for teratogenic effects.

43. **D**

   Closed system drug-transfer devices (CSTD) should be used to compound chemotherapy and other hazardous drugs. CSTDs minimize the risk of hazardous drug exposure to the employees compounding and nurses when administering to a patient. They also protect the patient from accidental spilling or leakage.

44. **C**

   Pepcid (famotidine) can be therapeutically substituted by ranitidine as they are both H2 receptor blockers.

45. **C**

   Benzodiazepines can be habit forming.

46. **A**

   Nitroglycerin sublingual tablets can be given every 5 minutes up to 3 times in 15 minutes.

47. **B**

Prescribing errors occur from the written order of a provider, either a prescription or a medication order. This includes errors in prescribed dosage or drug strength, quantity (excessive or insufficient) needed for drug therapy, route or dosage form, rate of infusion or drug ordered. A prescribing error can also include omitting necessary refills or approving early refills that may alter appropriate therapy. Incorrect patient errors can also occur during prescribing, including writing an order for a medication to a patient with a known allergy or contraindication.

48. **A**

0.003g.

$$\frac{x \text{ g}}{60\text{mL}} = \frac{0.005\text{g}}{100\text{mL}}$$

$$(x)(100) = (60)(0.005)$$

$$\frac{0.3}{100} = 0.003\text{g}$$

49. **B**

21 tabs.

Day 1 = 6 tabs

Day 2 = 5 tabs

Day 3 = 4 tabs

Day 4 = 3 tabs

Day 5 = 2 tabs

Day 6 = 1 tab

$$6 + 5 + 4 + 3 + 2 + 1 = 21 \text{ tabs}$$

50. **B**

Saint John's wort can prevent the elimination of serotonin. Sertraline is a selective serotonin reuptake inhibitor, which increases levels of serotonin. The interaction of the two can cause a dangerously high level of serotonin in the body.

51. **A**

Nitroglycerin is indicated for prophylaxis, management, and treatment of angina.

52. **A**

A physical incompatibility is the interaction of two or more substances that results in a change in color, odor, taste, viscosity, or physical structure.

53. **C**

   2°C to 8°C is the temperature range for refrigerated medications.

54. **B**

   Furosemide is a diuretic that increases excretion of water. Increased urination is a side effect of increased water output.

55. **C**

   The FDA uses a voluntary reporting system known as MedWatch for adverse and safety events. Healthcare professionals, consumers, or patients can all report through this online program. MedWatch reporting can include drugs, biologics, medical devices, dietary supplements, or cosmetics. This can also include suspected counterfeit medications.

56. **D**

   When a medication error occurs, it may require a more thorough investigation, or root cause analysis (RCA) to identify any underlying issues that could result in additional errors.

57. **C**

   0.26mL.

   $$\frac{x \text{ mL}}{26 \text{ units}} = \frac{1\text{mL}}{100 \text{ units}}$$

   $$(x)(100) = (26)(1)$$

   $$\frac{26}{100} = 0.26\text{mL}$$

58. **C**

   17.5mL.

   $$\frac{x \text{ mL}}{875\text{mg}} = \frac{5\text{mL}}{250\text{mg}}$$

   $$(x)(250) = (875)(5)$$

   $$\frac{4,375}{250} = 17.5\text{mL}$$

59. **C**

   A monitoring error is when a drug treatment plan for a patient is not evaluated for appropriate prescribing. It can occur when a patient's response to therapy is not monitored appropriately, such as through lab results or signs of drug toxicity. Monitoring errors include a lack of response if a patient requires a modification to the prescribed dosing.

60. **B**

6 tabs.

$$\frac{x\text{ mg}}{60\text{mL}} = \frac{1\text{mg}}{1\text{mL}}$$

$$(x)(1) = (60)(1) = 60\text{mg}$$

$$\frac{x\text{ tab}}{60\text{mg}} = \frac{1\text{tab}}{10\text{mg}}$$

$$(x)(10) = (60)(1)$$

$$\frac{60}{10} = 6 \text{ tabs}$$

61. **D**

5.7mL diluent is added to 14.3mL stock.

$$C1 = 21$$

$$V1 = x$$

$$C2 = 15$$

$$V2 = 20$$

$$(21)(x) = (15)(20)$$

$$\frac{300}{21} = 14.3\text{mL of stock solution}$$

This question also asks for quantity of diluent needed with the stock solution. This can be found by taking the final volume and subtracting the stock volume calculated.

$$20\text{mL} - 14.3\text{mL} = 5.7\text{mL}$$

14.3mL stock solution and 5.7mL of diluent to get a final volume of 20mL.

62. **B**

Sildenafil (Viagra) interacts with nitroglycerin and causes a dangerous hypotensive effect.

63. **A**

Lisinopril is an ACE inhibitor and has a potassium-sparing effect. Additional potassium supplements may increase potassium levels, causing hyperkalemia.

64. **C**

Return to stock (RTS) drugs are put back into the pharmacy inventory and can be dispensed to another patient. RTS drugs should never be dumped back into the original stock bottle.

65. **C**

    Unit doses are dispensed most commonly in the institutional setting, because it allows reuse of a medication if the package has not been opened.

66. **C**

    177.8g of the 0.5% and 22.2g of the 5%.

5		0.5
	1	
0.5		4

    Total parts = 4.5.

    5% hydrocortisone:

    $$\frac{x \text{ g}}{200\text{g}} = \frac{0.5 \text{ parts}}{4.5 \text{ parts}}$$

    $$(x)(4.5) = (200)(0.5)$$

    $$\frac{100}{4.5} = 22.2\text{g}$$

    22.2 grams of the 5% hydrocortisone is needed.

    0.5% hydrocortisone:

    $$\frac{x\text{ g}}{200\text{g}} = \frac{4\text{ parts}}{4.5\text{ parts}}$$

    $$(x)(4.5) = (200)(4)$$

    $$\frac{800}{4.5} = 177.8g$$

    177.8g of the 0.5% hydrocortisone is needed.

67. **D**

    meclizine is indicated to control vertigo and motion sickness.

68. **A**

    hydroxyzine is indicated for the treatment of pruritis.

69. **C**

    A DUR can be considered prospective (screening of medication before it is dispensed) or retrospective (ongoing review of claims data).

70. **B**

    Misuse of a prescription is when a patient intentionally or unintentionally takes a medication outside of the prescribed directions.

71. **B**

    Prednisone is indicated for allergy and inflammatory disease.

72. **B**

    Crestor (rosuvastatin) is a statin that can be therapeutically substituted by atorvastatin.

73. **B**

    The Beers list provides recommendations on prescribing these drug classes to prevent ADEs for geriatric patients.

74. **B**

    Aripiprazole is indicated for schizophrenia and bipolar disorder.

75. **C**

    Counting trays should be cleaned with 70% isopropyl alcohol (IPA).

76. **C**

    In the ante area outside the buffer area, the air should be no higher than ISO class 8. The buffer room must have a level no higher than ISO class 7, and within the PEC, the ISO level cannot be greater than ISO class 5.

77. **B**

    Sumatriptan is indicated for the treatment of migraines.

78. **A**

    Black cohosh is a supplement used for menopausal symptoms such as hot flashes, night sweats, or vaginal dryness.

79. **A**

    For hazardous drug compounding, a vertical flow hood or biological safety cabinet is used, which provides a vertical flow of air down after HEPA filtration.

80. **C**

    After completion of sterile compounding, doffing or removing garb should be in the reverse order of the garbing steps, starting with removal of sterile gloves and ending with removing shoe covers.

81. **C**

    Fluconazole is indicated for the treatment of vaginal candidiasis (yeast infection), esophageal candidiasis, oropharyngeal candidiasis.

82. **A**

    Levofloxacin is indicated to treat pneumonia, sinusitis, chronic bronchitis, prostatitis, UTI, and anthrax.

83. **B**

    Diphenhydramine is an antihistamine that has side effects of drowsiness and dry mouth.

84. **D**

100%.

$$90 \text{ day supply filled twice} = (90)(2) = 180 \text{ days' supply of patient fills}$$

$$6 \text{ months} \times 30 \frac{\text{days}}{\text{month}} = 180 \text{ total days}$$

$$\frac{180 \text{ total days' supply}}{180 \text{ total days}} \times 100 = 100\%$$

85. **C**

Any broken glass, such as the broken container of an ampule, should be disposed of in the sharps container.

86. **D**

Nitrofurantoin can cause urine discoloration as a side effect.

87. **B**

To prevent liver damage: max dose for healthy adult for acetaminophen is 4,000mg/day, renal or liver impairment should be max 3,000mg/day.

88. **D**

Amoxicillin has 14-day stability after reconstitution.

89. **B**

Antibiotic fluoroquinolones end in *-floxacin*.

90. **A**

Most insulin is stable for 28 days after opening, including insulin aspart.

Practice Test 4

The following practice exam tests your readiness for the PTCE. To best prepare, give yourself only 1 hour 50 minutes to complete the exam.

1. Which of the following is a corticosteroid?
    A. montelukast
    B. albuterol
    C. fluticasone
    D. hydrochlorothiazide

2. Which of the following would be considered by the ISMP to be high risk/alert?
    A. fluoxetine
    B. ranitidine
    C. amoxicillin
    D. insulin

3. Adderall is which schedule controlled substance?
    A. I
    B. II
    C. III
    D. IV

4. The third set of numbers in an NDC is known as the
    A. product code
    B. package code
    C. labeler code
    D. drug code

5. Which of the following is a selective serotonin reuptake inhibitor?

   A. alprazolam

   B. escitalopram

   C. prednisone

   D. pravastatin

6. The generic for Fosamax is

   A. latanoprost

   B. alendronate

   C. budesonide

   D. spironolactone

7. Which of the following is the appropriate way to write two milligrams?

   A. 2.0mg

   B. 2mcg

   C. 2mg

   D. 2.0mcg

8. A 13% w/v solution has how many mg of active ingredient?

   A. 0.013mg

   B. 13mg

   C. 130mg

   D. 13,000mg

9. Schedule III controlled substances have

   A. no accepted medical use

   B. high abuse potential

   C. low to moderate abuse potential

   D. no abuse potential

10. Which of the following is a direct oral anticoagulant?

   A. sumatriptan

   B. amitriptyline

   C. apixaban

   D. quetiapine

11. Keflex is which type of antibiotic?

   A. penicillin

   B. cephalosporin

   C. tetracycline

   D. fluoroquinolone

12. How many grams are in 450mL of a 7% solution?

    A. 18.4g

    B. 22.8g

    C. 31.5g

    D. 42.9g

13. Which of the following is a tool with a rounded end that is used to crush tablets into powder?

    A. pestle

    B. mortar

    C. beaker

    D. spatula

14. Which of the following is a benefit of BCMA?

    A. Nurses have to scan medications in emergent situations.

    B. Scanning the bar code at bedside alerts the retail pharmacy to fill the prescription.

    C. The nurse does not need to complete five rights if scanning.

    D. Medications are confirmed prior to administration.

15. Which of the following is one of the five rights of medication administration?

    A. right pharmacy

    B. right tubing

    C. right insurance

    D. right time

16. Zolpidem is which schedule controlled substance?

    A. I

    B. II

    C. III

    D. IV

17. The generic for Intuniv is

    A. methylphenidate

    B. guanfacine

    C. mirtazapine

    D. docusate

18. A prescription has been written for APAP 500mg PO TID PRN. The pharmacy technician is unsure what this abbreviation is. The provider should be called to confirm the drug is
    A. acetaminophen
    B. magnesium sulfate
    C. aspirin
    D. hydrochlorothiazide

19. Which of the following is a syringe tip and has a threading mechanism used for attaching needles securely?
    A. slip tip
    B. Luer lock
    C. plunger
    D. shaft

20. How many grams of active ingredient are in 35mL of a 17% solution?
    A. 2.45g
    B. 5.95g
    C. 6.82g
    D. 10.4g

21. How many times can a prescription for testosterone be refilled?
    A. up to 5 times within 6 months
    B. as many as issued by the provider
    C. no refills
    D. 12 times in 1 year

22. Baclofen is the generic for
    A. Lioresal
    B. Zetia
    C. Altace
    D. Diovan

23. Which of the following medications would not be stocked in the fast mover section of a pharmacy inventory?
    A. ACE inhibitors
    B. LASA drugs
    C. antibiotic suspensions
    D. statins

24. The generic of Tradjenta is

    A. lansoprazole
    B. glyburide
    C. linagliptin
    D. cefdinir

25. What does QS mean in the following prescription?

    1. Crush tablets to a fine powder.

    2. Add a small amount of water and mix well.

    3. QS to 100mL with distilled water.

    A. stir rapidly
    B. mix gently
    C. sufficient quantity
    D. allow to disintegrate

26. A patient is admitted to the hospital with the diagnoses of HTN, CHF, and COPD. What is this patient suffering from?

    A. headache, coronary artery disease, and chronic obstructive pulmonary disorder
    B. hypertension, gastroesophageal reflux disease, and chronic obstructive pulmonary disorder
    C. heart attack, congestive heart failure, and chronic obstructive pulmonary disorder
    D. hypertension, congestive heart failure, and chronic obstructive pulmonary disorder

27. DEA Form 41 is used for

    A. theft or loss of a controlled substance
    B. ordering Schedule I or II controlled substances
    C. registration of a new DEA number
    D. destruction of a controlled substance

28. An unwanted and undesirable effect of a medication that occurs during the standard clinical use or dose is a(n)

    A. near miss
    B. ADR
    C. medication error
    D. monitoring error

29. A patient fills a 30-day supply of a medication 5 times in 9 months. What is the adherence rate for this patient?

    A. 72%

    B. 42%

    C. 56%

    D. 95%

30. REMS is a program designed to

    A. inform patients of safety concerns or specific practices for safe use of certain medications

    B. allow patients to return unused medications safely

    C. help report opioid prescriptions

    D. inform healthcare workers of safe disposal methods

31. Which of the following TE codes represents extended-release dosage forms of which bioequivalence data are not submitted?

    A. AB

    B. AP

    C. BC

    D. CE

32. The generic of Cleocin is

    A. norethindrone

    B. gemfibrozil

    C. clindamycin

    D. ezetimibe

33. VAERS is used as a reporting system for which of the following?

    A. anticoagulants

    B. medical devices

    C. vaccines

    D. insulin

34. Which of the following can be compounded using the punch method?

    A. suppository

    B. capsule

    C. elixir

    D. enema

35. Which of the following are designed to reduce the frequency and severity of adverse events of FDA approved medications by informing patients of safety concerns of specific medications?

    A. USP<797>
    B. REMS
    C. unit of use
    D. OSHA

36. A patient has the following prescription:

    Novolin 70/30 Insulin 1,000 units/10mL

    Inject 30 units subcutaneously twice daily before meals

    How many vials will the patient need for a 30-day supply?

    A. 2 vials
    B. 3 vials
    C. 4 vials
    D. 5 vials

37. How much active ingredient is required to make 75mL of a 0.3% solution?

    A. 22.25g
    B. 2.25mg
    C. 26.25mg
    D. 60.5g

38. Which medication has a narrow therapeutic index?

    A. cetirizine
    B. ondansetron
    C. amoxicillin
    D. warfarin

39. If a medication is administered intra-articular, it is injected into the

    A. cartilage
    B. joint
    C. artery
    D. spinal column

40. Which of the following drugs will require a medication guide to be dispensed?

    A. rosuvastatin
    B. valsartan
    C. naproxen
    D. amoxicillin

41. Which of the following would be an acceptable purchase under the CMEA?

    A. 4 boxes of 10 tablets, 30mg pseudoephedrine in one day

    B. 3 boxes of 90 tablets, 60mg pseudoephedrine in one day

    C. 5 boxes of 30 tablets, 90mg pseudoephedrine in one month

    D. 2 boxes of 90 tablets, 90mg pseudoephedrine in one month

42. In order to dispense, prescribe and take isotretinoin, pharmacies, providers, and patients must all participate in which REMS?

    A. Clozaril

    B. iPLEDGE

    C. CMEA

    D. thalidomide

43. A drug administered over a quick period, often to bring a blood concentration to a therapeutic level quickly, is known as an

    A. IV piggybck

    B. IV bolus

    C. IA

    D. intrathecal

44. Olmesartan, an ARB, can be therapeutically substituted by which of the following?

    A. Accupril

    B. Coreg

    C. Prinivil

    D. Cozaar

45. Special instructions for laxatives and stool softeners include

    A. may cause insomnia

    B. rinse mouth after administration

    C. may cause photosensitivity

    D. drink plenty of water to avoid dehydration

46. Which of the following is an example of an acute condition?

    A. diabetes

    B. sinus infection

    C. hypertension

    D. hyperlipidemia

47. A pharmacy technician accidentally fills a prescription for bupropion SR instead of XL. The pharmacist does not catch the error, and the patient picks up the incorrect prescription. Which type of error has occurred?

    A. dispensing
    B. prescribing
    C. monitoring
    D. administering

48. A prescriber writes an order for 2.5mg/kg for a 42kg patient. How many grams will be in each dose?

    A. 0.05g
    B. 0.105g
    C. 150g
    D. 175.5g

49. A patient has the following prescription:

    Prednisone 10mg. Take 5 tabs PO QD × 5 days, then 4 tabs PO QD × 4 days, then 3 tabs PO QD × 3 days, then 2 tabs PO QD × 2 days, then 1 tab PO QD × 2 days.

    How many 10mg tablets are required to fill this prescription?

    A. 52 tabs
    B. 56 tabs
    C. 62 tabs
    D. 64 tabs

50. Taking aspirin and warfarin together can cause excessive bleeding. This is which type of drug–drug interaction?

    A. additive
    B. antagonistic
    C. synergistic
    D. potentiated

51. Which of the following medications is indicated as an adjunctive therapy for reduction in total cholesterol?

    A. ezetimibe
    B. nifedipine
    C. nebivolol
    D. chlorthalidone

52. Two medications are mixed together and a precipitate forms. This is an example of which type of incompatibility?

    A. chemical

    B. therapeutic

    C. clinical

    D. physical

53. A drug that must be stored in the freezer should be within which temperature range?

    A. −13°F to 14°F

    B. 30°C to 40°C

    C. 36°F to 46°F

    D. 8°C to 15°C

54. Fatigue is a side effect of which medication?

    A. metoprolol

    B. prednisone

    C. albuterol

    D. methylphenidate

55. What three components of transactions must be stored for 6 years to provide tracking information under the DSCSA?

    A. transaction logs, transaction data, and transaction documentation

    B. transaction information, transaction history, and transaction statement

    C. transaction statement, transaction audits, and transaction licensing

    D. transaction history, transaction registration, and transaction licensing

56. A root cause analysis is designed to

    A. allow one person to conduct a thorough investigation

    B. recognize the problem and develop a way to prevent recurrence

    C. identify the problem only

    D. determine the punitive response needed

57. A pharmacy technician drawing up 74 units into an insulin U-100 syringe has drawn up how many mL?

    A. 0.74mL

    B. 7.4mL

    C. 0.074mL

    D. 74mL

58. What volume of amoxicillin 125mg/5mL suspension is needed for a 275mg dose?

    A. 15mL

    B. 7.5mL

    C. 24mL

    D. 11mL

59. Pharmacists who review lab results may help prevent which type of error?

    A. dispensing

    B. prescribing

    C. administering

    D. monitoring

60. How many 100mg atenolol tablets are needed to prepare atenolol 2mg/mL oral suspension and a final volume of 250mL?

    A. 9 tabs

    B. 15 tabs

    C. 5 tabs

    D. 2 tabs

61. An order is written for 50mL of a 10% solution. You have a 25% solution in stock. How much stock solution and how much diluent is needed to compound this order?

    A. 30mL diluent is added to 20mL stock

    B. 41.2mL diluent is added to 8.8mL stock

    C. 6mL diluent is added to 44mL stock

    D. 35.5mL diluent is added to 14.5mL stock

62. Which type of interaction occurs when a patient's condition alters the properties of the drug, such as excretion or metabolism?

    A. drug–laboratory

    B. drug–disease

    C. drug–nutrient

    D. drug–dietary supplement

63. A patient has an allergy to penicillin antibiotics. Which of the following could be an alternative for treatment of a bacterial infection?

    A. amoxicillin

    B. azithromycin

    C. valacyclovir

    D. ampicillin

64. Which of the following attaches to the end of a MDI so the medication can stay within the chamber for inhalation?

    A. nebulizer
    B. spacer
    C. lancet
    D. nebule

65. A steroid dose pack, which includes a full course of therapy in one pack, is considered

    A. repackaged
    B. unit dose
    C. unit-of-use
    D. bulk supply

66. Prepare 50 grams of 6% gabapentin cream using 20% gabapentin base and an inert cream base. How many grams of each are required to compound this order?

    A. 16g of the cream base and 34g of the 20%
    B. 4g of the cream base and 46g of the 20%
    C. 35g of the cream base and 15g of the 20%
    D. 12g of the cream base and 38g of the 20%

67. Docusate is indicated for

    A. diarrhea
    B. constipation
    C. nausea and vomiting
    D. migraine

68. Which of the following is indicated for the treatment of COPD?

    A. mometasone
    B. loratadine
    C. tiotropium
    D. benzonatate

69. Through which review would an allergy alert be identified?

    A. therapeutic interchange
    B. retrospective DUR
    C. claims review
    D. prospective DUR

70. A patient asks a pharmacy technician for recommendation for their itchy throat. The pharmacy technician should

   A. ask the pharmacist to assist the customer

   B. tell the customer which works best

   C. advise the customer that they can't help them

   D. show the customer to the allergy section since that is most likely what the issue is

71. A patient is suffering from anxiety and panic disorder. Which medication could be used as treatment?

   A. alprazolam

   B. citalopram

   C. amitriptyline

   D. trazodone

72. A patient is taking nebivolol upon hospital admission. Which of the following could be therapeutically substituted?

   A. Coreg

   B. Prinivil

   C. Diovan

   D. Zantac

73. Which of the following drugs is most likely to be misused or abused?

   A. metoprolol

   B. epinephrine

   C. lovastatin

   D. alprazolam

74. Which of the following is indicated for depression, OCD, bulimia, and panic disorder?

   A. lithium

   B. quetiapine

   C. gabapentin

   D. fluoxetine

75. Which of the following is important to use for cleaning counting trays after counting medications that have high allergy implications, such as a penicillin antibiotic?

   A. ammonia

   B. distilled water

   C. 0.5% sodium hypochlorite

   D. 70% IPA

76. If the PEC (laminar or vertical) has been shut off at any time, how long must it run for prior to use?

    A. 30 minutes

    B. 1 hour

    C. 10 minutes

    D. It can be used immediately after turning on.

77. ADHD and narcolepsy can be treated with

    A. sumatriptan

    B. dextroamphetamine and amphetamine

    C. tamsulosin

    D. mirabegron

78. Latanoprost is indicated for

    A. conjunctivitis

    B. rheumatoid arthritis

    C. elevated intraocular pressure

    D. ophthalmic infections

79. Cleaning of the hood should occur at what times?

    A. only if a spill occurs

    B. beginning of every shift and for all spills

    C. beginning of every shift, every 30 minutes while batching, and if a spill occurs

    D. end of the day and if a spill occurs

80. Which of the following is the last item to be garbed prior to compounding?

    A. shoe covers

    B. face mask

    C. gown

    D. sterile gloves

81. Cyclobenzaprine, methocarbamol, and tizanidine can all be used to treat

    A. osteoarthritis

    B. migraine

    C. insomnia

    D. muscle spasm

82. Tramadol is indicated for the treatment of
    A. narcolepsy
    B. moderate to severe pain
    C. alcohol withdrawal
    D. tetanus and muscle spasm

83. Nervousness and insomnia may be a side effect of which medication?
    A. ethinyl estradiol and desogestrel
    B. dextromethorphan
    C. insulin glargine
    D. albuterol

84. A patient fills a 30-day supply of a medication 4 times in 6 months. What is the adherence rate for this patient?
    A. 67%
    B. 30%
    C. 100%
    D. 80%

85. Which of the following prevents the spread of illness and maintains cleanliness in the pharmacy?
    A. cleaning counting trays
    B. garbing PPE
    C. good hand hygiene
    D. cleaning the hoods every 30 minutes

86. Constipation, nausea, and vomiting are side effects of which medication?
    A. oxycodone
    B. aspirin
    C. mupirocin
    D. fluconazole

87. Which of the following can be used for more than one dose?
    A. ampule
    B. SDV
    C. MDV
    D. enema

88. A patient has a prescription for Augmentin suspension. The medication is reconstituted in the pharmacy. How many days is the Augmentin stable after reconstituting?

    A. 14 days

    B. 10 days

    C. 3 days

    D. 6 months

89. Which of the following has a preservative to help prevent growth of microbials?

    A. epidural

    B. ampules

    C. SDV

    D. MDV

90. Which class of drugs end in -*prazole*?

    A. antiulcer agent—proton pump inhibitor

    B. antiulcer agent—histamine (H2) antagonist

    C. monoclonal antibody

    D. antiemetic

Practice Test 4 Answer Key

1. **C**
   Fluticasone is a corticosteroid.

2. **D**
   Insulin is on the ISMP high-alert/risk medication list for both subcutaneous and IV infusions.

3. **B**
   Adderall is a Schedule II controlled substance.

4. **B**
   The last set of numbers is the package code. This describes the package's size and type.

5. **B**
   Escitalopram is a selective serotonin reuptake inhibitor.

6. **B**
   Alendronate is the generic for Fosamax.

7. **C**
   2mg. Trailing zeros should never be used when writing doses.

8. **D**
   13,000mg

   $$w/v = g/100mL$$

   $$134 = 13g$$

   $$(13)(1,000) = 13,000mg$$

9. **C**
   Schedule III controlled substances have low to moderate abuse potential.

10. **C**
    Apixaban is a direct oral anticoagulant.

11. **B**
    Keflex is a cephalosporin antibiotic.

12. **C**
    31.5g.

    $$\frac{x \text{ g}}{450\text{mL}} = \frac{7\text{g}}{100\text{mL}}$$

    $$(x)(100) = (450)(7)$$

    $$\frac{(450)(7)}{100} = 31.5\text{g}$$

13. **A**
    A mortar is a bowl and a pestle is a tool with a rounded end that is used for crushing and grinding.

14. **D**
    The patient's medications are scanned and documented in the medication administration record (MAR) and confirmed prior to administration. The bar code of the manufacturer label or pharmacy label is scanned to confirm correct product selection. If the wrong medication is scanned, an alert will notify the nurse that there is a problem. BCMA should not take the place of the five rights, but help support medication safety.

15. **D**
    The five rights are:
    - Right patient
    - Right drug
    - Right dose
    - Right route
    - Right time

16. **D**
    Zolpidem is a Schedule IV controlled substance.

17. **B**
    Guanfacine is the generic for Intuniv.

18. **A**
    APAP is a confusing abbreviation for acetaminophen and should not be used.

19. **B**
    Luer-lock syringes have a threading mechanism that allows a needle to screw on tight and prevent it from falling off.

20. **B**

5.95g.

$$\frac{x \text{ g}}{35\text{mL}} = \frac{17\text{g}}{100\text{mL}}$$

$$(x)(100) = (35)(17)$$

$$\frac{595}{100} = 5.95\text{g}$$

21. **A**

Testosterone is a Schedule III controlled substance and can be refilled up to 5 times within 6 months.

22. **A**

Lioresal is the name brand of baclofen.

23. **B**

For medication safety, use signing programs that draws attention to LASA drugs and high-risk/alert medications, such as stickers or separate inventory and avoid stocking LASA drugs in "fast mover" sections.

24. **C**

Linagliptin is the generic for Tradjenta.

25. **C**

QS means to add sufficient quantity to reach the final volume of 100mL.

26. **D**

This patient is suffering from hypertension, congestive heart failure, and chronic obstructive pulmonary disorder.

HTN = hypertension

CHF = congestive heart failure

COPD = chronic obstructive pulmonary disorder

27. **D**

DEA Form 41 is used for destruction of a controlled substance.

28. **B**

An adverse drug reaction (ADR) is an unwanted and undesirable effect of a medication that occurs during the standard clinical use or dose.

29. **C**

56%

$$\text{30 day supply filled five times} = (30)(5) = 150 \text{ days' supply of patient fills}$$

$$9 \text{ months} \times 30 \frac{\text{days}}{\text{month}} = 270 \text{ total days}$$

$$\frac{150 \text{ total days' supply}}{270 \text{ total days}} \times 100 = 56\%$$

30. **A**

REMS are designed to reduce the frequency and severity of adverse events by informing patients of safety concerns or requiring specific practices for safe use.

31. **C**

TE Code BC represents extended release dosage forms with no bioequivalence data submitted.

32. **C**

Clindamycin is the generic for Cleocin.

33. **C**

Any concerns reported by patients for vaccines should be reported to the Vaccine Adverse Event Reporting System (VAERS). This system is designed to detect possible problems with US vaccines.

34. **B**

To compound capsules, a capsule-filling machine can be used, or the punch method. The punch method is used for a smaller quantity. In this method, the height of the active ingredient powder is the same height as the capsule base. The pharmacy technician compounding can then punch the capsule into this powder, which will fill the entire base.

35. **B**

REMS are designed to reduce the frequency and severity of adverse events by informing patients of safety concerns or requiring specific practices for safe use.

36. **A**

    2 vials.

    $$30 + 30 = 60 \text{ total units daily}$$

    $$\frac{x \text{ vial}}{60 \text{ units}} = \frac{1 \text{ vial}}{1,000 \text{ units}}$$

    $$(x)(1000) = (1)(60)$$

    $$\frac{60}{1,000} = 0.06 \text{ vial for 1 day}$$

    $$(0.06)(30) = 1.8 \text{ vials}$$

    $$1.8 \text{ vials} = 2 \text{ total vials needed}$$

37. **B**

    2.25mg.

    $$\frac{x \text{ g}}{75 \text{mL}} = \frac{0.003 \text{g}}{100 \text{mL}}$$

    $$(x)(100) = (75)(0.003)$$

    $$\frac{0.225}{100} = 0.00225 \text{g} = 2.25 \text{mg}$$

38. **D**

    Warfarin has a narrow therapeutic index.

39. **B**

    Intra-articular route is injected into a joint.

40. **C**

    Naproxen is an NSAID and requires a medication guide to be dispensed when filling a prescription.

41. **A**

    4 boxes of 10 tablets, 30mg pseudoephedrine in one day.

    $$(4)(10)(30) = 1,200 \text{mg} = 1.2 \text{g}, \text{ which is under the daily maximum of } 3.6 \text{g}$$

42. **B**

    The REMS program for isotretinoin is known as iPLEDGE. The goal of this REMS to prevent fetal exposure and inform pharmacist, providers and patients of the potential for teratogenic effects.

43. **B**

    IV bolus is administering a drug over quick period often to bring a patient's blood concentration to a therapeutic level quickly (loading dose).

44. **D**
Olmesartan is an ARB that can be therapeutically substituted to Cozaar (losartan).

45. **D**
Special instructions for laxatives and stool softeners include drinking plenty of water to avoid dehydration.

46. **B**
Acute conditions are those with a rapid onset and quick resolution, such as a cold or viral infection.

47. **A**
A dispensing error is a difference in what was prescribed and what is dispensed to a patient. Dispensing errors can be caused by anyone involved in this process, including both pharmacists and pharmacy technicians. It can result from a wrong product selection, including wrong strength or dosage form.

48. **B**
0.105g.

$$\frac{x\text{ mg}}{42\text{kg}} = \frac{2.5\text{mg}}{1\text{kg}}$$

$$(x)(1) = (42)(2.5) = 105\text{mg}$$

$$105\text{mg} = 0.105\text{g}$$

49. **B**
56 tabs.

$$(5\text{ tabs})(5\text{ days}) = 25\text{ tabs}$$

$$(4\text{ tabs})(4\text{ days}) = 16\text{ tabs}$$

$$(3\text{ tabs})(3\text{ days}) = 9\text{ tabs}$$

$$(2\text{ tabs})(2\text{ days}) = 4\text{ tabs}$$

$$(1\text{ tab})(2\text{ days}) = 2\text{ tabs}$$

$$25 + 16 + 9 + 4 + 2 = 56\text{ tabs}$$

50. **C**
Because aspirin and warfarin together have a greater effect than when each is taken separately, this would be considered a synergistic interaction.

51. **A**
Ezetimibe is indicated as an adjunctive therapy for reducing total cholesterol.

52. **D**

A physical incompatibility is the interaction of two or more substances, which results in a change in color, odor, taste, viscosity, or physical structure. An example of this would be a precipitate forming when two substances are mixed that are incompatible.

53. **A**

−13°F to 14°F is the temperature range for freezer storage.

54. **A**

Metoprolol is a beta blocker and a side effect of beta blockers is fatigue. Beta blockers slow the heart rate, and fatigue or drowsiness is a possible side effect.

55. **B**

All drugs must be accompanied by transaction information (TI), transaction history (TH), and a transaction statement (TS), and these must be stored for 6 years to provide tracking information.

56. **B**

An RCA is a process to find the "root cause" of a problem through a comprehensive review of all workflows and systems in place. This will then not only identify the problem, but help develop a way to prevent it from occurring again. Not all errors have one root cause, and a RCA can help identify additional causes if there is more than one. A RCA should be conducted in a team approach. It is typically more beneficial to have the team be consisting of those who were not involved in the original error itself, but familiar with the workflows, processes, and procedures in the area it occurred.

57. **A**

0.74mL.

$$\frac{x \text{ mL}}{74 \text{ units}} = \frac{1\text{mL}}{100 \text{ units}}$$

$$(x)(100) = (74)(1)$$

$$\frac{74}{100} = 0.74\text{mL}$$

58. **D**

11mL.

$$\frac{x\,\text{mL}}{275\text{mg}} = \frac{5\text{mL}}{125\text{mg}}$$

$$(x)(125) = (275)(5)$$

$$\frac{1,375}{125} = 11\text{mL}$$

59. **D**

Preventing monitoring errors start with proper training of providers on the potential negative effects of medications, which may indicate toxicity. Providers must also be trained in understanding monitoring methods, such as through vital signs and evaluating lab results, this includes pharmacists. Pharmacists often review lab results prior to initiating drug therapy, such as chemotherapy.

60. **C**

5 tabs.

$$\frac{x \text{ mg}}{250 \text{mL}} = \frac{2 \text{mg}}{1 \text{mL}}$$

$$(x)(1) = (250)(2) = 500 \text{mg}$$

$$\frac{x \text{ tab}}{500 \text{mg}} = \frac{1 \text{ tab}}{100 \text{mg}}$$

$$(x)(100) = (500)(1)$$

$$\frac{500}{100} = 5 \text{ tabs}$$

61. **A**

30mL diluent is added to 20mL stock.

$$C1 = 25$$

$$V1 = x$$

$$C2 = 10$$

$$V2 = 50$$

$$(25)(x) = (10)(50)$$

$$\frac{500}{25} = 20 \text{mL of stock solution}$$

This question also asks for quantity of diluent needed with the stock solution. This can be found by taking the final volume and subtracting the stock volume calculated.

$$50 \text{mL} - 20 \text{mL} = 30 \text{mL}$$

20mL stock solution and 30mL of diluent get a final volume of 50mL.

62. **B**

Drug–disease interaction occurs when a patient's disease alters the ADME properties of the drug, such as metabolism and excretion.

63. **B**

Azithromycin is a macrolide antibiotic and can be taken when a patient has an allergy to penicillin.

64. **B**

A spacer attaches to the end of the MDI so the aerosolized medication stays within the chamber, and then the patient breathes into the other end of the spacer to absorb more of the drug.

65. **C**

Unit-of-use packaging is packaging that allows for a medication to be dispensed directly to a patient without any manipulation except applying a label.

66. **C**

35g of the cream base and 15g of the 20%.

20		6
	6	
0		14

Total parts = 20

20% gabapentin

$$\frac{x \text{ g}}{50\text{g}} = \frac{6 \text{ parts}}{20 \text{ parts}}$$

$$(x)(20) = (50)(6)$$

$$\frac{300}{20} = 15\text{g}$$

15 grams of the 20% gabapentin is needed.

Cream base

$$\frac{x \text{ g}}{50\text{g}} = \frac{14 \text{ parts}}{20 \text{ parts}}$$

$$(x)(20) = (50)(14)$$

$$\frac{700}{20} = 35\text{g}$$

35g of the cream base is needed.

67. **B**

Docusate is a stool softener indicated for treating constipation.

68. **C**

Tiotropium is indicated to treat COPD.

69. **D**

Prospective DUR identify issues such as

- Therapeutic duplication
- Drug–disease interaction
- Drug–drug interaction
- Inappropriate prescribing, such as incorrect dosage, frequency, or duration
- Recommendations for substitutions and therapeutic interchange
- Allergies
- Misuse or abuse of a medication
- Appropriateness of medication for patient
- Pregnancy alert

70. **A**

Pharmacy technicians can assist in selection of OTC products by answering any nonclinical questions, asking the pharmacist for assistance, and helping patients locate specific products.

71. **A**

Alprazolam is indicated for the treatment of anxiety and panic disorder.

72. **A**

Nebivolol is a beta blocker and can be therapeutically substituted with Coreg (carvedilol).

73. **D**

Alprazolam is a sedative (benzodiazepine) that is frequently abused and is more likely to be abused than a beta blocker (metoprolol), epinephrine, or a statin (lovastatin).

74. **D**

Fluoxetine is indicated for the treatment of depression, OCD, bulimia, and panic disorder.

75. **D**

Counting trays should be cleaned with 70% isopropyl alcohol (IPA). Cleaning counting trays regularly helps prevent cross-contamination, which is the contamination of another medication due to residual residue left on a counting tray. Drugs that leave a powder on the tray can contaminate the next prescription if the tray is not cleaned in between prescriptions. This is especially true for medications that have allergy implications. For example, if a counting tray is not cleaned following the counting of amoxicillin, and a patient has a penicillin allergy, this could result in an allergic reaction if the residue remains on the tray when the next prescription is counted.

76. **A**

If the PEC has been shut off at any time, it should be turned on and left to run for 30 minutes prior to use.

77. **B**

Dextroamphetamine and amphetamine are indicated to treat ADHD and narcolepsy.

78. **C**

Latanoprost is indicated for elevated intraocular pressure.

79. **C**

Cleaning of the hood should be done at the beginning of every shift, every 30 minutes, or before every batch and if a spill occurs.

80. **D**

Here is the proper order of PPE donning for sterile compounding:

- Start by removing any jewelry, makeup, artificial nails or polish before donning PPE.
- Put on shoe covers.
- Don hair cover including beard cover if needed.
- Put on a face mask or shield. A face shield or goggles are typically only required when compounding hazardous drugs.
- Perform hand hygiene.
- Don nonshedding gown over clean scrubs.
- Use surgical (alcohol-based) hand scrub prior to putting on gloves. Allow to dry.
- Don sterile gloves. Two pairs of chemotherapy gloves should be used if compounding a hazardous drug.

81. **D**

Cyclobenzaprine, methocarbamol, and tizanidine are all muscle relaxants indicated for the treatment of muscle spasm.

82. **B**

Tramadol is indicated for the treatment of moderate to severe pain.

83. **D**

Albuterol may cause nervousness, insomnia and palpitations.

84. **A**

67%.

$$\text{30 day supply filled three times} = (30)(4) = 120 \text{ days' supply of patient fills}$$

$$6 \text{ months} \times 30 \frac{\text{days}}{\text{month}} = 180 \text{ total days}$$

$$\frac{120 \text{ total days' supply}}{180 \text{ total days}} \times 100 = 67\%$$

85. **C**

Good handwashing and hand hygiene prevents the spread of illness and also helps maintain cleanliness within a pharmacy.

86. **A**

Oxycodone and other narcotic analgesics may cause constipation, nausea, and vomiting

87. **C**

A MDV or multidose vial can be used for more than one dose.

88. **B**

Augmentin suspension is good for 10 days after reconstitution.

89. **D**

MDVs do contain a preservative, and this prevents the growth of microbials. MDVs, once opened, typically have a BUD of 28 days.

90. **A**

Antiulcer agent proton pump inhibitor has the stem *-prazole* such as esomeprazole, lansoprazole, and omeprazole.

Notes

Notes

Notes

Notes

Notes

Notes

Notes

Notes